EVERYMAN, I will go with thee,

and be thy guide,

In thy most need to go by thy side

A Century of
Humorous Verse
1850-1950

EDITED BY
ROGER LANCELYN GREEN
M.A., B. LITT.

DENT: LONDON
EVERYMAN'S LIBRARY
DUTTON: NEW YORK

PR
1195
H8
G7
1959

No. 813   Hardback ISBN 0 460 00813 7
No. 1813   Paperback ISBN 0 460 01813 2

THIS BOOK IS DEDICATED

TO THE MEMORY

OF

PATRICK REGINALD CHALMERS

BY HIS

Little Pagan Faun

WHERE Thames falls over Streatley Weir
   And down to Pangbourne speeds,
I hear a whisper murmuring clear
   Of wind among the reeds.

Two shadows fall across the grass
   And leave my open page:
One that I knew in life to pass
   Through my own Golden Age;

And with him there a mightier shade
   On whom I did not gaze,
Though at his side my feet have strayed
   Through many Dreaming Days.

The Wind among the Willows' gold
   Of Badger, Mole, and Toad
And Rat, is telling as of old
   Beside the Roman Road;

But there a Little Pagan Faun
   Comes leading by the hand
A Piper from the Gates of Dawn
   Who sang of faery land.

                           R. L. G.

PREFACE

'TO BE GAY is almost a lost form of the literary art,' wrote Andrew Lang in 1907, and the reiteration of some such statement in every period must be my excuse for the shortcomings of the present volume.

Any anthology must suffer to a greater or less extent from personal taste and prejudice, and a collection of humorous verse is particularly liable to be marked by the taste of its editor. Humour has a dimension beyond criticism: it is possible, for example, to acknowledge the fact that *The Wrong Box* and *Three Men in a Boat* are masterpieces of humour—but to be amused by one and bored by the other.

In the *Century of Humorous Verse* from 1850 to 1950 I have found the most amusement in the middle of the period, and least towards the end. This does not, however, come amiss, for the object of the present volume is to include representative works by the acknowledged masters of humorous verse (accompanied by a sprinkling of more personal choices)—and naturally few contemporary writers have yet qualified for the distinctions which we hand unhesitatingly to Lear, Lewis Carroll, W. S. Gilbert, or Calverley, though some are drawing near to the class in which such writers as Godley, Seaman, Quiller-Couch, and Belloc have already taken a permanent place.

The main object being to include the most famous verse writers and their best-known poems, no excuse is needed for the majority of items in this volume. Among the giants, Lewis Carroll and Lear are not, however, represented by their most famous verses—which may already be found in other volumes of Everyman's Library; but Gilbert and Calverley, since this is their only appearance, by as many as seemed possible without overweighting my anthology.

While a number of the authors and poems were inevitable, wide reading over the period—aided greatly by *Punch*, which covers the whole of it—has added many names and sets of verses which may be new to the majority of readers. Several writers, such as Du Maurier, Andrew Lang, F. Anstey, St John Hankin, and Patrick Barrington, have demanded an unexpectedly large allowance of space, and may one day be classed as major writers of humorous verse; while several poems by writers quite unknown, or known for utterly different kinds of writing, have demanded a place with equal insistency—though often no other poem by the author in question could be considered for an instant.

The inclusion of Lear and Lewis Carroll, although I have been able to choose mainly poems written for an adult audience, raises the question of the inclusion of verse written primarily for children. Anthologies of humorous verse usually boast such pieces as 'The Walrus and the Carpenter' and 'The Owl and the Pussy Cat,' and sometimes a stray set of verses from the nursery volumes of Eugene Field. This has given me sufficient precedent for including so famous a writer as W. B. Rands, author of *Lilliput Levee*, and that forgotten genius Elizabeth Anna Hart. These are, however, my only borrowings from the junior bookshelf, except in the obvious cases of Hilaire Belloc and A. A. Milne—the modern equivalents of Lear and Dodgson.

The arbitrary division of dates—1850 to 1950—to which I have adhered strictly, has not proved as much of a hardship as at first I expected. The most serious omissions from before my period are *Rejected Addresses*, *The Ingoldsby Legends*, the poetry of the *Anti-Jacobin*, and the writings of Praed and Hood—all easily obtainable. With regard to the authors included, the restriction has only seemed irksome in the cases of Thomas Love Peacock and Oliver Wendell Holmes, whose best humorous verse was written early—one regrets, for example, 'Paper Money Lyrics' and that 'The Mysterious Visitor' could not be included.

The arrangement of this anthology has caused considerable thought. Ideally the poems should stand in the order in which they were written, or at least published. But it has seemed better to group them together under their respective authors, who have therefore been arranged strictly in the chronological order of their birth.

I have, however, added the dates of first publication of each poem included. In some early cases, and in a few American instances, it has been impossible to give more than the date of publication in book form. But in every possible case the date given is that of periodical publication. This attempt at exact dating seems to be new in anthologies of humorous verse; if the dating, and the bibliographical notes included in the Index of Authors seem too academic for some readers, they are reminded of their ancient prerogative of skipping. 'Mankind,' as an Oxford don remarked sadly not long ago, 'is now divided into three classes instead of two: the Literate, the Illiterate—and the B.Litt-erate.'

Another feature of this collection is the second part or appendix. In it I have included a selection of Limericks by known authors; a collection (mainly from memory) of the most famous Limericks by authors unknown; a number of short pieces of verse, both famous and of personal choice; and a final medley of 'Rootless Rhymes,' mainly transmitted orally. There also will be found a number of quatrains from *The Masque of Balliol*.

My personal debts are of two kinds. Firstly, to those who have helped directly or indirectly with this anthology—in which class I must first mention the dedicatee of this book, who first interested me in humorous verse. I have still vivid recollections of Patrick Chalmers in his home at Goring-on-Thames, standing beneath the picture which inspired 'My Woodcock' and reading or reciting verses by Quiller-Couch, Owen Seaman, J. K. Stephen, Kipling, and many others; also of the days when one flew week by week to *Punch* for the latest of his charming verses or prose sketches. In the same category comes my late father, who recited *Departmental Ditties* to me before I could read them to myself, and read choice verses from *Punch*, which, remembering, I have now hunted out and recovered with great delight— and occasionally used in this book.

Secondly I must record my debt to earlier anthologists of humorous verse. My first list—three-quarters of the present volume—was made before having recourse to any of these; but later reference to those edited by J. C. Squire, Michael Roberts, Guy Boas, and J. M. Cohen introduced me to a number of new authors—though not always to what seemed to me their best or most amusing poems.

Finally I must express my gratitude for the many hours, days, weeks of entertainment which the eighty-three authors, from Peacock, Holmes, and Thackeray, to Ogden Nash, C. S. Lewis, and Patrick Barrington, have given me while supplying the body of this book—not forgetting the many writers known and unknown who have dropped 'Stray Verses' and 'Limericks' to form the sediment of *A Century of Humorous Verse*.

ROGER LANCELYN GREEN.

1959.

INDEX OF AUTHORS AND
ACKNOWLEDGMENTS

For permission to reprint copyright material, the cordial thanks of the editor and publishers are offered to the persons named at the foot of each author's entry.

Items printed in *italic* are short pieces gathered separately as *Stray Verses*, *Limericks*, and *The Masque of Balliol*

xi

THOMAS LOVE PEACOCK

(1785–1866)

A New Order of Chivalry

SIR MOSES, Sir Aaron, Sir Jamramajee,
Two stock-jobbing Jews, and a shroffing Parsee,
Have girt on the armour of old Chivalrie,
And, instead of the Red Cross, have hoisted Balls Three.

Now fancy our sovereign, so gracious and bland,
With the sword of Saint George in her royal right hand,
Instructing this trio of marvellous Knights
In the mystical meanings of Chivalry's rites.

'You have come from the bath, all in milk-white array,
To show you have washed worldly feelings away,
And, pure as your vestments from secular stain,
Renounce sordid passions and seekings for gain.

'This scarf of deep red o'er your vestments I throw,
In token, that down them your life-blood shall flow,
Ere Chivalry's honour, or Christendom's faith,
Shall meet through your failure, or peril or scaith.

'These slippers of silk, of the colour of earth,
Are in sign of remembrance of whence you had birth:
That from earth you have sprung, and to earth you return,
But stand for the faith, life immortal to earn.

'This blow of the sword on your shoulder-blade true
Is the mandate of homage, where homage is due,
And the sign that your swords from the scabbard shall fly
When "St George and the Right" is the rallying cry.

'This belt of white silk, which no speck has defaced,
Is the sign of a bosom with purity graced,
And binds you to prove, whatsoever betides,
Of damsels distressed the friends, champions, and guides.

1

'These spurs of pure gold are the symbols which say,
As your steeds obey them, you the Church shall obey,
And speed at her bidding, through country and town,
To strike, with your falchions, her enemies down.'

Now fancy these Knights, when the speech they have heard,
As they stand, scarfed, shoed, shoulder-dubbed, belted and
    spurred,
With the cross-handled sword duly sheathed on the thigh,
Thus simply and candidly making reply:

'By your Majesty's grace we have risen up Knights,
But we feel little relish for frays and for fights:
There are heroes enough, full of spirit and fire,
Always ready to shoot and be shot at for hire.

'True with bulls and with bears we have battled our cause;
And the bulls have no horns, and the bears have no paws;
And the mightiest blow which we ever have struck
Has achieved but the glory of laming a duck.

'With two nations in arms, friends impartial to both,
To raise each a loan we shall be nothing loth;
We will lend them the pay, to fit men for the fray;
But shall keep ourselves carefully out of the way.

'We have small taste for championing maids in distress:
For State we care little: for Church we care less:
To Premium and Bonus our homage we plight:
"Percentage!" we cry: and "A fig for the right!"

''Twixt Saint George and the Dragon we settle it thus:
Which has scrip above par is the Hero for us:
For a turn in the market, the Dragon's red gorge
Shall have our free welcome to swallow Saint George.'

Now, God save our Queen, and if aught should occur
To peril the crown or the safety of her,
God send that the leader, who faces the foe,
May have more of King Richard than Moses and Co.

                                                    (1860)

JAMES ROBINSON PLANCHÉ
(1796–1880)

A Literary Squabble

THE Alphabet rejoiced to hear
That Monckton Milnes was made a Peer;
For in this present world of letters
But few, if any, are his betters:
So an address by acclamation,
They voted of congratulation,
And H, O, U, G, T, and N,
Were chosen the address to pen;
Possessing each an interest vital
In the new Peer's baronial title.
'Twas done in language terse and telling,
Perfect in grammar and in spelling:
But when 'twas read aloud, oh, mercy!
There sprang up such a controversy
About the true pronunciation
Of said baronial appellation.
The vowels O and U averred
They were entitled to be *heard*;
The consonants denied their claim,
Insisting that they *mute* became.
Johnson and Walker were applied to,
Sheridan, Bailey, Webster, tried too;
But all in vain, for each picked out
A word that left the case in doubt.
O, looking round upon them all,
Cried, 'If it be correct to call,
T H R O U G H, *throo*,
H O U G H, must be *Hoo*,
Therefore there can be no dispute on
The question, we should say, "Lord *Hoo*ton."'
U brought 'bought,' 'fought,' and 'sought,' to show
He should be doubled and not O,
For sure if 'ought' was '*awt*,' then 'nought' on
Earth could the title be but '*Haw*ton,'
H, on the other hand, said he,
In 'cough' and 'trough,' stood next to G,
And like an F was thus looked soft on,
Which made him think it should be '*Hof*ton.'

But G corrected H, and drew
Attention other cases to,
'Tough,' 'rough,' and 'chough' more than 'enough'
To prove O U G H spent '*uff*,'
And growled out in a sort of gruff tone,
They must pronounce the title '*Huff*ton.'
N said emphatically 'No!'
There is D O U G H '*doh*,'
And *though* (look here again) that stuff
At sea, for fun, they nicknamed 'duff,'
They should propose they took a vote on
The question, 'Should it not be *Ho*ton?'
Besides in French 'twould have such force,
A lord was of 'Haut ton,' of course.
Higher and higher contention rose,
From words they almost came to blows,
Till T, as yet who hadn't spoke,
And dearly loved a little joke,
Put in his word and said 'Look there!
"Plough" in this *row* must have its *share*.'
At this atrocious pun each page
Of Johnson whiter turned with rage,
Bailey looked desperately cut up,
And Sheridan completely shut up,
Webster, who is no idle talker,
Made a sign indicating 'Walker'!
While Walker, who had been used badly,
Just shook his dirty dog's-ears sadly.
But as we find in prose or rhyme
A joke made happily in time,
However poor, will often tend
The hottest argument to end,
And smother anger in a laugh,
So T succeeded with his chaff
(Containing, as it did, some wheat)
In calming this fierce verbal heat.
Authorities were all conflicting,
And T there was no contradicting;
P L O U G H was *plow*,
Even 'enough' was called '*enow*,'
And no one who preferred 'enough'
Would dream of saying 'Speed the Pluff!'
So they considered it more wise
With T to make a compromise,
And leave no loop to hang a doubt on

By giving three cheers for 'Lord $\left\{ \begin{matrix} \text{Hough} \\ \text{How} \end{matrix} \right\}$ ton!'

(1863)

SAMUEL LOVER
(1797–1868)

The Quaker's Meeting

A TRAVELLER wended the wilds among,
With a purse of gold and a silver tongue;
His hat it was broad, and all drab were his clothes,
For he hated high colours—except on his nose,
And he met with a lady, the story goes,
   Heigho! *yea* thee and *nay* thee.

The damsel she cast him a merry blink,
And the traveller nothing was loath, I think,
Her merry black eye beamed her bonnet beneath,
And the Quaker, he grinned, for he'd very good teeth,
And he asked: 'Art thee going to ride on the heath?'
   Heigho! *yea* thee and *nay* thee.

'I hope you'll protect me, kind sir,' said the maid,
'As to ride this heath over, I'm sadly afraid;
For robbers, they say, here in numbers abound,
And I wouldn't for anything I should be found,
For, between you and me, I have five hundred pound.'
   Heigho! *yea* thee and *nay* thee.

'If that is thee own, dear,' the Quaker he said,
'I ne'er saw a maiden I sooner would wed;
And I have another five hundred just now,
In the padding that's under my saddle-bow,
And I'll settle it all upon thee, I vow!'
   Heigho! *yea* thee and *nay* thee.

The maiden she smil'd, and her rein she drew,
'Your offer I'll take, but I'll not take you,'
A pistol she held at the Quaker's head—
'Now give me your gold, or I'll give you my lead,
'Tis under the saddle, I think you said.'
   Heigho! *yea* thee and *nay* thee.

The damsel she ripped up the saddle-bow,
And the Quaker was never a quaker till now!
And he saw, by the fair one he wished for a bride,
His purse borne away with a swaggering stride,
And the eye that shamm'd tender, now only defied.
   Heigho! *yea* thee and *nay* thee.

'The spirit doth move me, friend Broadbrim,' quoth she,
'To take all this filthy temptation from thee,
For Mammon deceiveth, and beauty is fleeting,
Accept from thy maiden this right-loving greeting,
For much doth she profit by this Quaker's meeting!
    Heigho! *yea* thee and *nay* thee.

'And hark! jolly Quaker, so rosy and sly,
Have righteousness, more than a wench, in thine eye;
Don't go again peeping girls' bonnets beneath,
Remember the one that you met on the heath,
Her name's Jimmy Barlow, I tell to your teeth.'
    Heigho! *yea* thee and *nay* thee.

'Friend James,' quoth the Quaker, 'pray listen to me,
For thou canst confer a great favour, d'ye see;
The gold thou hast taken is not mine, my friend,
But my master's; and truly on thee I depend
To make it appear I my trust did defend.
    Heigho! *yea* thee and *nay* thee.   .

'So fire a few shots thro' my clothes, here and there,
To make it appear 'twas a desperate affair.'
So Jim he popp'd first through the skirt of his coat,
And then through his collar—quite close to his throat;
'Now one thro' my broadbrim,' quoth Ephraim, 'I vote.'
    Heigho! *yea* thee and *nay* thee.

'I have but a brace,' said bold Jim, 'and they're spent,
And I won't load again for a make-believe rent.'—
'Then!'—said Ephraim, producing his pistols, 'just give
My five hundred pounds back, or, as sure as you live
I'll make of your body a riddle or sieve.'
    Heigho! *yea* thee and *nay* thee.

Jim Barlow was diddled—and, tho' he was game,
He saw Ephraim's pistol so deadly in aim,
That he gave up the gold, and he took to his scrapers,
And when the whole story got into the papers,
They said that '*the thieves were no match for the Quakers.*'
    Heigho! *yea* thee and *nay* thee.

                                        (1860)

OLIVER WENDELL HOLMES
(1809–1894)

Aunt Tabitha

WHATEVER I do, and whatever I say,
Aunt Tabitha tells me that isn't the way;
When *she* was a girl (forty summers ago)
Aunt Tabitha tells me they never did so.

Dear aunt! If I only would take her advice!
But I like my own way, and I find it *so* nice!
And besides, I forget half the things I am told;
But they all will come back to me—when I am old.

If a youth passes by, it may happen, no doubt,
He may chance to look in as I chance to look out;
She would never endure an impertinent stare—
It is *horrid*, she says, and I mustn't sit there.

A walk in the moonlight has pleasures, I own,
But it isn't quite safe to be walking alone;
So I take a lad's arm—just for safety, you know—
But Aunt Tabitha tells me *they* didn't do so.

How wicked we are, and how good they were then!
They kept at arm's length those detestable men;
What an era of virtue she lived in!—But stay—
Were the *men* all such rogues in Aunt Tabitha's day?

If the men *were* so wicked, I'll ask my papa
How he dared to propose to my darling mamma?
Was he like the rest of them? Goodness! Who knows?
And what shall *I* say, if a wretch should propose?

I am thinking if aunt knew so little of sin,
What a wonder Aunt Tabitha's aunt must have been!
And her grand-aunt—it scares me—how shockingly sad
That we girls of to-day are so frightfully bad!

A martyr will save us, and nothing else can;
Let *me* perish—to rescue some wretched young man!
Though when to the altar a victim I go,
Aunt Tabitha'll tell me *she* never did so!

(1871)

William Makepeace Thackeray
(1811–1863)

Little Billee

There were three sailors of Bristol city
Who took a boat and went to sea.
But first with beef and captain's biscuits
And pickled pork they loaded she.

There was gorging Jack and guzzling Jimmy,
And the youngest he was little Billee.
Now when they got as far as the Equator
They'd nothing left but one split pea.

Says gorging Jack to guzzling Jimmy,
'I am extremely hungaree.'
To gorging Jack says guzzling Jimmy,
'We've nothing left, us must eat we.'

Says gorging Jack to guzzling Jimmy,
'With one another we shouldn't agree!
There's little Bill, he's young and tender,
We're old and tough, so let's eat he.

'Oh! Billy, we're going to kill and eat you,
So undo the button of your chemie.'
When Bill received this information
He used his pocket handkerchie.

'First let me say my catechism,
Which my poor mamy taught to me.'
'Make haste, make haste,' says guzzling Jimmy,
While Jack pulled out his snickersnee.

So Billy went up to the maintop gallant mast,
And down he fell on his bended knee.
He scarce had come to the twelfth commandment
When up he jumps. 'There's land I see:

'Jerusalem and Madagascar,
And North and South Amerikee:
There's the British flag a riding at anchor,
With Admiral Napier, K.C.B.'

So when they got aboard of the Admiral's
He hanged fat Jack and flogged Jimmee;
But as for little Bill he made him
The Captain of a Seventy-three.

(1855)

The Willow-tree

I

KNOW ye the willow-tree
   Whose grey leaves quiver,
Whispering gloomily
   To yon pale river;
Lady, at eventide
   Wander not near it,
They say its branches hide
   A sad, lost spirit!

Once to the willow-tree
   A maid came fearful,
Pale seemed her cheek to be,
   Her blue eye tearful;
Soon as she saw the tree,
   Her step moved fleeter,
No one was there—ah me!
   No one to meet her!

Quick beat her heart to hear
   The far bell's chime
Toll from the chapel-tower
   The trysting time:
But the red sun went down
   In golden flame,
And though she looked round,
   Yet no one came!

Presently came the night,
   Sadly to greet her—
Moon in her silver light,
   Stars in their glitter;
Then sank the moon away
   Under the billow,
Still wept the maid alone—
   There by the willow!

Through the long darkness,
   By the stream rolling,
Hour after hour went on
   Tolling and tolling.

Long was the darkness,
    Lonely and stilly;
Shrill came the night-wind,
    Piercing and chilly.

Shrill blew the morning breeze,
    Biting and cold,
Bleak peers the grey dawn
    Over the wold.
Bleak over moor and stream
    Looks the grey dawn,
Grey, with dishevelled hair,
Still stands the willow there—
    THE MAID IS GONE!

Domine, Domine!
    Sing we a litany,—
Sing for poor maiden-hearts broken and weary;
    Domine, Domine!
Sing we a litany,
    Wail we and weep we a wild Miserere!

II

LONG by the willow-trees
    Vainly they sought her,
Wild rang the mother's screams
    O'er the grey water:
'Where is my lovely one?
    Where is my daughter?

'Rouse thee, sir constable—
    Rouse thee and look;
Fisherman, bring your net,
    Boatman your hook.
Beat in the lily-beds,
    Dive in the brook!'

Vainly the constable
    Shouted and called her;
Vainly the fisherman
    Beat the green alder,
Vainly he flung the net,
    Never it hauled her!

Mother beside the fire
    Sat, her nightcap in;
Father, in easy-chair,
    Gloomily napping,
When at the window-sill
    Came a light tapping!

And a pale countenance
  Looked through the casement.
Loud beat the mother's heart,
  Sick with amazement,
And at the vision which
  Came to surprise her,
Shrieked in an agony—
  'Lor'! it's Elizar!'

Yes, 'twas Elizabeth—
  Yes, 'twas their girl;
Pale was her cheek, and her
  Hair out of curl.
'Mother!' the loving one,
  Blushing, exclaimed,
'Let not your innocent
  Lizzy be blamed.

'Yesterday, going to aunt
  Jones's to tea,
Mother, dear mother, I
  Forgot the door-key!
And as the night was cold,
  And the way steep,
Mrs Jones kept me to
  Breakfast and sleep.'

Whether her Pa and Ma
  Fully believed her,
That we shall never know,
  Stern they received her;
And for the work of that
  Cruel, though short, night,
Sent her to bed without
  Tea for a fortnight.

MORAL

Hey diddle diddlety,
  Cat and the Fiddlety,
Maidens of England take caution by she!
  Let love and suicide
  Never tempt you aside,
And always remember to take the door-key.

(1855)

Sorrows of Werther

WERTHER had a love for Charlotte
  Such as words could never utter;
Would you know how first he met her?
  She was cutting bread and butter.

Charlotte was a married lady,
  And a moral man was Werther,
And, for all the wealth of Indies,
  Would do nothing for to hurt her.

So he sighed and pined and ogled,
  And his passion boiled and bubbled,
Till he blew his silly brains out,
  And no more was by it troubled.

Charlotte, having seen his body
  Borne before her on a shutter,
Like a well-conducted person,
  Went on cutting bread and butter.

                    (1855)

EDWARD LEAR

(1812–1888)

The Akond of Swat

WHO or why, or which, or *what*,
    Is the Akond of SWAT?

Is he tall or short, or dark or fair?
Does he sit on a stool or a sofa or chair,
      or SQUAT,
    The Akond of Swat?

Is he wise or foolish, young or old?
Does he drink his soup and his coffee cold,
      or HOT,
    The Akond of Swat?

Does he sing or whistle, jabber or talk,
And when riding abroad does he gallop or walk,
    or TROT,
      The Akond of Swat?

Does he wear a turban, a fez, or a hat?
Does he sleep on a mattress, a bed, or a mat,
    or a COT,
      The Akond of Swat?

When he writes a copy in round-hand size,
Does he cross his T's and finish his I's
    with a DOT,
      The Akond of Swat?

Can he write a letter concisely clear
Without a speck or a smudge or smear
    or BLOT,
      The Akond of Swat?

Do his people like him extremely well?
Or do they, whenever they can, rebel,
    or PLOT,
      At the Akond of Swat?

If he catches them then, either old or young,
Does he have them chopped in pieces or hung,
    or SHOT,
      The Akond of Swat?

Do his people prig in the lanes or park?
Or even at times, when days are dark,
    GAROTTE?
      O the Akond of Swat!

Does he study the wants of his own dominion?
Or doesn't he care for public opinion
    a JOT,
      The Akond of Swat?

To amuse his mind do his people show him
Pictures, or anyone's last new poem,
    or WHAT,
      For the Akond of Swat?

At night if he suddenly screams and wakes,
Do they bring him only a few small cakes,
    or a LOT,
      For the Akond of Swat?

Does he live on turnips, tea, or tripe?
Does he like his shawl to be marked with a stripe,
     or a DOT,
      The Akond of Swat?

Does he like to lie on his back in a boat
Like the lady who lived in that isle remote,
     SHALLOTT,
      The Akond of Swat?

Is he quiet, or always making a fuss?
Is his steward a Swiss or a Swede or a Russ,
     or a SCOT,
      The Akond of Swat?

Does he like to sit by the calm blue wave?
Or to sleep and snore in a dark green cave,
     or a GROTT,
      The Akond of Swat?

Does he drink small beer from a silver jug?
Or a bowl? or a glass? or a cup? or a mug?
     or a POT,
      The Akond of Swat?

Does he beat his wife with a gold-topped pipe,
When she lets the gooseberries grow too ripe,
     or ROT,
      The Akond of Swat?

Does he wear a white tie when he dines with friends,
And tie it neat in a bow with ends,
     or a KNOT,
      The Akond of Swat?

Does he like new cream, and hate mince-pies?
When he looks at the sun does he wink his eyes,
     or NOT,
      The Akond of Swat?

Does he teach his subjects to roast and bake?
Does he sail about on an inland lake,
     in a YACHT,
      The Akond of Swat?

Someone, or nobody, knows, I wot,
Who or which or why or what
     Is the Akond of Swat!

               (1877)

The Dong with a Luminous Nose

WHEN awful darkness and silence reign
Over the great Gromboolian plain,
    Through the long, long wintry nights;
When the angry breakers roar
As they beat on the rocky shore;
    When Storm-clouds brood on the towering heights
Of the Hills of the Chankly Bore:

Then, through the vast and gloomy dark,
There moves what seems a fiery spark,
    A lonely spark with silvery rays
        Piercing the coal-black night—
    A meteor strange and bright—
Hither and thither the vision strays,
    A single lurid light.

Slowly it wanders—pauses, creeps—
Anon it sparkles—flashes and leaps;
And ever as onward it gleaming goes
A light on the Bong-tree stems it throws.
And those who watch at that midnight hour
From Hall or Terrace, or lofty Tower,
Cry, as the wild light passes along—
    'The Dong!—the Dong!
    The wandering Dong through the forest goes!
        The Dong! the Dong!
    The Dong with a luminous Nose!'

        Long years ago
    The Dong was happy and gay,
Till he fell in love with a Jumbly Girl
    Who came to those shores one day.
For the Jumblies came in a Sieve, they did—
Landing at eve near the Zemmery Fidd
    Where the Oblong Oysters grow,
    And the rocks are smooth and grey.
And all the woods and the valleys rang
With the Chorus they daily and nightly sang:
    '*Far and few, far and few,*
        Are the lands where the Jumblies live;
        Their heads are green, and their hands are blue
        And they went to sea in a Sieve.'

Happily, happily passed those days!
　　While the cheerful Jumblies staid;
　　They danced in circlets all night long,
　　To the plaintive pipe of the lively Dong,
　　　In moonlight, shine, or shade.
For day and night he was always there
By the side of the Jumbly Girl so fair,
With her sky-blue hands, and her sea-green hair,
Till the morning came of that hateful day
When the Jumblies sailed in their Sieve away,
And the Dong was left on the cruel shore
Gazing—gazing for evermore—
Ever keeping his weary eyes on
That pea-green sail on the far horizon—
Singing the Jumbly Chorus still
As he sate all day on the grassy hill—
　　　'Far and few, far and few,
　　　Are the lands where the Jumblies live;
　　　Their heads are green, and their hands are blue,
　　　And they went to sea in a Sieve.'

But when the sun was low in the West,
　　The Dong arose and said:
　'What little sense I once possessed
　Has quite gone out of my head!'
And since that day he wanders still
By lake and forest, marsh and hill,
Singing: 'Oh somewhere, in valley or plain
Might I find my Jumbly Girl again!
For ever I'll seek by lake and shore
Till I find my Jumbly Girl once more!'

　　Playing a pipe with silvery squeaks,
　　Since then his Jumbly Girl he seeks,
　　And because by night he could not see,
　　He gathered the bark of the Twangum Tree
　　　On the flowery plain that grows.
　　And he wove him a wondrous Nose—
　　A Nose as strange as a Nose could be!
Of vast proportions and painted red,
And tied with cords to the back of his head.
　—In a hollow rounded space it ended
　With a luminous lamp within suspended
　　All fenced about
　　With a bandage stout
　　　To prevent the wind from blowing it out;
　And with holes all round to send the light,
In gleaming rays on the dismal night.

And now each night, and all night long,
Over those plains still roams the Dong;
And above the wail of the Chimp and Snipe
You may hear the squeak of his plaintive pipe
While ever he seeks, but seeks in vain
To meet with his Jumbly Girl again;
Lonely and wild—all night he goes—
The Dong with a luminous Nose!
And all who watch at the midnight hour,
From Hall or Terrace, or lofty Tower,
Cry, as they trace the Meteor bright,
Moving along through the dreary night,
 'This is the hour when forth he goes,
 The Dong with a luminous Nose!
 Yonder—over the plain he goes;
  He goes!
  He goes;
The Dong with a luminous Nose!'

(1871)

The Cummerbund

AN INDIAN POEM

SHE sate upon her Dobie,
 To watch the Evening Star,
And all the Punkahs as they passed
 Cried: 'My! how fair you are!'
Around her bower, with quivering leaves
 The tall Kamsamahs grew,
And Kitmutgars in wild festoons
 Hung down from Tchokis blue.

Below her home the river rolled
 With soft meloobious sound,
Where golden-finned Chuprassies swam,
 In myriads circling round.
Above, on tallest trees remote,
 Green Ayahs perched alone,
And all night long the Mussak moan'd
 Its melancholy tone.

And where the purple Nullahs threw
 Their branches far and wide—
And silvery Goreewallahs flew
 In silence, side by side—

The little Bheesties' twittering cry
    Rose on the fragrant air,
And oft the angry Jampan howled
    Deep in his hateful lair.

She sate upon her Dobie—
    She heard the Nimmak hum—
When all at once a cry arose:
    'The Cummerbund is come!'
In vain she fled;—with open jaws
    The angry monster followed,
And so (before assistance came),
    That Lady Fair was swallowed.

They sought in vain for even a bone
    Respectfully to bury—
They said: 'Hers was a dreadful fate!'
    (And Echo answered 'Very.')
They nailed her Dobie to the wall,
    Where last her form was seen,
And underneath they wrote these words,
    In yellow, blue, and green:

Beware, ye Fair! Ye Fair, beware!
    Nor sit out late at night—
Lest horrid Cummerbunds should come,
    And swallow you outright.

                                    (1874)

A Sonnet

COLD are the crabs that crawl on yonder hills,
    Cold are the cucumbers that grow beneath,
    And colder still the brazen chops that wreathe
The tedious gloom of philosophic pills!
For when the tardy film of nectar fills
    The ample bowls of demons and of men,
    There lurks the feeble mouse, the homely hen,
And there the porcupine with all her quills.
Yet much remains—to weave a solemn strain
    That lingering sadly—slowly dies away,
    Daily departing with departing day.
A pea green gamut on a distant plain
    When wily walruses in congress meet—
    Such such is life—[the bitter and the sweet].

                              n.d. [1953]

WILLIAM EDMONDSTOUNE AYTOUN
(1813–1865)

The Massacre of the Macpherson

FHAIRSHON swore a feud
  Against the clan M'Tavish;
Marched into their land
  To murder and to rafish;
For he did resolve
  To extirpate the vipers,
With four-and-twenty men
  And five-and-thirty pipers.

But when he had gone
  Half-way down Strath Canaan,
Of his fighting tail
  Just three were remainin'.
They were all he had
  To back him in ta battle;
All the rest had gone
  Off, to drive ta cattle.

'Fery coot!' cried Fhairshon,
  'So my clan disgraced is;
Lads, we'll need to fight
  Before we touch the peasties.
Here's Mhic-Mac-Methusaleh
  Coming wi' his fassals,
Gillies seventy-three,
  And sixty Dhuinéwassails!'

'Coot tay to you, sir;
  Are you not ta Fhairshon?
Was you coming here
  To fisit any person?
You are a plackguard, sir!
  It is now six hundred
Coot long years, and more,
  Since my glen was plundered.'

'Fat is tat you say?
    Dare you cock your peaver?
I will teach you, sir,
    Fat is coot pehaviour!
You shall not exist
    For another day more;
I will shoot you, sir,
    Or stap you with my claymore!'

'I am fery glad
    To learn what you mention,
Since I can prevent
    Any such intention.'
So Mhic-Mac-Methusaleh
    Gave some war-like howls,
Trew his skhian-dhu,
    An' stuck it in his powels.

In this fery way
    Tied ta faliant Fhairshon,
Who was always thought
    A superior person.
Fhairshon had a son
    Who married Noah's daughter,
And nearly spoiled ta Flood,
    By trinking up ta water.

Which he would have done,
    I at least pelieve it,
Had ta mixture peen
    Only half Glenlivet.
This is all my tale:
    Sirs, I hope 'tis new t'ye!
Here's your fery good healths,
    And tamn ta whusky duty!

(1853)

THEODORE MARTIN
(1816–1909)

The Cry of the Lovelorn

COMRADES, you may pass the rosy.   With permission of the chair,
I shall leave you for a little, for I'd like to take the air.

Whether 'twas the sauce at dinner, or that glass of ginger-beer,
Or these strong cheroots, I know not, but I feel a little queer.

Let me go.   Nay, Chuckster, blow me, 'pon my soul, this is too bad!
When you want me, ask the waiter; he knows where I'm to be had.

Whew! this is a great relief now!   Let me but undo my stock;
Resting here beneath the porch, my nerves will steady like a rock.

In my ears I hear the singing of a lot of favourite tunes—
Bless my heart, how very odd!   Why, surely there's a brace of moons!

See! the stars! how bright they twinkle, winking with a frosty glare,
Like my faithless cousin Amy when she drove me to despair.

Oh, my cousin, spider-hearted!   Oh, my Amy!   No, confound it!
I must wear the mournful willow—all around my heart I've bound it.

Falser than the bank of fancy, frailer than a shilling glove,
Puppet to a father's anger, minion to a nabob's love.

Is it well to wish thee happy?   Having known me could you ever
Stoop to marry half a heart, and little more than half a liver?

Happy!   Damme!   Thou shalt lower to his level day by day,
Changing from the best of china to the commonest of clay.

As the husband is, the wife is—he is stomach-plagued and old;
And his curry soups will make thy cheek the colour of his gold.

When his feeble love is sated, he will hold thee surely then
Something lower than his hookah—something less than his
    cayenne.

What is this? His eyes are pinky. Was't the claret? Oh, no, no—
Bless your soul! it was the salmon—salmon always makes him so.

Take him to thy dainty chamber—soothe him with thy lightest
    fancies;
He will understand thee, won't he?—pay thee with a lover's
    glances?

Louder than the loudest trumpet, harsh as harshest ophicleide,
Nasal respirations answer the endearments of his bride.

Sweet response, delightful music! Gaze upon thy noble charge,
Till the spirit fill thy bosom that inspired the meek Laffarge.

Better thou wert dead before me, better, better that I stood,
Looking on thy murdered body, like the injured Daniel Good!

Better thou and I were lying, cold and timber-stiff and dead,
With a pan of burning charcoal underneath our nuptial bed!

Cursed be the Bank of England's notes, that tempt the soul to sin!
Cursed be the want of acres—doubly cursed the want of tin!

Cursed be the marriage-contract, that enslaved thy soul to greed!
Cursed be the sallow lawyer, that prepared and drew the deed!

Cursed be his foul apprentice, who the loathsome fees did earn!
Cursed be the clerk and parson—cursed be the whole concern!

   .   .   .   .   .

Oh, 'tis well that I should bluster—much I'm like to make of that;
Better comfort have I found in singing 'All around my Hat.'

But that song, so wildly plaintive, palls upon my British ears.
'Twill not do to pine for ever—I am getting up in years.

Can't I turn the honest penny, scribbling for the weekly press,
And in writing Sunday libels drown my private wretchedness?

Oh, to feel the wild pulsation that in manhood's dawn I knew,
When my days were all before me—and my years were twenty-
    two!

When I smoked my independent pipe along the Quadrant wide,
With the many larks of London flaring up on every side;

When I went the pace so wildly, caring little what might come;
Coffee-milling care and sorrow, with a nose-adapted thumb.

Felt the exquisite enjoyment, tossing nightly off, oh heavens!
Brandies at the Cider Cellars, kidneys smoking hot at Evans'!

Or in the Adelphi sitting, half in rapture, half in tears,
Saw the glorious melodrama conjure up the shades of years!

Saw Jack Sheppard, noble stripling, act his wondrous feats
again,
Snapping Newgate's bars of iron, like an infant's daisy chain.

Might was right, and all the terrors, which had held the world
in awe,
Were despised, and prigging prospered, spite of Laurie, spite
of law.

In such scenes as these I triumphed, ere my passions' edge was
rusted,
And my cousin's cold refusal left me very much disgusted!

Since, my heart is sere and withered, and I do not care a curse,
Whether worse shall be the better, or the better be the worse.

Hark! my merry comrades call me, bawling for another jorum;
They would mock me in derision, should I thus appear before
'em.

Womankind no more shall vex me, such at least as go arrayed
In the most expensive satins and the newest silk brocade.

I'll to Afric, lion-haunted, where the giant forest yields
Rarer robes and finer tissue than are sold at Spitalfields.

Or to burst all chains of habit, flinging habit's self aside,
I shall walk the tangled jungle in mankind's primeval pride;

Feeding on the luscious berries and the rich cassava root,
Lots of dates, and lots of guavas, clusters of forbidden fruit.

Never comes the trader thither, never o'er the purple main
Sounds the oath of British commerce, or the accent of Cockaigne.

There, methinks, would be enjoyment, where no envious rule
prevents;
Sink the steamboats! cuss the railways! rot, O rot the Three
per Cents!

There the passions, cramped no longer, shall have space to
breathe, my cousin!
I will wed some savage woman—nay, I'll wed at least a dozen.

There I'll rear my young mulattos, as no Bond Street brats are
reared:
They shall dive for alligators, catch the wild goats by the beard—

Whistle to the cockatoos, and mock the hairy-faced baboon,
Worship mighty Mumbo Jumbo in the Mountains of the Moon.

I, myself, in far Timbuctoo, Leopard's blood will daily quaff,
Ride a-tiger-hunting, mounted on a thoroughbred giraffe.

Fiercely shall I shout the war-whoop, as some sullen stream he
crosses,
Startling from their noonday slumbers iron-bound rhinoceroses.

Fool! again the dream, the fancy! But I know my words are
mad,
For I hold the grey barbarian lower than the Christian cad.

I the swell—the city dandy! I to seek such horrid places—
I to haunt with squalid Negroes, blubber-lips and monkey-faces!

I to wed with Coromantees! I, who managed—very near—
To secure the heart and fortune of the widow Shillibeer!

Stuff and nonsense! let me never fling a single chance away;
Maids, ere now, I know, have loved me, and another maiden
may.

Morning Post (*The Times* won't trust me), help me as I know
you can;
I will pen an advertisement—that's a never-failing plan.

'WANTED—by a bard, in wedlock, some young interesting
woman:
Looks are not so much an object, if the shiners be forthcoming!

'Hymen's chains the advertiser vows shall be but silken fetters;
Please address to A. T. Chelsea. N.B.—You must pay the
letters.'

That's the sort of thing to do it. Now I'll go and taste the
balmy—
Rest thee with thy yellow nabob, spider-hearted Cousin Amy!

(1853)

SHIRLEY BROOKS
(1816–1874)

The Philosopher and her Father

A SOUND came booming through the air---
  'What is that sound?' quoth I.
My blue-eyed pet, with golden hair,
  Made answer, presently,
'Papa, you know it very well—
That sound—it was Saint Pancras Bell.'

'My own Louise, put down that cat,
  And come and stand by me;
I'm sad to hear you talk like that,
  Where's your philosophy?
That sound—attend to what I tell—
That was *not* Saint Pancras Bell.

'Sound is the name the sage selects
  For the concluding term
Of a long series of effects,
  Of which the blow's the germ.
The following brief analysis
Shows the interpolations, Miss.

'The blow which, when the clapper slips
  Falls on your friend, the Bell,
Changes its circle to ellipse,
  (A word you'd better spell)
And then comes elasticity,
Restoring what it used to be.

'Nay, making it a little more,
  The circle shifts about,
As much as it shrunk in before
  The Bell, you see, swells out;
And so a new ellipse is made.
(You're not attending, I'm afraid.)

'This change of form disturbs the air,
  Which in its turn behaves
In like elastic fashion there,
  Creating waves on waves;
These press each other onward, dear,
Until the outmost finds your ear.'

'And then, papa, I hear the sound,
  Exactly what I said;
You 're only talking round and round,
  Just to confuse my head.
All that you say about the Bell
My Uncle George would call a "sell."'

'Not so, my child, my child, not so,
  Sweet image of your sire!
A long way farther we must go
  Before it's time to tire;
This wondrous, wandering wave, or tide,
Has only reached your ear's outside.

'Within that ear the surgeons find
  A *tympanum*, or drum,
Which has a little bone behind—
  Malleus it's called by some;
But those not proud of Latin Grammar,
Humbly translate it as the hammer.

'The Wave's vibrations this transmits,
  On to the *incus* bone,
(*Incus* means anvil, which it hits,)
  And this transfers the tone
To the small *os, orbiculare*,
The tiniest bone that people carry.

'The *stapes* next—the name recalls
  A stirrup's form, my daughter—
Joins three half-circular canals,
  Each fill'd with limpid water;
Their curious lining, you 'll observe,
Made of the auditory nerve.

'This vibrates next—and then we find
  The mystic work is crown'd,
For there my daughter's gentle mind
  First recognizes sound.
See what a host of causes swell
To make up what you call "the Bell."'

Awhile she paused, my bright Louise,
  And ponder'd on the case;
Then, settling that he meant to tease,
  She slapp'd her father's face,
'You bad old man to sit and tell
Such gibberybosh about a Bell!'

(1875)

JAMES THOMAS FIELDS
(1817–1881)

The Owl-Critic

'WHO stuffed that white owl?'   No one spoke in the shop.
The barber was busy, and he couldn't stop;
The customers, waiting their turns, were all reading
The *Daily*, the *Herald*, the *Post*, little heeding
The young man who blurted out such a blunt question;
No one raised a head, or even made a suggestion;
   And the barber kept on shaving.

'Don't you see, Mr Brown,'
Cried the youth, with a frown,
'How wrong the whole thing is,
How preposterous each wing is,
How flattened the head is, how jammed down the neck is—
In short, the whole owl, what an ignorant wreck 'tis!
I make no apology;
I've learned owl-eology.

'I've passed days and nights in a hundred collections,
And cannot be blinded to any deflections
Arising from unskilful fingers that fail
To stuff a bird right, from his beak to his tail.
Mister Brown!   Mister Brown!
Do take that bird down,
Or you'll soon be the laughing-stock all over town!'
   And the barber kept on shaving.

'I've studied owls,
And other night-fowls,
And I tell you
What I know to be true;
An owl cannot roost
With his limbs so unloosed;
No owl in this world
Ever had his claws curled,
Ever had his legs slanted,
Ever had his bill canted,
Ever had his neck screwed
Into that attitude.
He can't do it, because
'Tis against all bird-laws.

'Anatomy teaches,
Ornithology preaches,
An owl has a toe
That can't turn out so!
I've made the white owl my study for years,
And to see such a job almost moves me to tears!
Mr Brown, I'm amazed
You should be so gone crazed
As to put up a bird
In that posture absurd!
To look at that owl really brings on a dizziness;
The man who stuffed him don't half know his business!'
    And the barber kept on shaving.

'Examine those eyes.
I'm filled with surprise
Taxidermists should pass
Off on you such poor glass;
So unnatural they seem
They'd make Audubon scream,
And John Burroughs laugh
To encounter such chaff.
Do take that bird down;
Have him stuffed again, Brown!'
    And the barber kept on shaving.

'With some sawdust and bark
I could stuff in the dark
An owl better than that.
I could make an old hat
Look more like an owl
Than that horrid fowl,
Stuck up there so stiff like a side of coarse leather.
In fact, about him there's not one natural feather.'

Just then, with a wink and a sly normal lurch,
The owl, very gravely, got down from his perch,
Walked round, and regarded his fault-finding critic
(Who thought he was stuffed) with a glance analytic,
And then fairly hooted, as if he should say:
'Your learning's at fault this time, anyway;
Don't waste it again on a live bird, I pray;
I'm an owl; you're another.   Sir Critic, good day!'
    And the barber kept on shaving.

                                                    (1881)

On a Watchman asleep at Midnight

How sleep the brave who sink to rest,
By all the city rascals blest!
When Night, with snowy fingers cold,
Returns to freeze the watery mould,
She there shall meet a sounder sod,
Than Fancy's Feet have ever trod.

By fire-y hands our knell is rung,
By forms unseen our locks are sprung;
There burglars come—black, white, and grey—
To bless the steps that wrap their clay:
While watchmen do awhile repair,
And dwell, like sleeping hermits, there.

(1881)

FREDERICK LOCKER-LAMPSON

(1821–1895)

The Jester's Plea

THE World's a sorry wench, akin
    To all that's frail and frightful:
The World's as ugly—ay, as Sin,
    And nearly as delightful!
The World's a merry world (*pro tem.*),
    And some are gay, and therefore
It pleases them, but some condemn
    The World they do not care for.

The World's an ugly world.   Offend
    Good people, how they wrangle!
The manners that they never mend,
    The characters they mangle!
They eat, and drink, and scheme, and plod,
    And go to church on Sunday;
And many are afraid of God—
    And more of *Mrs Grundy*.

The time for Pen and Sword was when
   'My ladye fayre,' for pity
Could tend her wounded knight, and then
   Be tender at his ditty.
Some ladies now make pretty songs,
   And some make pretty nurses:
Some men are great at righting wrongs—
   And some at writing verses.

I wish we better understood
   The tax that poets levy!
I know the Muse is *goody good*,
   I think she's rather heavy:
She now compounds for winning ways
   By morals of the sternest,
Methinks the lays of nowadays
   Are painfully in earnest.

When Wisdom halts, I humbly try
   To make the most of Folly:
If Pallas be unwilling, I
   Prefer to flirt with Polly;
To quit the goddess for the maid
   Seems low in lofty musers;
But Pallas is a lofty jade—
   And beggars can't be choosers.

I do not wish to see the slaves
   Of party-stirring passion,
Or psalms quite superseding staves,
   Or piety 'the fashion.'
I bless the hearts where pity glows,
   Who, here together banded,
Are holding out a hand to those
   That wait so empty-handed!

A righteous Work.   My masters! may
   A Jester by confession,
Scarce noticed join, half sad, half gay,
   The close of your procession?
The motley here seems out of place
   With graver robes to mingle,
But if one tear bedews his face,
   Forgive the bells their jingle.

                      (1862)

On an Old Muff

TIME has a magic wand!
What is it meets my hand,
Moth-eaten, mouldy, and
    Cover'd with fluff?
Faded, and stiff, and scant;
Can it be? no, it can't—
Yes—I declare, it's Aunt
    Prudence's Muff!

Years ago, twenty-three,
Old Uncle Barnaby
Gave it to Aunty P.
    Laughing and teasing—
'Pru., of the breezy curls,
Whisper those solemn churls,
What holds a pretty girl's
    Hand without squeezing?'

Uncle was then a lad
Gay, but, I grieve to add,
Sinful; if smoking bad
    Baccy's a vice:
Glossy was then this mink
Muff, lined with pretty pink
Satin, which maidens think
    'Awfully nice!'

I seem to see again
Aunt in her hood and train,
Glide, with a sweet disdain,
    Gravely to Meeting:
Psalm-book, and kerchief new,
Peep'd from the Muff of Pru.;
Young men, and pious too,
    Giving her greeting.

Sweetly her Sabbath sped
Then; from this Muff, it's said,
Tracts she distributed:—
    Converts (till Monday!)
Lured by the grace they lack'd,
Follow'd her.   One, in fact,
Ask'd for—and got his tract
    Twice of a Sunday!

Love has a potent spell;
Soon this bold ne'er-do-well,
Aunt's too susceptible
    Heart undermining,
Slipt, so the scandal runs,
Notes in the pretty nun's
Muff, triple-corner'd ones,
    Pink as its lining.

Worse follow'd, soon the jade
Fled (to oblige her blade!)
Whilst her friends thought that they'd
    Lock'd her up tightly:
After such shocking games
Aunt is of wedded dames
Gayest, and now her name's
    Mrs Golightly.

In female conduct flaw
Sadder I never saw,
Faith still I've in the law
    Of compensation.
Once Uncle went astray,
Smoked, joked, and swore away,
Sworn by he's now, by a
    Large congregation.

Changed is the Child of Sin,
Now he's (he once was thin)
Grave, with a double chin—
    Blest be his fat form!
Changed is the garb he wore,
Preacher was never more
Prized than is Uncle for
    Pulpit or platform.

If all's as best befits
Mortals of slender wits,
Then beg the Muff and its
    Fair Owner pardon:
All's for the best, indeed
Such is *my* simple creed,
Still I must go and weed
    Hard in my garden.

(1865)

An Old Buffer

'A KNOCK-ME-DOWN sermon, and worthy of Birch,'
Says I to my wife, as we toddle from church;
'Convincing, indeed,' is the lady's remark;
'How logical, too, on the size of the Ark!'
Then Blossom cut in, without begging our pardons,
'Pa, was it as big as the 'Logical Gardens?'

'Miss Blossom,' said I, to my dearest of dearies,
'Papa disapproves of nonsensical queries;
The Ark was an Ark, and had people to build it,
Enough that we read Noah built it and fill'd it:
Mamma does not ask how he caught his opossums.'
Said she: 'That remark is as foolish as Blossom's.'

Thus talking and walking the time is beguiled
By my orthodox wife and my sceptical child;
I act as their *buffer*, whenever I can,
And you see I'm of use as a family-man.
I parry their blows, and I've plenty to do—
I think that the child's are the worst of the two!

My wife has a healthy aversion for sceptics,
She vows that they're bad when they're only dyspeptics!
May Blossom prove neither the one nor the other,
But do what she's bid by her excellent mother.
She thinks I'm a Solon; perhaps, if I huff her,
She'll think I'm a—something that's denser and tougher!

MAMMA *loquitur*

'If Blossom's a sceptic, or saucy, I'll search,
And I'll find her a wholesome corrective in Birch.'

(1870)

ELIZABETH ANNA HART

(1822–*c*.1886)

Mother Tabbyskins

SITTING at a window
In her cloak and hat,
I saw Mother Tabbyskins,
The *real* old cat!

Very old, very old,
Crumplety and lame;
Teaching kittens how to scold—
Is it not a shame?

Kittens in the garden
Looking in her face,
Learning how to spit and swear—
Oh, what a disgrace!
Very wrong, very wrong,
Very wrong, and bad;
Such a subject for our song,
Makes us all too sad.

Old Mother Tabbyskins,
Sticking out her head,
Gave a howl, and then a yowl,
Hobbled off to bed.
Very sick, very sick,
Very savage, too;
Pray send for a doctor quick—
Any one will do!

Doctor Mouse came creeping,
Creeping to her bed;
Lanced her gums and felt her pulse,
Whispered she was dead.
Very sly, very sly,
The *real* old cat
Open kept her weather eye—
Mouse! beware of that!

Old Mother Tabbyskins,
Saying 'Serves him right,'
Gobbled up the doctor, with
Infinite delight.
Very fast, very fast,
Very pleasant, too—
'What a pity it can't last!
Bring another, do!'

Doctor Dog comes running,
Just to see her begs;
Round his neck a comforter,
Trousers on his legs.
Very grand, very grand—
Golden-headed cane
Swinging gaily from his hand,
Mischief in his brain!

'Dear Mother Tabbyskins,
  And how are you now?
Let me feel your pulse—so, so;
  Show your tongue—bow, wow.
    'Very ill, very ill,
      Please attempt to purr;
    Will you take a draught or pill?
      Which do you prefer?'

Ah, Mother Tabbyskins,
  Who is now afraid?
Of poor little Doctor Mouse
  You a mouthful made.
    Very nice, very nice
      Little doctor he,
    But for Doctor Dog's advice
      You must pay the fee.

Doctor Dog comes nearer,
  Says she must be bled;
I heard Mother Tabbyskins
  Screaming in her bed.
    Very near, very near,
      Scuffling out and in;
    Doctor Dog looks full and queer—
      Where is Tabbyskin?

I will tell the Moral
  Without any fuss:
Those who lead the young astray
  Always suffer thus.
    Very nice, very nice,
      Let our conduct be;
    For all doctors are not mice,
      Some are dogs, you see!

(1868)

Sweeping the Skies

BLUE are the beautiful skies!
  Bright each particular star!
Children, who see with such innocent eyes,
  Ask what the pretty things are.

One little Darling is told,
  If she can give them a tap,
Plates of sky-china, embossed with star-gold,
  Softly will slide to her lap.

All in a flutter at this,
　　Eager such treasures to win,
Light little laughters, inviting a kiss,
　　Dimple her delicate chin.

Darling has gathered a rose
　　(Scarce can her hand get so high),
Stands on the tips of her little fat toes,
　　Thinks she can reach to the sky.

Seizes on grandpapa's stick
　　(Oft she bestrode it in play),
Jumps on a garden-chair, holds it up quick,
　　Lest they should snatch her away.

Darling is dumb with despair:
　　What can a little child do?
With the bad stick she can beat the bad chair,
　　Break the bad rose-bud in two.

Up to the attic she crept,
　　Mounted the laddery stair,
Out on the roof in a rapture she stept,
　　Brandished a broom in the air!

　　　·　　　·　　　·

Searching through house and through wood,
　　Calling and calling again,
'Darling! O naughty! O Darling! be good!'
　　Searching and calling in vain.

One, from the others aloof
　　Standing, bewildered in gloom,
Sees little Darling step out on the roof,
　　Sweeping the skies with Ann's broom,

Dares not to speak or to move,
　　Fears lest a breath should betray;
Wonderful silence of wonderful love,
　　Keeping his anguish at bay.

Sweet little figure in white
　　Perched on the roof all alone,
Sweeping the skies with a scream of delight,
　　Begging a star for her own.

Softly he enters the house,
　　Softly ascendeth the stair,
Steals up the ladder as still as a mouse:
　　Oh, is it hope or despair?

Through the trap-window he peeps,
  Peeps at the dear little maid;
Through the trap-window a sturdy arm creeps,
  Creeps like a creature afraid.

Darling is sweeping the skies,
  Eager for platters of blue;
Gazing aloft with her heart in her eyes,
  Swaying and tottering too.

On, under steady command,
  On creeps that desperate arm,
Clutches a fat little leg in its hand,
  Snatches its Darling from harm.

What though a dusty old broom
  Brushes his face and his eyes?
What though his Darling, in resolute gloom,
  Sweeps *him* instead of the skies?

Gratitude—rapture—delight—
  Prayer from a satisfied heart;
Tears he would hide from her wondering sight,
  But which she sees as they start.

Out come her lips for a kiss,
  Thinking he cries from the pain;
Sweet eager promises bind her to this—
  Never to sweep *him* again.

Kissing his face in distress,
  Feeling she merits reproof;
Utterly hopeless to make her confess
  Girls should not climb on the roof;

What can they do in this strait?
  How keep her down from the skies?
Lock the trap-windows, and patiently wait
  Till the wee Darling grows wise.

(1869)

WILLIAM BRIGHTY RANDS

(1823–1882)

Lilliput Levee

WHERE does Pinafore Palace stand?
Right in the middle of Lilliput-land!
There the Queen eats bread-and-honey,
There the King counts up his money!

Oh, the Glorious Revolution!
Oh, the Provisional Constitution!
Now that the Children, clever bold folks,
Have turned the tables upon the Old Folks!

Easily the thing was done,
For the Children were more than two to one;
Brave as lions, quick as foxes,
With hoards of wealth in their money-boxes!

They seized the keys, they patrolled the street,
They drove the policeman off his beat,
They built barricades, they stationed sentries—
You must give the word, when you come to the entries!

They dressed themselves in the Riflemen's clothes,
They had pea-shooters, they had arrows and bows,
So as to put resistance down—
Order reigns in Lilliput-town!

They made the baker bake hot rolls,
They made the wharfinger send in coals,
They made the butcher kill the calf,
They cut the telegraph-wires in half.

They went to the chemist's, and with their feet
They kicked the physic all down the street;
They went to the schoolroom and tore the books,
They munched the puffs at the pastry-cook's.

They sucked the jam, they lost the spoons,
They sent up several fire-balloons,
They let off crackers, they burnt a guy,
They piled a bonfire ever so high.

They offered a prize for the laziest boy,
And one for the most Magnificent toy,
They split or burnt the canes off-hand,
They made new laws in Lilliput-land.

Never do to-day what you can
Put off till to-morrow, one of them ran;
Late to bed and late to rise,
Was another law which they did devise.

They passed a law to have always plenty
Of beautiful things: we shall mention twenty:
A magic lantern for all to see,
Rabbits to keep, and a Christmas-tree.

A boat, a house that went on wheels,
An organ to grind, and sherry at meals,
Drums and wheelbarrows, Roman candles,
Whips with whistles let into the handles,

A real live giant, a roc to fly,
A goat to tease, a copper to sky,
A garret of apples, a box of paints,
A saw and a hammer and no complaints.

Nail up the door, slide down the stairs,
Saw off the legs of the parlour-chairs—
That was the way in Lilliput-land,
The Children having the upper hand.

They made the Old Folks come to school,
All in pinafores—that was the rule—
Saying, *Eener-deener-diner-duss,*
Kattler-wheeler-whiler-wuss;

They made them learn all sorts of things
That nobody liked. They had catechizings;
They kept them in, they sent them down
In class, in school, in Lilliput-town.

Oh but they gave them tit-for-tat!
Thick bread and butter, and all that;
Stick-jaw pudding that tires your chin
With the marmalade spread ever so thin!

They governed the clock in Lilliput-land,
They altered the hour or the minute-hand,
They made the day fast, they made the day slow,
Just as they wished the time to go.

They never waited for king or for cat;
They never wiped their shoes on the mat;
Their joy was great! their joy was greater;
They rode in the baby's perambulator!

There was a Levee in Lilliput-town,
At Pinafore Palace.　Smith and Brown,
Jones and Robinson had to attend—
All to whom they cards did send.

Everyone rode in a cab to the door;
Everyone came in a pinafore;
Lady and gentleman, rat-tat-tat,
Loud knock, proud knock, opera hat!

The place was covered with silver and gold,
The place was as full as it ever could hold;
The ladies kissed her Majesty's hand;
Such was the custom in Lilliput-land.

．　　　．　　　．　　　．

(1864)

A Fishing Song

THERE was a boy whose name was Phinn,
　　And he was fond of fishing;
His father could not keep him in,
　　Nor all his mother's wishing.

His life's ambition was to land
　　A fish of several pound weight;
The chief thing he could understand,
　　Was hooks, or worms for ground-bait.

The worms crept out, the worms crept in,
　　From every crack and pocket;
He had a worm-box made of tin,
　　With proper worms to stock it.

He gave his mind to breeding worms
　　As much as he was able;
His sister spoke in angry terms
　　To see them on the table.

You found one walking up the stairs,
　　You found one in a bonnet,
Or, in the bedroom, unawares,
　　You set your foot upon it.

Worms, worms, worms for bait!
    Roach, and dace, and gudgeon!
With rod and line to Twickenham Ait
    To-morrow he is trudging!

O worms and fishes day and night!
    Such was his sole ambition;
I'm glad to think you are not quite
    So very fond of fishing!

                                            (1864)

CHARLES GODFREY LELAND

(1824–1903)

Hans Breitmann's Barty

HANS BREITMANN gife a barty;
    Dey had biano-blayin';
I felled in lofe mit a Merican frau,
    Her name vas Madilda Yane.
She hat haar as prown ash a pretzel,
    Her eyes vas himmel-plue,
Und vhen dey looket indo mine,
    Dey shplit mine heart in dwo.

Hans Breitmann gife a barty,
    I vent dere you'll pe pound;
I valtzet mit Madilda Yane,
    Und vent shpinnen' round und round.
De pootiest Fraulein in de house,
    She vayed 'pout dwo hoondred pound,
Und efery dime she gife a shoomp
    She make de vindows sound.

Hans Breitmann gife a barty,
    I dells you it cost him dear;
Dey rolled in more ash sefen kecks
    Of foost-rate lager beer.
Und vhenefer dey knocks de shpicket in
    De Deutschers gifes a cheer:
I dinks dat so vine a barty
    Nefer coom to a het dis year.

Hans Breitmann gife a barty;
  Dere all vas Souse and Brouse,
Vhen de sooper comed in, de gompany
  Did make demselfs to house;
Dey ate das Brot and Gensy broost,
  De Bratwurst and Braten vine,
Und vash der Abendessen down
  Mit four parrels of Neckarwein.

Hans Breitmann gife a barty;
  Ve all cot troonk ash bigs.
I poot mine mout' to a parrel of beer,
  Und emptied it oop mit a schwigs;
Und den I gissed Madilda Yane,
  Und she shlog me on de kop,
Und de gompany vighted mit daple-lecks
  Dill de coonshtable made oos shtop.

Hans Breitmann gife a barty—
  Vhere ish dat barty now?
Vhere ish de lofely golden cloud
  Dat float on de moundain's prow?
Vhere ish de himmelstrahlende stern—
  De shtar of de shpirit's light?
All goned afay mit de lager beer—
  Afay in de ewigkeit!

                                              (1857)

Ballad by Hans Breitmann

DER noble Ritter Hugo
  Von Schwillensaufenstein,
Rode out mit shper and helmet,
  Und he coom to de panks of de Rhine.

Und opp dere rose a meermaid,
  Vot hadn't got nodings on,
Und she say: 'Oh, Ritter Hugo,
  Vhere you goes mit yourself alone?'

And he says: 'I rides in de creenwood,
  Mit helmet und mit shpeer,
Till I cooms into em Gasthaus,
  Und dere I trinks some beer.'

Und den outshpoke de maiden
   Vot hadn't got nodings on:
'I tont dink mooch of beoplesh
   Dat goes mit demselfs alone.

'You'd petter coom down in de wasser,
   Vhere dere's heaps of dings to see,
Und hafe a shplendid tinner
   Und drafel along mit me.

'Dere you sees de fisch a schwimmin',
   Und you catches dem efery von'—
So sang dis wasser maiden
   Vot hadn't got nodings on.

'Dere ish drunks all full mit money
   In ships dat vent down of old;
Und you helpsh yourself, by dunder!
   To shimmerin' crowns of gold.

'Shoost look at dese shpoons und vatches!
   Shoost see dese diamant rings!
Coom down and fill your bockets,
   Und I'll giss you like efery dings.

'Vot you vantsh mit your schnapps und lager?
   Coom down into der Rhine!
Der ish pottles der Kaiser Charlemagne
   Vonce filled mit gold-red wine!'

Dat fetched him—he shtood all shpell pound;
   She pooled his coat-tails down,
She drawed him oonder der wasser,
   De maiden mit nodings on.

                      (1869)

MORTIMER COLLINS
(1827–1876)

Salad—After Tennyson

KING ARTHUR, growing very tired indeed
Of wild Tintagel, now that Lancelot
Had gone to Jersey or to Jericho,
And there was nobody to make a rhyme,
And Cornish girls were christened Jennifer,
And the Round Table had grown rickety,
Said unto Merlin (who had been asleep
For a few centuries in Broceliande,
But woke, and had a bath, and felt refreshed):
'What shall I do to pull myself together?'
Quoth Merlin: 'Salad is the very thing,
And you can get it at the Cheshire Cheese.'
King Arthur went there: *verily*, I believe
That he has dined there every day since then.
Have you not marked the portly gentleman
In his cool corner, with his plate of greens?
The great knight Lancelot prefers the Cock,
Where port is excellent (in pints), and waiters
Are portlier than kings, and steaks are tender,
And poets have been known to meditate . . .
Ox-fed orating ominous octastichs.

(1872)

CHARLES STUART CALVERLEY
(1831–1884)

Striking

IT WAS a railway passenger,
    And he lept out jauntilie.
'Now up and bear, thou stout portèr,
    My two chattèls to me.

'Bring hither, bring hither my bag so red,
    And portmanteau so brown:
(They lie in the van, for a trusty man
    He labelled them London town.)

'And fetch me eke a cabman bold,
    That I may be his fare, his fare;
And he shall have a good shilling,
If by two of the clock he do me bring
    To the Terminus, Euston Square.'

'Now—so to thee the saints alway,
    Good gentleman, give luck—
As never a cab may I find this day,
    For the cabman wights have struck:
And now, I wis, at the Red Post Inn,
    Or else at the Dog and Duck,
Or at Unicorn Blue, or at Green Griffin,
The nut-brown ale and the fine old gin
    Right pleasantly they do suck.'

'Now rede me aright, thou stout portèr,
    What were it best that I should do:
For woe is me, an' I reach not there
    Or ever the clock strike two.'

'I have a son, a lytel son;
    Fleet is his foot as the wild roebuck's:
Give him a shilling, and eke a brown,
And he shall carry thy fardels down
To Euston, or half over London town,
    On one of the station trucks.'

Then forth in a hurry did they twain fare,
The gent, and the son of the stout portèr,
Who fled like an arrow, nor turned a hair,
    Through all the mire and muck:
'A ticket, a ticket, sir clerk, I pray:
For by two of the clock must I needs away.'
'That may hardly be,' the clerk did say,
    'For indeed—the clocks have struck.'

(1862)

Beer

IN those old days which poets say were golden—
    (Perhaps they laid the gilding on themselves:
And, if they did, I'm all the more beholden
    To those brown dwellers in my dusty shelves,
Who talk to me 'in language quaint and olden'
    Of gods and demigods and fauns and elves,
Pan with his pipes, and Bacchus with his leopards,
And staid young goddesses who flirt with shepherds:)

In those old days, the Nymph called Etiquette
  (Appalling thought to dwell on) was not born.
They had their May, but no Mayfair as yet,
  No fashions varying as the hues of morn.
Just as they pleased they dressed and drank and ate,
  Sang hymns to Ceres (their John Barleycorn)
And danced unchaperoned, and laughed unchecked,
And were no doubt extremely incorrect.

Yet do I think their theory was pleasant:
  And oft, I own, my 'wayward fancy roams'
Back to those times, so different from the present;
  When no one smoked cigars, nor gave At-homes,
Nor smote, a billiard-ball, nor winged a pheasant,
  Nor 'did' her hair by means of long-tailed combs,
Nor migrated to Brighton once a year,
Nor—most astonishing of all—drank Beer.

No, they did not drink Beer, 'which brings me to'
  (As Gilpin said) 'the middle of my song.'
Not that 'the middle' is precisely true,
  Or else I should not tax your patience long:
If I had said 'beginning,' it might do;
  But I have a dislike to quoting wrong:
I was unlucky—sinned against, not sinning—
When Cowper wrote down 'middle' for 'beginning.'

So to proceed. That abstinence from Malt
  Has always struck me as extremely curious.
The Greek mind must have had some vital fault,
  That they should stick to liquors so injurious—
(Wine, water, tempered p'raps with Attic salt)—
  And not at once invent that mild, luxurious,
And artful beverage, Beer. How the digestion
Got on without it, is a startling question.

Had they digestions? and an actual body
  Such as dyspepsia might make attacks on?
Were they abstract ideas (like Tom Noddy
  And Mr Briggs) or men, like Jones and Jackson?
Then nectar—was that beer, or whisky-toddy?
  Some say the Gaelic mixture, *I* the Saxon:
I think a strict adherence to the latter
Might make some Scots less pig-headed, and fatter.

Besides, Bon Gaultier definitely shews
  That the real beverage for feasting gods on
Is a soft compound, grateful to the nose
  And also to the palate, known as 'Hodgson.'

I know a man—a tailor's son—who rose
   To be a peer: and this I would lay odds on,
(Though in his Memoirs it may not appear)
That that man owed his rise to copious Beer.

O Beer!   O Hodgson, Guinness, Allsop, Bass!
   Names that should be on every infant's tongue!
Shall days and months and years and centuries pass,
   And still your merits be unrecked, unsung?
Oh! I have gazed into my foaming glass,
   And wished that lyre could yet again be strung
Which once rang prophetic-like through Greece, and taught her
Misguided sons that the best drink was water.

How would he now recant that wild opinion,
   And sing—as would that I could sing—of you!
I was not born (alas!) the 'Muses' minion,'
   I'm not poetical, not even blue:
And he, we know, but strives with waxen pinion,
   Whoe'er he is that entertains the view
Of emulating Pindar, and will be
Sponsor at last to some now nameless sea.

Oh! when the green slopes of Arcadia burned
   With all the lustre of the dying day,
And on Cithaeron's brow the reaper turned,
   (Humming, of course, in his delightful way,
How Lycidas was dead, and how concerned
   The Nymphs were when they saw his lifeless clay;
And how rock told to rock the dreadful story
That poor young Lycidas was gone to glory:)

What would that lone and labouring soul have given,
   At that soft moment for a pewter pot!
How had the mists that dimmed his eye been riven,
   And Lycidas and sorrow all forgot!
If his own grandmother had died unshriven,
   In two short seconds he'd have recked it not;
Such power hath Beer.   The heart which Grief hath canker'd
Hath one unfailing remedy—the Tankard.

Coffee is good, and so no doubt is cocoa;
   Tea did for Johnson and the Chinamen:
When 'Dulce est desipere in loco'
   Was written, real Falernian winged the pen.
When a rapt audience has encored 'Fra Poco!
   Or 'Casta Diva,' I have heard that then
The Prima Donna, smiling herself out,
Recruits her flagging powers with bottled stout.

But what is coffee, but a noxious berry,
   Born to keep used-up Londoners awake?
What is Falernian, what is Port or Sherry,
   But vile concoctions to make dull heads ache?
Nay stout itself (though good with oysters, very)—
   Is not a thing your reading man should take.
He that would shine, and petrify his tutor,
Should drink draught Allsop in its 'native pewter.'

But hark! a sound is stealing on my ear—
   A soft and silvery sound—I know it well.
Its tinkling tells me that a time is near
   Precious to me—it is the Dinner Bell.
O blessed Bell! Thou bringest beef and beer,
   Thou bringest good things more than tongue may tell:
Seared is, of course, my heart—but unsubdued
Is, and shall be, my appetite for food.

I go. Untaught and feeble is my pen:
   But on one statement I may safely venture:
That few of our most highly gifted men
   Have more appreciation of the trencher.
I go. One pound of British beef, and then
   What Mr Swiveller called a 'modest quencher';
That home-returning, I may 'soothly say,'
'Fate cannot touch me: I have dined to-day.'

                                   (1862)

Lines on Hearing the Organ

GRINDER, who serenely grindest
   At my door the Hundredth Psalm,
Till thou ultimately findest
   Pence in thy unwashen palm:

Grinder, jocund-hearted Grinder,
   Near whom Barbary's nimble son,
Poised with skill upon his hinder
   Paws, accepts the proffered bun:

Dearly do I love thy grinding;
   Joy to meet thee on thy road
Where thou prowlest through the blinding
   Dust with that stupendous load,

'Neath the baleful star of Sirius,
   When the postmen slowlier jog,
And the ox becomes delirious,
   And the muzzle decks the dog.

Tell me by what art thou bindest
  On thy feet those ancient shoon:
Tell me, Grinder, if thou grindest
  Always, always out of tune.

Tell me if, as thou art buckling
  On thy straps with eager claws,
Thou forecastest, inly chuckling,
  All the rage that thou wilt cause.

Tell me if at all thou mindest
  When folks flee, as if on wings,
From thee as at ease thou grindest:
  Tell me fifty thousand things.

Grinder, gentle-hearted Grinder!
  Ruffians who led evil lives,
Soothed by thy sweet strains, are kinder
  To their bullocks and their wives.

Children, when they see thy supple
  Form approach, are out like shots;
Half a bar sets several couple
  Waltzing in convenient spots;

Not with clumsy Jacks or Georges:
  Unprofaned by grasp of man
Maidens speed those simple orgies,
  Betsey Jane with Betsey Ann.

As they love thee in St Giles's
  Thou art loved in Grosvenor Square:
None of those engaging smiles is
  Unreciprocated there.

Often, ere yet thou hast hammer'd
  Through thy four delicious airs,
Coins are flung thee by enamour'd
  Housemaids upon area stairs:

E'en the ambrosial-whisker'd flunkey
  Eyes thy boots and thine unkempt
Beard and melancholy monkey
  More in pity than contempt.

Far from England, in the sunny
  South, where Anio leaps in foam,
Thou wast rear'd, till lack of money
  Drew thee from thy vineclad home:

And thy mate, the sinewy Jocko,
  From Brazil or Afric came,
Land of simoom and sirocco—
  And he seems extremely tame.

There he quaff'd the undefilèd
  Spring, or hung with apelike glee,
By his teeth or tail or eyelid,
  To the slippery mango-tree:

There he woo'd and won a dusky
  Bride, of instinct like his own;
Talk'd of love till he was husky
  In a tongue to us unknown:

Side by side 'twas theirs to ravage
  The potato ground, or cut
Down the unsuspecting savage
  With the well-aim'd coconut:

Till the miscreant Stranger tore him
  Screaming from his blue-faced fair;
And they flung strange raiment o'er him,
  Raiment which he could not bear:

Sever'd from the pure embraces
  Of his children and his spouse,
He must ride fantastic races
  Mounted on reluctant sows:

But the heart of wistful Jocko
  Still was with his ancient flame
In the nutgroves of Morocco;
  Or if not it's all the same.

Grinder, winsome grinsome Grinder!
  They who see thee and whose soul
Melts not at thy charms, are blinder
  Than a trebly bandaged mole:

They to whom thy curt (yet clever)
  Talk, thy music and thine ape,
Seem not to be joys for ever,
  Are but brutes in human shape.

'Tis not that thy mien is stately
  'Tis not that thy tones are soft;
'Tis not that I care so greatly
  For the same thing play'd so oft:

But I've heard mankind abuse thee;
　And perhaps it's rather strange,
But I thought that I would choose thee
　For encomium, as a change.

(1872)

Wanderers

As o'er the hill we roam'd at will,
　My dog and I together,
We mark'd a chaise, by two bright bays
　Slow-moved along the heather:

Two bays arch neck'd, with tails erect
　And gold upon their blinkers;
And by their side an ass I spied;
　It was a travelling tinker's.

The chaise went by, nor aught cared I;
　Such things are not in my way:
I turn'd me to the tinker, who
　Was loafing down a byway:

I ask'd him where he lived—a stare
　Was all I got in answer,
As on he trudged: I rightly judged
　The stare said: 'Where I can, sir.'

I ask'd him if he'd take a whiff
　Of 'bacco; he acceded;
He grew communicative too
　(A pipe was all he needed),
Till of the tinker's life, I think,
　I knew as much as he did.

'I loiter down by thorp and town;
　For any job I'm willing;
Take here and there a dusty brown,
　And here and there a shilling.

'I deal in every ware in turn,
　I've rings for buddin' Sally
That sparkle like those eyes of her'n;
　I've liquor for the valet.

'I steal from th' parson's strawberry-plots,
　I hide by th' squire's covers;
I teach the sweet young housemaids what's
　The art of trapping lovers.

'The things I've done 'neath moon and stars
   Have got me into messes:
I've seen the sky through prison bars,
   I've torn up prison dresses:

'I've sat, I've sigh'd, I've gloom'd, I've glanced
   With envy at the swallows
That through the window slid, and danced
   (Quite happy) round the gallows;

'But out again I come, and show
   My face nor care a stiver
For trades are brisk and trades are slow,
   But mine goes on for ever.'

Thus on he prattled like a babbling brook.
Then I, 'The sun hath slipt behind the hill,
And my aunt Vivian dines at half past six.'
So in all love we parted; I to the Hall,
They to the village.   It was noised next noon
That chickens had been miss'd at Syllabub Farm.

(1872)

Ballad

PART I

THE auld wife sat at her ivied door,
   (*Butter and eggs and a pound of cheese*)
A thing she had frequently done before;
   And her spectacles lay on her apron'd knees.

The piper he piped on the hill-top high,
   (*Butter and eggs and a pound of cheese*)
Till the cow said 'I die,' and the goose ask'd 'Why?'
   And the dog said nothing, but search'd for fleas.

The farmer he strode through the square farmyard;
   (*Butter and eggs and a pound of cheese*)
His last brew of ale was a trifle hard—
   The connection of which with the plot one sees.

The farmer's daughter hath frank blue eyes;
   (*Butter and eggs and a pound of cheese*)
She hears the rooks caw in the windy skies,
   As she sits at her lattice and shells her peas.

The farmer's daughter hath ripe red lips;
   (*Butter and eggs and a pound of cheese*)
If you try to approach her, away she skips
   Over tables and chairs with apparent ease.

The farmer's daughter hath soft brown hair;
  (*Butter and eggs and a pound of cheese*)
And I met with a ballad, I can't say where,
  Which wholly consisted of lines like these.

PART II

She sat, with her hands 'neath her dimpled cheeks,
  (*Butter and eggs and a pound of cheese*)
And spake not a word.   While a lady speaks
  There is hope, but she didn't even sneeze.

She sat, with her hands 'neath her crimson cheeks;
  (*Butter and eggs and a pound of cheese*)
She gave up mending her father's breeks,
  And let the cat roll in her new chemise.

She sat, with her hands 'neath her burning cheeks,
  (*Butter and eggs and a pound of cheese*)
And gazed at the piper for thirteen weeks;
  Then she follow'd him out o'er the misty leas.

Her sheep follow'd her, as their tails did them.
  (*Butter and eggs and a pound of cheese*)
And this song is consider'd a perfect gem,
  And as to the meaning, it's what you please.

                                              (1872)

Disaster

'Twas ever thus from childhood's hour!
  My fondest hopes would not decay:
I never loved a tree or flower
  Which was the first to fade away!
The garden, where I used to delve
  Short-frock'd, still yields me pinks in plenty:
The pear-tree that I climb'd at twelve
  I see still blossoming, at twenty.

I never nursed a dear gazelle;
  But I was given a parroquet—
(How I did nurse him if unwell!)
  He's imbecile, but lingers yet.
He's green, with an enchanting tuft;
  He melts me with his small black eye:
He'd look inimitable stuff'd,
  And knows it—but he will not die!

I had a kitten—I was rich
    In pets—but all too soon my kitten
Became a full-sized cat, by which
    I've more than once been scratch'd and bitten.
And when for sleep her limbs she curl'd
    One day beside her untouch'd plateful,
And glided calmly from the world,
    I freely own that I was grateful.

And then I bought a dog—a queen!
    Ah Tiny, dear departing pug!
She lives, but she is past sixteen
    And scarce can crawl across the rug.
I loved her beautiful and kind;
    Delighted in her pert Bow-wow:
But now she snaps if you don't mind;
    'Twere lunacy to love her now.

I used to think, should e'er mishap
    Betide my crumple-visaged Ti,
In shape of prowling thief, or trap,
    Or coarse bull-terrier—I should die.
But ah! disasters have their use;
    And life might e'en be too sunshiny:
Nor would I make myself a goose,
    If some big dog should swallow Tiny.

(1875)

EDWARD BURNETT TYLOR (1832–1917)
AND ANDREW LANG (1844–1912)

Double Ballade of Primitive Man

HE lived in a cave by the seas,
He lived upon oysters and foes,
But his list of forbidden degrees,
An extensive morality shows;
Geological evidence goes
To prove he had never a pan,
But he shaved with a shell when he chose—
'Twas the manner of Primitive Man.

He worshipp'd the rain and the breeze,
He worshipp'd the river that flows,
And the Dawn, and the Moon, and the trees,
And bogies, and serpents, and crows;

He buried his dead with their toes
Tucked-up, an original plan,
Till their knees came right under their nose—
'Twas the manner of Primitive Man.

His communal wives, at his ease,
He would curb with occasional blows;
Or his State had a queen, like the bees
(As another philosopher trows):
When he spoke, it was never in prose,
But he sang in a strain that would scan,
For (to doubt it, perchance, were morose)
'Twas the manner of Primitive Man!

On the coasts that incessantly freeze,
With his stones, and his bones, and his bows;
On luxuriant tropical leas,
Where the summer eternally glows,
He is found, and his habits disclose
(Let theology say what she can)
That he lived in the long, long agos,
'Twas the manner of Primitive Man!

From a status like that of the Crees,
Our society's fabric arose—
Develop'd, evolved, if you please,
But deluded chronologists chose,
In a fancied accordance with Mos
es, 4000 B.C. for the span
When he rushed on the world and its woes—
'Twas the manner of Primitive Man!

But the mild anthropologist—*he*'s
Not *recent* inclined to suppose
Flints Palaeolithic like these,
Quaternary bones such as those!
In Rhinoceros, Mammoth and Co.'s,
First epoch, the Human began,
Theologians all to expose—
'Tis the *mission* of Primitive Man.

ENVOY

MAX, proudly your Aryans pose,
But their rigs they undoubtedly ran,
For, as every Darwinian knows,
'Twas the manner of Primitive Man!

(1880)

'LEWIS CARROLL'
(CHARLES LUTWIDGE DODGSON)
(1832–1898)

She's All My Fancy Painted Him

SHE'S all my fancy painted him
   (I make no idle boast);
If he or you had lost a limb,
   Which would have suffered most?

He said that you had been to her,
   And seen me here before;
But, in another character,
   She was the same of yore.

There was not one that spoke to us,
   Of all that thronged the street:
So he sadly got into a bus,
   And pattered with his feet.

They sent him word I had not gone
   (We know it to be true);
If she should push the matter on,
   What would become of you?

They gave her one, they gave me two,
   They gave us three or more;
They all returned from him to you,
   Though they were mine before.

If I or she should chance to be
   Involved in this affair,
He trusts to you to set them free,
   Exactly as we were.

It seemed to me that you had been
   (Before she had this fit)
An obstacle, that came between
   Him, and ourselves, and it.

Don't let him know she liked them best,
   For this must ever be
A secret, kept from all the rest,
   Between yourself and me.

(1855)

Hiawatha's Photographing

[*Introduction by the Author.* In these days of imitation I can claim no sort of merit for this slight attempt at doing what is known to be so easy. Anyone who knows what verse is, with the smallest ear for rhythm, can throw off a composition in an easy running metre like *The Song of Hiawatha.* Having, then, made it quite clear that I challenge no attention in the following little poem to its merely verbal jingle, I must beg the candid reader to confine his criticism to its treatment of the subject.]

FROM his shoulder Hiawatha
Took the camera of rosewood—
Made of sliding, folding rosewood—
Neatly put it all together.
   In its case it lay compactly,
Folded into nearly nothing;
But he opened out its hinges,
Pushed and pulled the joints and hinges
Till it looked all squares and oblongs,
Like a complicated figure
In the second book of Euclid.
   This he perched upon a tripod,
And the family, in order
Sat before him for their pictures—
Mystic, awful, was the process.
   First, a piece of glass he coated
With collodion, and plunged it
In a bath of lunar caustic
Carefully dissolved in water—
There he left it certain minutes.
   Secondly, my Hiawatha
Made with cunning hand a mixture
Of the acid pyrro-gallic,
And of glacial-acetic,
And of alcohol and water—
This developed all the picture.
   Finally, he fixed each picture
With a saturate solution
Which was made of hyposulphite,
Which, again, was made of soda.
(Very difficult the name is
For a metre like the present
But periphrasis has done it.)
   All the family, in order,
Sat before him for their pictures;
Each in turn, as he was taken,

Volunteered his own suggestions—
His invaluable suggestions.
   First, the governor—the father—
He suggested velvet curtains
Looped about a massy pillar,
And the corner of a table—
Of a rosewood dining-table.
He would hold a scroll of something—
Hold it firmly in his left hand;
He would keep his right hand buried
(Like Napoleon) in his waistcoat;
He would gaze upon the distance—
(Like a poet seeing visions,
Like a man that plots a poem,
In a dressing gown of damask,
At 12.30 in the morning,
Ere the servants bring in luncheon)—
With a look of pensive meaning,
As of ducks that die in tempests.
   Grand, heroic was the notion:
Yet the picture failed entirely,
Failed because he moved a little—
Moved because he couldn't help it.
   Next his better half took courage—
She would have her picture taken:
She came dressed beyond description,
Dressed in jewels and in satin,
Far too gorgeous for an empress.
Gracefully she sat down sideways,
With a simper scarcely human,
Holding in her hand a nosegay
Rather larger than a cabbage.
All the while that she was taking,
Still the lady chattered, chattered,
Like a monkey in the forest.
'Am I sitting still?' she asked him;
'Is my face enough in profile?
Shall I hold the nosegay higher?
Will it come into the picture?'
And the picture failed completely.
   Next the son, the stunning Cantab.,
He suggested curves of beauty,
Curves pervading all his figure,
Which the eye might follow onward
Till it centred in the breast-pin—
Centred in the golden breast-pin.
He had learnt it all from Ruskin
(Author of *The Stones of Venice*,

Seven Lamps of Architecture,
Modern Painters, and some others)—
And perhaps he had not fully
Understood the author's meaning;
But, whatever was the reason,
All was fruitless, as the picture
Ended in a total failure.
    After him the eldest daughter:
She suggested very little,
Only begged she might be taken
With her look of 'passive beauty.
Her idea of passive beauty
Was a squinting of the left eye,
Was a drooping of the right eye,
Was a smile that went up sideways
To the corner of the nostrils.
    Hiawatha, when she asked him,
Took no notice of the question,
Looked as if he hadn't heard it;
But, when pointedly appealed to,
Smiled in a peculiar manner,
Coughed, and said it 'didn't matter,'
Bit his lips, and changed the subject.
    Nor in this was he mistaken,
As the picture failed completely.
    So, in turn, the other daughters:
All of them agreed on one thing,
That their pictures came to nothing,
Though they differed in their causes,
From the eldest, Grinny-haha,
Who, throughout her time of taking
Shook with sudden, ceaseless laughter,
With a silent fit of laughter,
To the youngest, Dinny-wawa,
Shook with sudden, causeless weeping—
Anything but silent weeping:
And their pictures failed completely.
Last, the youngest son was taken:
'John' his Christian name had once been;
But his overbearing sisters
Called him names he disapproved of—
Called him Johnny, 'Daddy's Darling'—
Called him Jacky, 'Scrubby Schoolboy.'
Very rough and thick his hair was,
Very dusty was his jacket,
Very fidgety his manner,
And, so fearful was the picture,
In comparison the others

Might be thought to have succeeded—
To have partially succeeded—
   Finally, my Hiawatha
Tumbled all the tribe together
('Grouped' is not the right expression),
And, as happy chance would have it,
Did at last obtain a picture
Where the faces all succeeded:
Each came out a perfect likeness.
   Then they joined and all abused it—
Unrestrainedly abused it—
As 'the worst and ugliest picture
That could possibly be taken
Giving one such strange expressions!
Sulkiness, conceit, and meanness!
Really any one would take us
(Any one who did not know us)
For the most unpleasant people!'
(Hiawatha seemed to think so—
Seemed to think it not unlikely).
All together rang their voices—
Angry, hard, discordant voices—
As of dogs that howl in concert,
As of cats that wail in chorus.
   But my Hiawatha's patience,
His politeness and his patience,
Unaccountably had vanished,
And he left that happy party.
Neither did he leave them slowly,
With the calm deliberation,
The intense deliberation
Of a photographic artist:
But he left them in a hurry,
Left them in a mighty hurry,
Stating that he would not stand it,
Stating in emphatic language
What he'd be before he'd stand it.
Hurriedly he packed his boxes:
Hurriedly the porter trundled
On a barrow all his boxes:
Hurriedly he took his ticket:
Hurriedly the train received him:
Thus departed Hiawatha.

(1857)

A Sea Dirge

THERE are certain things—as, a spider, a ghost,
  The income-tax, gout, an umbrella for three—
That I hate, but the thing that I hate the most
    Is a thing they call the Sea.

Pour some salt water over the floor—
  Ugly I'm sure you'll allow it to be:
Suppose it extended a mile or more,
    That's very like the Sea.

Beat a dog till it howls outright—
  Cruel, but all very well for a spree:
Suppose that he did so day and night,
    That would be like the Sea.

I had a vision of nursery-maids;
  Tens of thousands passed by me—
All leading children with wooden spades,
    And this was by the Sea.

Who invented those spades of wood?
  Who was it cut them out of the tree?
None, I think, but an idiot could—
    Or one that loved the Sea.

It is pleasant and dreamy, no doubt, to float
  With 'thoughts as boundless, and souls as free':
But, suppose you are very unwell in the boat,
    How do you like the Sea?

'But it makes the intellect clear and keen'—
  Prove it! prove it! how can that be?
'Why, what does "B sharp" (in music) mean,
    If not "the natural C"?'

What! keen? with such questions as 'When's high tide?'
  'Is shelling shrimps an improvement to tea?'
'Were donkeys intended for Man to ride?'
    Such are our thoughts by the Sea.

There is an insect that people avoid
  (Whence is derived the verb 'to flee').
Where have you been by it most annoyed?
    In lodgings by the Sea.

If you like your coffee with sand for dregs,
    A decided hint of salt in your tea,
And a fishy taste in the very eggs—
    By all means choose the Sea.

And if, with these dainties to drink and eat,
    You prefer not a vestige of grass or tree,
And a chronic state of wet in your feet,
    Then—I recommend the Sea.

For *I* have friends who dwell by the coast—
    Pleasant friends they are to me!
It is when I am with them I wonder most
    That anyone likes the Sea.

They take me a walk: though tired and stiff,
    To climb the heights I madly agree;
And, after a tumble or so from the cliff,
    They kindly suggest the Sea.

I try the rocks, and I think it cool
    That they laugh with such an excess of glee,
As I heavily slip into every pool
    That skirts the cold cold Sea.

Once I met a friend in the street,
    With wife, and nurse, and children three:
Never again such a sight may I meet
    As that party from the Sea.

Their cheeks were hollow, their steps were slow,
    Convicted felons they seemed to be:
'Are you going to prison, dear friend?' 'Oh, no!
    We're returning from the Sea!'

(1860)

Disillusionized

I PAINTED her a gushing thing,
    With years perhaps a score;
I little thought to find they were
    At least a dozen more;
My fancy gave her eyes of blue,
    A curly auburn head:
I came, to find the blue a green,
    The auburn turned to red.

I painted her a lip and cheek
  In colour like the rose;
I little thought the selfsame hue
  Extended to her nose!
I dreamed of rounded features,
  A smile of ready glee—
But it was not *fat* I wanted,
  Nor a *grin* I hoped to see!

She boxed my ears this morning,
  They tingled very much;
I own that I could wish her
  A somewhat lighter touch;
And if you were to ask me how
  Her charms might be improved,
I would not have them *added to*,
  But just a few *removed*!

She has the bear's ethereal grace,
  The bland hyena's laugh,
The footstep of the elephant,
  The neck of the giraffe;
I love her still, believe me,
  Though my heart its passion hides;
'She's all my fancy painted her,'
  But oh! how much *besides*!

                                        (1862)

Atalanta in Camden-Town

AY, 'twas here, on this spot,
  In that summer of yore,
Atalanta did not
  Vote my presence a bore,
Nor reply to my tenderest talk 'She had
  heard all that nonsense before.'

She'd the brooch I had bought
  And the necklace and sash on,
And her heart, as I thought,
  Was alive to my passion;
And she'd done up her hair in the style that
  the Empress had brought into fashion.

I had been to the play
    With my pearl of a Peri—
But, for all I could say,
    She declared she was weary,
That 'the place was so crowded and hot, and
she couldn't abide that Dundreary.'

Then I thought 'Lucky boy!
    'Tis for *you* that she whimpers!'
And I noted with joy
    Those sensational simpers:
And I said 'This is scrumptious!'—a phrase I had
learned from the Devonshire shrimpers.

And I vowed ''Twill be said
    I'm a fortunate fellow,
When the breakfast is spread,
    When the topers are mellow,
When the foam of the bride-cake is white, and the
fierce orange-blossoms are yellow!'

O that languishing yawn!
    O those eloquent eyes!
I was drunk with the dawn
    Of a splendid surmise—
I was stung by a look, I was slain by a tear, by a
tempest of sighs.

Then I whispered 'I see
    The sweet secret thou keepest.
And the yearning for *ME*
    That thou wistfully weepest!
And the question is "Licence or Banns?" though
undoubtedly Banns are the cheapest.

'Be my Hero,' said I,
    'And let *me* be Leander!'
But I lost her reply—
    Something ending with 'gander'—
For the omnibus rattled so loud that no mortal could
quite understand her.

(1867)

GEORGE DU MAURIER
(1834–1896)

A Legend of Camelot

PART I

TALL Braunighrindas left her bed
At cock-crow, with an aching head.
     O miserie!
'I yearn to suffer and to do,'
She cried, 'ere sunset, something new!
     O miserie!
To do and suffer, ere I die,
I care not what. I know not why.
     O miserie!
Some quest I crave to undertake,
Or burden bear, or trouble make.'
She shook her hair about her form
In waves of colour bright and warm.
It rolled and writhed, and reached the floor:
A silver wedding-ring she wore.
She left her tower, and wandered down
Into the High Street of the town.
Her pale feet glimmered, in and out,
Like tombstones as she went about.
From right to left, and left to right;
And blue veins streakt her insteps white;
And folks did ask her in the street
'How fared it with her long pale feet?'
And blinkt, as though 'twere hard to bear
The red-heat of her blazing hair!
Sir Galahad and Sir Launcelot
Came hand-in-hand down Camelot;
Sir Gauwaine followèd close behind;
A weight hung heavy on his mind.
'Who knows this damsel, burning bright,'
Quoth Launcelot, 'like a northern light?'
Quoth Sir Gauwaine: '*I* know her not!'
'Who quoth you *did*?' quoth Launcelot.
'''Tis Braunighrindas!' quoth Sir Bors
(Just then returning from the wars).
Then quoth the pure Sir Galahad:
'She seems, methinks, but lightly clad!
The winds blow somewhat chill to-day;
Moreover, what would Arthur say!'

She thrust her chin towards Galahad
Full many an inch beyond her head . . .
But when she noted Sir Gauwaine
She wept, and drew it in again!
She wept: 'How beautiful am I!'
He shook the poplars with a sigh.
Sir Launcelot was standing near;
Him kist he thrice behind the ear.
'Ah, me!' sighed Launcelot where he stood,
'I cannot fathom it!' . . . (who could?)
Hard by his wares a weaver wove,
And weaving with a will, he throve;
Him beckoned Galahad, and said:
'Gaunt Blaunighrindas wants your aid . . .
Behold the wild growth from her nape!
Good weaver, weave it into shape!'
The weaver straightway to his loom
Did lead her, whilst the knights made room;
And wove her locks, both web and woof,
And made them wind and waterproof;
Then with his shears he opened wide
An arm-hole neat on either side,
And bound her with his handkerchief
Right round the middle like a sheaf.
'Are you content, knight?' quoth Sir Bors
To Galahad; quoth he, 'Of course!'
　　　O miserie!
'Ah, me! those locks,' quoth Sir Gauwaine,
'Will never know the comb again!'
　　　O miserie!
The bold Sir Launcelot quoth he nought;
So (haply) all the more he thought.
　　　O miserie!

PART II

An one-eyed Eastern past, who sold
And bought, and bartered garments old;
　　　O miserie!
His yellow garb did show the thread,
A triple head-dress crowned his head;
　　　O miserie!
And, ever and anon, his throat,
Thick-bearded, gave a solemn note;
　　　O miserie!
The knights were gathered in a knot;
Rapt in a trance, they heard him not;
Before them Braunighrindas stood

In native growth of gown and hood;
Fresh from a cunning weaver's hand,
She lookt, not gaudy, but so grand!
Not gaudy, gentles, but so neat!
For chaste and knightly eyes a treat!
The Pilgrim eyed her shapely dress
With curious eye to business:
Then whispered he to Launcelot,
'I'll give five shekels for the lot!'
Gauwaine his battle-axe he drew . . .
Once and again he clove him through!
'No man of many words am I!'
Quoth he, and wope his weapon dry.
A butcher caught the sounds and said,
'There go two cracks upon one head!'
A baker whispered in his fun:
'Butcher, more heads are crackt than one!'
'The moon is up to many tricks!'
Quoth he who made the candlesticks! . . .
Dead-limp, the unbeliever lay
Athwart the flags and stopt the way. . . .
The bold Sir Launcelot mused a bit,
And smole a bitter smile at it.
Gauwaine, he gave his orders brief:
'*Manants: emportez-moi ce Juif!*'
Some heard the knight not: they that heard
Made answer to him none, nor stirred.
But Braunighrindas was not dumb;
Her opportunity had come.
Her accents tinkled ivory-sweet—
'*Je vays l'emporter tout de suite!*' . . .
She bowed her body, slenderly,
And lifted him full tenderly:
Full silverly her stretchèd throat
Intoned the wonted Hebrew note:
Right broke-in-halfenly she bent;
Jew-laden on her way she went!
The knights all left her one by one,
And, leaving, cried in unison—
'*Voyez ce vilain Juif qui pend
Par derrière et par devant!*' . . .
Yet bearing it she journeyed forth,
Selecting north-north-east by north.
The knights (most wisely) with one mouth,
Selected south-south-west by south.
The butcher, baker, and the rest,
Said: 'Let them go where they like best!'
      O miserie!

And many a wink they wunk, and shook
Their heads; but further more they took
        O miserie!
No note: it was a way they had,
In Camelot, when folks went mad. . . .
        O miserie!

PART III

She bore her burden all that day
Half-faint; the unconverted clay
        O miserie!
A burden grew, beneath the sun,
In many a manner more than one.
        O miserie!
Half-faint the whitening road along
She bore it, singing (in her song)—
        O miserie!
    'The locks you loved, Gauwaine, Gauwaine,
        Will never know the comb again! . . .
    The man you slew, Gauwaine, Gauwaine,
        Will never come to life again!
    So when they do, Gauwaine, Gauwaine,
        Then take me back to town again!' . . .
The shepherds gazed, but marvelled not;
They knew the ways of Camelot!
She heeded neither man nor beast:
Her shadow lengthened toward the east.
A little castle she drew nigh,
With seven towers twelve inches high. . . .
A baby castle, all a-flame
With many a flower that hath no name.
It had a little moat all round:
A little drawbridge too she found,
On which there stood a stately maid,
Like her in radiant locks arrayed . . .
Save that her locks grew rank and wild,
By weaver's shuttle undefiled! . . .
Who held her brush and comb, as if
Her faltering hands had waxèd stiff
With baulkt endeavour! whence she sung
A chant, the burden whereof rung:
    'These hands have striven in vain
        To part
    These locks that won Gauwaine
        His heart!'
All breathless, Blaunighrindas stopt
To listen, and her load she dropt,

And rolled in wonder wild and blear
The whites of her eyes grown green with fear:
'What is your name, young person, pray?'
'Knights call me Fidele-strynges-le-Fay.'
'You wear a wedding-ring, I see!'
'I do . . . Gauwaine he gave it me . . .'
'Are you Gauwaine his wedded spouse?
Is this Gauwaine his . . . country-house?'
'I am . . . it is . . . we are . . . oh who,
That you should greet me thus, are you?'
'I am ANOTHER! . . since the morn
The fourth month of the year was born!' . . .
'What! that which followed when the last
Bleak night of bitter March had past?' . . .
'The same.'—'*That day for both hath done!
And you, and he, and I, are* ONE!' . . .
Then hand in hand, most woefully,
They went, the willows weeping nigh;
Left hand in left was left to cling!
On each a silver wedding-ring.
And having walkt a little space,
They halted, each one in her place:
And chanted loud a wondrous plaint
Well chosen: wild, one-noted, quaint:
 'Heigho! the Wind and the Rain!
  The Moon's at the Full, Gauwaine, Gauwaine!
 Heigho! the Wind and the Rain
  On gold-hair woven, and gold-hair plain!
 Heigho! the Wind and the Rain!
  Oh when shall we Three meet again!'
Atween the river and the wood,
Knee-deep 'mid whispering reeds they stood:
  O miserie!
The green earth oozing soft and dank
Beneath them, soakt and suckt and sank! . . .
  O miserie!
Yet soak-and-suck-and-sink or not,
They, chanting, craned towards Camelot. . . .
  O miserie!

PART IV

The pale wet moon did rise and ride,
O'er misty wolds and marshes wide.
  O miserie!
Sad earth slept underneath the yew,
Lapt in the death-sweat men call dew.
  O miserie!

O raven ringlets, ringing wet!
O bright eyes rolling black as jet!
        O miserie!
O matted locks about the chin!
O towering head-piece, battered in!
Three hats that fit each other tight,
Are worth the helmet of a knight!
He rose all shapeless from the mud,
His yellow garb was stained with blood;
'Vat ish thish schwimming in mine head?
Thish turning round and round?' he said.
He took three paces through the night,
He saw red gold that glittered bright!
Two Royal Heads of Hair he saw!
And One was Woven, and One was Raw!
'O Sholomon! if there ain't a pair
Of dead young damshels shinking there!
O Moshesh! vat a precioush lot
Of beautiful red hair they've got!
The prishe of it would compenshate
Most handshome for my broken pate!
How much their upper lipsh do pout!
How very much their chins shtick out!
How dreadful shtrange they shtare! they sheem
Half to be dead, and half to dream!
The Camelot peoplesh alvaysh try
To look like that! I vonder vy?
Yet each hath got a lovely fashe!
Good Father Jacob shend them grashe!
O Jacob! blesh the lovely light,
That lit the moon that shtruck the knight,
That married the maid that carried the Jew,
That shold (as he intensh to do)
The golden locks and shilver rings
Of Braunighrinde and Fiddleshtrings!'
Thus having given thanks, he drew
His twofold weapon cutting true;
And close he clipt, and clean and clear,
From crown and temple, nape and ear.
The wind in pity soughed and sighed!
The river beat the river side!
The willows wept to stand and see
The sweetest, softest heads that be,
In ghastliest baldness gleam dead-white,
And sink unhallowed out of sight!
But, lo, you! Ere kind earth could fold
Their shame within its bosom cold,
The moon had laught in mockery down,

And stampt a high-light on each crown! . . .
Thrice muttering deep his mystic note,
The stillness of the night he smote:
Then, with a treasure dangling slack
From either shoulder adown his back,
O miserie!
He, whistling in his whistle, strode,
Nor felt he faint upon the road!
O miserie!
You may be sure that it was not
The road that leads to Camelot!
O miserie!

PART V

The castle weeds have grown so tall
Knights cannot see the red brick wall.
O miserie!
The little drawbridge hangs awry,
The little flowery moat is dry!
O miserie!
And the wind, it soughs and sighs alway
Through the grey willows, night and day!
O miserie!
And evermore two willows there
Do weep, whose boughs are always bare:
At all times weep they, in and out
Of season, turn and turn about!
But later, when the year doth fall,
And other willows, one and all,
In yellowing and dishevelled leaf
Sway haggard with their autumn grief,
Then do these leafless willows now
Put forth a rosebud from each bough!
What time Gauwaine, with spurless heels,
Barefoot (but not bare-headed) kneels
Between! . . . as fits a bigamous knight
Twice widowed in a single night:
And then, for that promiscuous way
Of axing Hebrews in broad day,
He ever uttereth a note
Of Eastern origin remote. . . .
A well-known monochord, that tells
Of one who, wandering, buys and sells!
What time the knights and damsels fair,
Of Arthur's court come trooping there,
They come in dresses of dark green,
Two damsels take a knight between:

One sad and sallow knight is fixt
Dyspeptic damsels twain betwixt!
They speak not, but their weary eyes
And wan white eyelids droop and rise
With dim dead gaze of mystic woe!
They always take their pleasures so
In Camelot. . . .   It doth not lie
With us to ask, or answer, why!
Yet, seeing them so fair and good,
Fain would we cheer them, if we could!
And every time they find a bud,
They pluck it, and it bleeds red blood.
And when they pluck a full blown rose,
And breathe the same, its colour goes!
But with Gauwaine alone at night,
The willows dance in their delight!
The rosebuds wriggle in their bliss,
And lift them for his lips to kiss!
And if he kiss a rose instead,
It blushes of a deeper red!
And if he like it, let him be!
It makes no odds to you or me!
O many-headed multitude,
Who read these rhymes that run so rude,
Strive not to fathom their intent!
But say your prayers, and rest content
　　　　O miserie!
That, notwithstanding those two cracks
He got from Gauwaine's battle-axe,
　　　　O miserie!
The Hebrew had the best of it!
So, Gentles, let us rest a bit.
　　　　O miserie!

　　　　　　　　　　　　　(1866)

A Lost Illusion

THERE was a young woman, and what do you think?
She lived upon nothing but paper and ink!
For ink and for paper she only did care,
Though they wrinkle the forehead and rumple the hair.

And she bought a gold pen, and she plied it so fast
That she brought forth her three-volume novel at last;
And she called it *The Ghoul of Mayfair*, by 'Sirène';
And I read it, reread it, and read it again.

'Twas about a young girl, whom the gods, in their grace,
Had endowed with a balefully beautiful face;
While her lithe, supple body and limbs were as those
Of a pantheress (*minus* the spots, I suppose).

And oh! reader, her eyes! and oh! reader, her hair!
They were red, green, blue, lustreless, lava-like. . . .   There!
I can't screw my muse to the exquisite pitch
For adjusting exactly the whichness of which!

I may mention at once that she'd dabbled in vice
From her cradle—and found it exceedingly nice:
That she doated on sin—that her only delight
Was in breaking commandments from morning till night.

And moreover, to deepen her wonderful spell,
She was not only vicious, but artful as well;
For she managed three husbands at once—to begin—
(Just by way of a trifle to keep her hand in).

The first, a bold indigo-broker was he;
Not young, but as wealthy as wealthy could be—
The next a fond burglar—and last, but not least,
The third was a strapping young Catholic priest!

Now, three doating husbands to start with in life
Seems a decent allowance for *any* young wife;
But legitimate trigamy very soon palled
Upon Barbara Blackshepe (for so she was called).

And it took but a very few pages to tell
How by means of a rope, and a knife, and a well,
And some charcoal, and poison, and powder and shot,
She effectually widowed herself of the lot.

Then she suddenly found that she couldn't control
The yearning for love of her ardent young soul,
So—(this is the cream of the story—prepare)
She took a large house in the midst of Mayfair:

Where she started a kind of a sort of a—eh?
Well, a sort of a kind of a—what shall I say!
Like *Turkey*, you know—only just the reverse;
Which, if possible, makes it a little bit worse!

There were tenors, priests, poets, and parsons—a host!
And Horseguards, and Coldstreams regardless of cost;
While a Leicester Square agent provided a tale
Of select refugees on a liberal scale.

The nobility, gentry, and public all round
Her immediate vicinity threatened and frowned;
Some went so far as to call and complain;
But they never went back to their spouses again!

Nay, the very policemen that knocked at the door
To remonstrate were collared, and never seen more;
And 'tis rumoured that *bishops* deserted their lambs
To enrol among 'Barbara's Rollicking Rams.'

And their dowdy, respectable, commonplace wives
And ridiculous daughters all fled for their lives,
And all died with disgusting decorum elsewhere,
To the scorn of 'Sirène' and her 'Ghoul of Mayfair'!

(This light—I might even add *frivolous*—tone
Isn't that of the author, 'tis fair I should own;
Passion hallows each page—guilt ennobles each line;
All this flippant facetiousness, reader, is mine.)

To our muttons. Who dances, the piper must pay,
And we can't eat our cake and yet have it, they say;
So we learn with regret that this duck of a pet
Of a dear little widow, she ran into debt.

And the Hebrew came down like the wolf on the fold
(With his waistcoat all gleaming in purple and gold),
And the auctioneer's hammer rang loud in the hall,
And they sold her up—harem and scar'em and all!

Then, says she: 'There are no more commandments to break;
I have lived—I have loved—I have eaten my cake!'
(Which she had, with a vengeance); so what does she do?
Why, she takes a revolver, and stabs herself through!

.   .   .   .   .

Now, this naughty but nice little Barbara B.
Had, I own, amongst others, demoralized me—
And the tale of her loves had excited me so
That I longed its fair passionate author to know.

For, oh! what's more seductive than vice, when you find
It with youth, beauty, genius, and culture combined!
Sweet 'Sirène'! How I yearned—how I burned for her! nay
I went secretly, silently wasting away!

Well, at last I beheld her—it did thus befall:
I was wasting away at the Tomkins's ball,
Half inclined to be sick, in my loathing profound
For the mild goody-goody flirtations all round—

When my hostess said suddenly: '*So* glad you came,
Tho' you *may* find us somewhat insipid and tame!
I've a great treat in store for you—turn, and look there!
That's 'Sirène,' who indited *The Ghoul of Mayfair*.'

Oh! the wild thrill that shot thro' this passionate heart!
There—before me—alone in her glory—apart
From that milksoppy, maudlin, contemptible throng,
Sat the being I'd yearned for and burned for so long!

I respectfully gazed one brief moment—but stop!
For particulars, *vide* design at the top:[1]
She's that sweet, scornful pet in black velvet you see
Near the nice little man in blue goggles.   That's me.

(1886)

TOM HOOD
['The Younger']

(1835–1874)

All in the Downs

I WOULD I had something to do—or to think!
Or something to read, or to write!
I am rapidly verging on Lunacy's brink,
Or I shall be dead before night.

In my ears has been ringing and droning all day,
Without ever a stop or a change,
That poem of Tennyson's—heart-cheering lay!—
Of the Moated Monotonous Grange!

The stripes in the carpet and paper alike
I have counted, and counted, all through.
And now I've a fervid ambition to strike
Out some path of wild pleasure that's new.

They say if a number you count, and re-count,
That the time imperceptibly goes:—
Ah, I wish—how I wish!—I'd ne'er learnt the amount
Of my aggregate fingers and toes.

'Enjoyment is fleeting,' the proverbs all say,
'Even that, which it feeds upon, fails.'
I've arrived at the truth of the saying to-day,
By devouring the whole of my nails.

[1] Du Maurier's drawing for the original. 'Sirène' appears as an elderly,
severe dowager, ugly and commonplace.

I have numbered the minutes, so heavy and slow,
Till of that dissipation I tire.
And as for exciting amusements—you know
One can't *always* be stirring the fire!

(1861)

A Catch

BY A MIMIC OF MODERN MELODY

If you were queen of bloaters
    And I were king of soles,
The sea we'd wag our fins in,
Nor heed the crooked pins in
The water, dropped by boaters
    To catch our heedless joles;
If you were queen of bloaters
    And I were king of soles.

If you were Lady Mile-End
    And I were Duke of Bow,
We'd marry and we'd quarrel,
And then, to point the moral,
Should Lord Penzance his file lend,
    Our chains to overthrow;
If you were Lady Mile-End
    And I were Duke of Bow.

If you were chill November
    And I were sunny June;
I'd not with love pursue you;
For I should be to woo you
(You're foggy, pray remember)
    A most egregious spoon;
If you were chill November
    And I were sunny June.

If you were cook to Venus
    And I were J. 19;
When missus was out dining,
Our suppertites combining,
We'd oft contrive between us
    To keep the platter clean;
If you were cook to Venus
    And I were J. 19.

If you were but a jingle
   And I were but a rhyme;
We'd keep this up for ever,
Nor think it very clever
A grain of sense to mingle
   At times with simple chime;
If you were but a jingle
   And I were but a rhyme.

                               (1877)

Poets and Linnets

WHERE'ER there's a thistle to feed a linnet
And linnets are plenty, thistles rife—
Or an acorn cup to catch dew-drops in it,
There's ample promise of further life.
Now, mark how we begin it.

Now linnets will follow, if linnets are minded,
As blows the white feather parachute;
And ships will reel by the tempest blinded—
By ships, and shiploads of men to boot!
How deep whole fleets you'll find hid.

And we'll blow the thistledown hither and thither,
Forgetful of linnets and men, and God.
The dew! for its want an oak will wither—
By the dull hoof into the dust is trod,
And then who strikes the cithar?

But thistles were only for donkeys intended,
And that donkeys are common enough is clear.
And that drop! what a vessel it might have befriended,
Does it add any flavour to Glugabib's beer?
Well, there's my musing ended.

                               (1877)

WILLIAM JEFFERY PROWSE
('Nicholas')
(1836–1870)

The City of Prague

I DWELT in a city enchanted,
   And lonely, indeed, was my lot;
Two guineas a week, all I wanted,
   Was certainly all that I got.

Well, somehow I found it was plenty;
    Perhaps you may find it the same,
If—*if* you are just five-and-twenty,
    With industry, hope, and an aim:
        Though the latitude's rather uncertain,
            And the longitude also is vague,
        The persons I pity who know not the City,
            The beautiful city of Prague!

Bohemian, of course, were my neighbours,
    And not of a pastoral kind!
Our pipes were of clay, and our tabors
    Would scarcely be easy to find.
Our Tabors?   Instead of such mountains
    Ben Holborn was all we could share,
And the nearest available fountains
        Were the horrible things in the square:
            Does the latitude still seem uncertain?
                Or think ye the longitude vague?
            The persons I pity who know not the City,
                The beautiful City of Prague!

How we laughed as we laboured together!
    How well I remember, to-day,
Our 'outings' in midsummer weather,
    Our winter delights at the play!
We were not over-nice in our dinners;
    Our 'rooms' were up rickety stairs;
But if hope be the wealth of beginners,
    By Jove, we were all millionaires!
        Our incomes were very uncertain,
            Our prospects were equally vague;
        Yet the persons I pity who know not the City,
            The beautiful City of Prague!

If at times the horizon was frowning,
    Or the ocean of life looking grim,
Who dreamed, do you fancy, of drowning?
    Not we, for we knew we could swim . . .
Oh, Friends, by whose side I was breasting
    The billows that rolled to the shore,
Ye are quietly, quietly resting,
    To laugh and to labour no more!
        Still, in accents a little uncertain,
            And tones that are possibly vague,
        The persons I pity who know not the City,
            The beautiful City of Prague!

L'ENVOI

As for me, I have come to an anchor;
    I have taken my watch out of pawn;
I keep an account with a banker,
    Which at present is *not* overdrawn.
Though my clothes may be none of the smartest,
    The 'snip' has receipted the bill;
But the days I was poor and an artist
    Are the dearest of days to me still!
        Though the latitude's rather uncertain
            And the longitude also is vague,
        The persons I pity who know not the City,
            The beautiful City of Prague!

(1870)

WALTER BESANT

(1836–1901)

The Day is Coming

COME hither, lads, and hearken, for a tale there is to tell
Of the wonderful days a-coming, when all shall be better than
    well.

Not one of all the millions, in the days that are to come,
Shall have any hope of the morrow, or joy in the ancient home.
Then a man who works shall remember that to work at his level
    best,
Would be but the part of a fool, since the worst is done by the rest.
I tell you this for a wonder: that no man then shall dare
To think himself better than others, or look for a larger share;
And whether he work like a master, or like to a 'prentice raw,
No profit or loss shall be his, by the new and the righteous law.
Wherefore good work shall die, and the contest of wits be killed,
(By this equal law and just), and the voice of the boss be stilled,
And whether we work at all, or whether we lie in the sun,
Shall be by the will of all: and, as they will, shall be done.
For strong and for weak alike, for good as well as for bad,
An equal reward shall be meted, and an equal wage be paid.
Then the cry of the rough will be 'Grab!' and the cry of the
    poor, 'Divide!'
And no man shall have any money, and no man shall have any
    pride.

Then all that is thine shall be mine, when this pitiful age is o'er,
And nobody then so caitiff for himself to save and store.
And never a gentleman left—Oh! listen, and understand!—
And never a gracious lady in all this blessed land.
And Art, which the poor man now with wonder passes by,
When all shall be poor alike, shall wither and droop and die.
Hear, ye generous hearts! when working men shall be kings,
We will burn, for their sakes, our treasures of Art and our
     beautiful things;
Make no more ballads and songs; yea, even I will refrain,
Though I still would babble on in my own monotonous strain.
And since *they* desire no more, let knowledge and learning cease,
And the science and skill of the present be buried in peace.
Nor any be left at all to boast of his learning and lore;
And the libraries pitched in the fire, and no booksellers' shops
     any more.
Ah! such the days that shall be!   No more great houses then;
But endless streets of cottages plain, and fit for the working-men;
After the self-same pattern all, and square and complete,
Two windows atop and one below, and a door with a knocker
     neat.
And when all is devoured remains, with wide and welcome gates,
The universal workhouse, with no one to pay the rates.

Is it too much, this dream?   Does it fill the soul like wine,
To think that men shall be equal, and all that is thine shall be
     mine?
But the voices of all good men, the living and dead beside,
Call on us to fight for this glorious cause, and the great Divide.

Ah! come, cast off all fooling, for this at least you know—
That the dawn of the day is coming, and forth the banners go.

                                                  (1885)

WILLIAM SCHWENCK GILBERT

(1836–1911)

The Rival Curates

LIST while the poet trolls
    Of MR CLAYTON HOOPER,
Who had a cure of souls
    At Spiffton-extra-Sooper.

He lived on curds and whey,
    And daily sang their praises,
And then he'd go and play
    With buttercups and daisies.

Wild croquet HOOPER banned,
    And all the sports of Mammon,
He warred with cribbage, and
    He exorcized backgammon.

His helmet was a glance
    That spoke of holy gladness;
A saintly smile his lance,
    His shield a tear of sadness.

His vicar smiled to see
    This armour on him buckled;
With pardonable glee
    He blessed himself and chuckled:

'In mildness to abound
    My curate's sole design is,
In all the country round
    There's none so mild as mine is!'

And HOOPER, disinclined
    His trumpet to be blowing,
Yet didn't think you'd find
    A milder curate going.

A friend arrived one day
    At Spiffton-extra-Sooper,
And in this shameful way,
    He spoke to MR HOOPER:

'You think your famous name
    For mildness can't be shaken,
That none can blot your fame—
    But, HOOPER, you're mistaken!

'Your mind is not as blank
    As that of HOPLEY PORTER,
Who holds a curate's rank
    At Assesmilk-cum-Worter.

'*He* plays the airy flute,
    And looks depressed and blighted,
Doves round about him "toot,"
    And lambkins dance delighted.

'*He* labours more than you
　　At worsted work, and frames it;
In old maids' albums, too,
　　Sticks seaweed—yes, and names it!'

The tempter said his say,
　　Which pierced him like a needle—
He summoned straight away
　　His sexton and his beadle.

These men were men who could
　　Hold liberal opinions:
On Sundays they were good—
　　On week-days they were minions.

'To HOPLEY PORTER go,
　　Your fare I will afford you—
Deal him a deadly blow,
　　And blessings shall reward you.

'But stay—I do not like
　　Undue assassination,
And so, before you strike,
　　Make this communication:

'I'll give him this one chance—
　　If he'll more gaily bear him,
Play croquet, smoke, and dance,
　　I willingly will spare him.'

They went, those minions true,
　　To Assesmilk-cum-Worter,
And told their errand to
　　The REVEREND HOPLEY PORTER.

'What?' said that reverend gent,
　　'Dance through my hours of leisure?
Smoke?—bathe myself with scent?—
　　Play croquet?   Oh, with pleasure!

'Wear all my hair in curl?
　　Stand at my door, and wink—so—
At every passing girl?
　　My brothers, I should think so!

'For years I've longed for some
　　Excuse for this revulsion:
Now that excuse has come—
　　I do it on compulsion!!!'

He smoked and winked away—
   This REVEREND HOPLEY PORTER—
The deuce there was to pay
   At Assesmilk-cum-Worter.

And HOOPER holds his ground,
   In mildness daily growing—
They think him, all around,
   The mildest curate going.

                    (1869)

The Yarn of the 'Nancy Bell'

'TWAS on the shores that round our coast
   From Deal to Ramsgate span,
That I found alone on a piece of stone
   An elderly naval man.

His hair was weedy, his beard was long,
   And weedy and long was he,
And I heard this wight on the shore recite,
   In a singular minor key:

'Oh, I am a cook and a captain bold,
   And the mate of the *Nancy* brig,
And a bo'sun tight, and a midshipmite,
   And the crew of the captain's gig.'

And he shook his fists and he tore his hair,
   Till I really felt afraid,
For I couldn't help thinking the man had been drinking,
   And so I simply said:

'Oh, elderly man, it's little I know
   Of the duties of men of the sea,
But I'll eat my hand if I understand
   How you can possibly be

'At once a cook, and a captain bold,
   And the mate of the *Nancy* brig,
And a bo'sun tight, and a midshipmite,
   And the crew of the captain's gig.'

Then he gave a hitch to his trousers, which
   Is a trick all seamen larn,
And having got rid of a thumping quid,
   He spun this painful yarn:

''Twas in the good ship *Nancy Bell*
  That we sailed to the Indian sea,
And there on a reef we come to grief,
  Which has often occurred to me.

'And pretty nigh all o' the crew was drowned
  (There was seventy-seven o' soul),
And only ten of the *Nancy*'s men
  Said "Here!" to the muster-roll.

'There was me and the cook and the captain bold,
  And the mate of the *Nancy* brig,
And the bo'sun tight, and a midshipmite,
  And the crew of the captain's gig.

'For a month we'd neither wittles nor drink,
  Till a-hungry we did feel,
So we drawed a lot, and accordin' shot
  The captain for our meal.

'The next lot fell to the *Nancy*'s mate,
  And a delicate dish he made;
Then our appetite with the midshipmite
  We seven survivors stayed.

'And then we murdered the bo'sun tight,
  And he much resembled pig;
Then we wittled free, did the cook and me,
  On the crew of the captain's gig.

'Then only the cook and me was left,
  And the delicate question, "Which
Of us two goes to the kettle?" arose
  And we argued it out as sich.

'For I loved that cook as a brother, I did,
  And the cook he worshipped me;
But we'd both be blowed if we'd either be stowed
  In the other chap's hold, you see.

'"I'll be eat if you dines off me," says TOM,
  "Yes, that," says I, "you'll be,"—
"I'm boiled if I die, my friend," quoth I,
  And "Exactly so," quoth he.

'Says he, "Dear JAMES, to murder me
  Were a foolish thing to do,
For don't you see that you can't cook *me*,
  While I can—and will—cook *you*!"

'So he boils the water, and takes the salt
    And the pepper in portions true
(Which he never forgot), and some chopped shallot,
    And some sage and parsley too.

'"Come here," says he, with a proper pride,
    Which his smiling features tell,
"'Twill soothing be if I let you see,
    How extremely nice you'll smell."

'And he stirred it round and round and round,
    And he sniffed at the foaming froth;
When I ups with his heels, and smothers his squeals
    In the scum of the boiling broth.

'And I eat that cook in a week or less,
    And—as I eating be
The last of his chops, why, I almost drops,
    For a wessel in sight I see!

> .   .   .   .

'And I never grin, and I never smile,
    And I never larf nor play,
But I sit and croak, and a single joke
    I have—which is to say:

'Oh, I am a cook and a captain bold,
    And the mate of the *Nancy* brig,
And a bo'sun tight, *and* a midshipmite,
    And the crew of the captain's gig!'

(1869)

The Bishop of Rum-ti-Foo

FROM east and south the holy clan
Of Bishops gathered, to a man;
To Synod, called Pan-Anglican,
    In flocking crowds they came.
Among them was a Bishop, who
Had lately been appointed to
The balmy isle of Rum-ti-Foo,
    And PETER was his name.

His people—twenty-three in sum—
They played the eloquent tum-tum,
And lived on scalps served up in rum—
    The only sauce they knew.

When first good Bishop PETER came
(For PETER was that Bishop's name),
To humour them, he did the same
      As they of Rum-ti-Foo.

His flock, I've often heard him tell,
(His name was PETER) loved him well,
And summoned by the sound of bell,
      In crowds together came.
'Oh, massa, why you go away?
Oh, Massa PETER, please to stay.'
(They called him PETER, people say,
Because it was his name.)

He told them all good boys to be,
And sailed away across the sea,
At London Bridge that Bishop he
      Arrived one Tuesday night—
And as forthwith he homeward strode
To his pan-Anglican abode,
He passed along the Borough Road
      And saw a gruesome sight.

He saw a crowd assembled round
A person dancing on the ground,
Who straight began to leap and bound
      With all his might and main.
To see that dancing man he stopped,
Who twirled and wriggled, skipped and hopped,
Then down incontinently dropped,
      And then sprang up again.

The Bishop chuckled at the sight,
'This style of dancing would delight
A simple Rum-ti-Foozleite,
      I'll learn it if I can,
To please the tribe when I get back.'
He begged the man to teach his knack.
'Right Reverend Sir, in half a crack,'
      Replied that dancing man.

The dancing man he worked away—
And taught the Bishop every day—
The dancer skipped like any fay—
      Good PETER did the same.
The Bishop buckled to his task
With *battements*, cuts, and *pas de basque*
(I'll tell you, if you care to ask,
      That PETER was his name).

'Come, walk like this,' the dancer said,
'Stick out your toes—stick in your head,
Stalk on with quick, galvanic tread—
   Your fingers thus extend;
The attitude's considered quaint.'
The weary Bishop, feeling faint,
Replied, 'I do not say it ain't,
   But Time, my Christian friend.'

'We now proceed to something new—
Dance as the PAYNES and LAURIS do,
Like this—one, two—one, two—one, two.'
   The Bishop, never proud,
But in an overwhelming heat
(His name was PETER, I repeat)
Performed the PAYNE and LAURI feat,
   And puffed his thanks aloud.

Another game the dancer planned—
'Just take your ankle in your hand,
And try, my lord, if you can stand—
   Your body stiff and stark.
If, when revisiting your see,
You learnt to hop on shore—like me—
The novelty would striking be,
   And must attract remark.'

'No,' said the worthy Bishop, 'No,
That is a length to which, I trow,
Colonial Bishops cannot go.
   You may express surprise
At finding Bishops deal in pride—
But, if that trick I ever tried,
I should appear undignified
   In Rum-ti-Foozle's eyes.

'The islanders of Rum-ti-Foo
Are well-conducted persons, who
Approve a joke as much as you,
   And laugh at it as such;
But if they saw their Bishop land,
His leg supported in his hand,
The joke they wouldn't understand—
   'Twould pain them very much!'

(1869)

The King of Canoodle-Dum

THE story of FREDERICK GOWLER,
  A mariner of the sea,
Who quitted his ship, the *Howler*,
  A-sailing in Caribee.
For many a day he wandered,
  Till he met, in a state of rum,
CALAMITY POP VON PEPPERMINT DROP,
  The King of Canoodle-Dum.

That monarch addressed him gaily,
  'Hum!   Golly de do to-day?
Hum!   Lily-white Buckra sailee'—
  (You notice his playful way?)—
'What dickens you doin' here, sar?
  Why debbil you want to come?
Hum!   Picaninnee, dere isn't no sea
  In City Canoodle-Dum!'

And GOWLER he answered sadly,
  'Oh, mine is a doleful tale!
They've treated me very badly
  In Lunnon, from where I hail.
I'm one of the Family Royal—
  No common Jack Tar you see;
I'm WILLIAM THE FOURTH, far up in the North,
  A King in my own countree!'

Bang-bang!   How the tom-toms thundered!
  Bang-bang!   How they thumped the gongs!
Bang-bang!   How the people wondered!
  Bang-bang!   At it, hammer and tongs!
Alliance with Kings of Europe
  Is an honour Canoodlers seek;
Her monarchs don't stop with PEPPERMINT DROP
  Every day in the week!

FRED told them that he was *un*done,
  For his people all went insane,
And fired the Tower of London,
  And Grinnidge's Naval Fane.
And some of them racked St James's,
  And vented their rage upon
The Church of St Paul, the Fishmongers' Hall,
  And the Angel at Islington.

CALAMITY POP implored him
   At Canoodle-Dum to remain
Till those people of his restored him
   To power and rank again.
CALAMITY POP he made him
   A Prince of Canoodle-Dum,
With a couple of caves, some beautiful slaves,
   And the run of the royal rum.

POP gave him his only daughter,
   HUM PICKITY WIMPLE TIP:
FRED vowed that if over the water
   He went, in an English ship,
He'd make her his queen—though truly,
   It is an unusual thing
For a Caribee brat who's as black as your hat
   To be wife of an English King.

And all the Canoodle-Dummers
   They copied his rolling walk,
His method of draining rummers,
   His emblematical talk.
For his dress and his graceful breeding,
   His delicate taste in rum,
And his nautical way, were the talk of the day
   In the Court of Canoodle-Dum.

CALAMITY POP most wisely
   Determined in everything
To model his Court precisely
   On that of the English King;
And ordered that every lady
   And every lady's lord
Should masticate jacky (a kind of tobaccy)
   And scatter its juice abroad.

They signified wonder roundly
   At any astounding yarn,
By darning their dear eyes soundly
   ('Twas all that they had to darn).
They 'hoisted their slacks,' adjusting
   Garments of plantain-leaves,
With nautical twitches (as if they wore stitches—
   Instead of a dress like Eve's!)

They shivered their timbers proudly,
   At phantom fore-locks dragged,
And called for a hornpipe loudly
   Whenever amusement flagged.

'Hum!   Golly! him POP resemble,
    Him Britisher sov'reign, hum!
CALAMITY POP VON PEPPERMINT DROP,
    De King of Canoodle-Dum!'

The mariner's lively 'Hollo!'
    Enlivened Canoodle's plain
(For blessings unnumbered follow
    In Civilization's train).
But Fortune, who loves a bathos,
    A terrible ending planned,
For ADMIRAL D. CHICKABIDDY, C.B.,
    Placed foot on Canoodle land!

That officer seized KING GOWLER;
    He threatened his royal brains,
And put him aboard the *Howler*,
    And fastened him down with chains.
The *Howler* she weighed her anchor,
    With FREDERICK nicely nailed,
And off to the North with WILLIAM THE FOURTH
    That Admiral slowly sailed.

CALAMITY said (with folly)
    'Hum! nebber want him again—
Him civilize all of us, golly!
    CALAMITY such him brain!'
The people, however, were pained when
    They saw him aboard the ship,
But none of them wept for their FREDDY, except
    HUM PICKITY WIMPLE TIP.

                                            (1869)

Etiquette

THE *Ballyshannon* foundered off the coast of Cariboo,
And down in fathoms many went the captain and the crew;
Down went the owners—greedy men whom hope of gain allured:
Oh, dry the starting tear, for they were heavily insured.

Besides the captain and the mate, the owners and the crew,
The passengers were also drowned excepting only two:
Young PETER GRAY, who tasted teas for BAKER, CROOP, AND Co.,
And SOMERS, who from Eastern shores imported indigo.

These passengers, by reason of their clinging to a mast,
Upon a desert island were eventually cast.
They hunted for their meals, as ALEXANDER SELKIRK used,
But they couldn't chat together—they had not been introduced.

For PETER GRAY, and SOMERS too, though certainly in trade,
Were properly particular about the friends they made;
And somehow thus they settled in without a word of mouth—
That GRAY should take the northern half, while SOMERS took
   the south.

On PETER'S portion oysters grew—a delicacy rare,
But oysters were a delicacy PETER couldn't bear.
On SOMERS' side was turtle, on the shingle lying thick,
Which SOMERS couldn't eat, because it always made him sick.

GRAY gnashed his teeth with envy as he saw a mighty store
Of turtle unmolested on his fellow-creature's shore:
The oysters at his feet aside impatiently he shoved,
For turtle and his mother were the only things he loved.

And SOMERS sighed in sorrow as he settled in the south,
For the thought of PETER'S oysters brought the water to his
   mouth.
He longed to lay him down upon the shelly bed, and stuff:
He had often eaten oysters, but had never had enough.

How they wished an introduction to each other they had had
When on board the *Ballyshannon*!   And it drove them nearly
   mad
To think how very friendly with each other they might get,
If it wasn't for the arbitrary rule of etiquette!

One day, when out a-hunting for the *mus ridiculus*,
GRAY overheard his fellow-man soliloquizing thus:
'I wonder how the playmates of my youth are getting on,
M'CONNELL, S. B. WALTERS, PADDY BYLES, and ROBINSON?'

These simple words made PETER as delighted as could be,
Old chummies at the Charterhouse were ROBINSON and he!
He walked straight up to SOMERS, then he turned extremely red,
Hesitated, hummed and hawed a bit, then cleared his throat, and
   said:

'I beg your pardon—pray forgive me if I seem too bold,
But you have breathed a name I knew familiarly of old.
You spoke of ROBINSON—I happened to be by—
You know him?'   'Yes, extremely well.'   'Allow me—so do I!'

It was enough: they felt they could more sociably get on,
For (ah, the magic of the fact!) they each knew ROBINSON!
And MR SOMERS' turtle was at PETER's service quite,
And MR SOMERS punished PETER's oyster-beds all night.

They soon became like brothers from community of wrongs:
They wrote each other little odes and sang each other songs;
They told each other anecdotes disparaging their wives;
On several occasions, too, they saved each other's lives.

They felt quite melancholy when they parted for the night,
And got up in the morning soon as ever it was light;
Each other's pleasant company they reckoned so upon,
And all because it happened that they both knew ROBINSON!

They lived for many years on that inhospitable shore,
And day by day they learned to love each other more and more,
At last, to their astonishment, on getting up one day,
They saw a vessel anchored in the offing of the bay!

To PETER an idea occurred.   'Suppose we cross the main?
So good an opportunity may not occur again.'
And SOMERS thought a minute, then ejaculated, 'Done!
I wonder how my business in the City's getting on?'

'But stay,' said MR PETER: 'when in England, as you know,
I earned a living tasting teas for BAKER, CROOP, AND CO.,
I may be superseded—my employers think me dead!'
'Then come with me,' said SOMERS, 'and taste indigo instead.'

But all their plans were scattered in a moment when they found
The vessel was a convict ship from Portland, outward bound!
When a boat came off to fetch them, though they felt it very kind,
To go on board they firmly but respectfully declined.

As both the happy settlers roared with laughter at the joke,
They recognized an unattractive fellow pulling stroke:
'Twas ROBINSON—a convict, in an unbecoming frock!
Condemned to seven years for misappropriating stock!!!

They laughed no more, for SOMERS thought he had been rather
    rash
In knowing one whose friend had misappropriated cash;
And PETER thought a foolish tack he must have gone upon
In making the acquaintance of a friend of ROBINSON.

At first they didn't quarrel very openly, I've heard;
They nodded when they met, and now and then exchanged a
    word:
The word grew rare, and rarer still the nodding of the head,
And when they meet each other now, they cut each other dead.

To allocate the island they agreed by word of mouth,
And PETER takes the north again, and SOMERS takes the south;
And PETER has the oysters, which he loathes with horror grim,
And SOMERS has the turtle—turtle disagrees with him.

(1869)

Captain Reece

OF all the ships upon the blue
No ship contained a better crew
Than that of worthy CAPTAIN REECE,
Commanding of the *Mantelpiece*.

He was adored by all his men,
For worthy CAPTAIN REECE, R.N.,
Did all that lay within him to
Promote the comfort of his crew.

If ever they were dull or sad,
Their captain danced to them like mad,
Or told, to make the time pass by,
Droll legends of his infancy.

A feather bed had every man,
Warm slippers and hot-water can,
Brown windsor from the captain's store,
A valet, too, to every four.

Did they with thirst in summer burn?
Lo, seltzogenes at every turn,
And on all very sultry days
Cream ices handed round on trays.

Then currant wine and ginger pops
Stood handily on all the 'tops';
And, also, with amusement rife,
A 'Zoetrope, or Wheel of Life.'

New volumes came across the sea
From MISTER MUDIE's libraree;
The Times and *Saturday Review*
Beguiled the leisure of the crew.

Kind-hearted CAPTAIN REECE, R.N.,
Was quite devoted to his men;
In point of fact, good CAPTAIN REECE
Beatified the *Mantelpiece*.

One summer eve, at half-past ten,
He said (addressing all his men):
'Come, tell me, please, what I can do
To please and gratify my crew?

'By any reasonable plan
I'll make you happy, if I can;
My own convenience count as *nil*;
It is my duty, and I will.'

Then up and answered WILLIAM LEE
(The kindly captain's coxswain he,
A nervous, shy, low-spoken man),
He cleared his throat and thus began:

'You have a daughter, CAPTAIN REECE,
Ten female cousins, and a niece,
A ma, if what I'm told is true,
Six sisters, and an aunt or two.

'Now, somehow, sir, it seems to me,
More friendly-like we all should be
If you united of 'em to
Unmarried members of the crew.

'If you'd ameliorate our life,
Let each select from them a wife;
And as for nervous me, old pal,
Give me your own enchanting gal!'

Good CAPTAIN REECE, that worthy man,
Debated on his coxswain's plan:
'I quite agree,' he said, 'O BILL;
It is my duty, and I will.

'My daughter, that enchanting gurl,
Has just been promised to an earl,
And all my other familee,
To peers of various degree.

'But what are dukes and viscounts to
The happiness of all my crew?
The word I gave you I'll fulfil;
It is my duty, and I will.

'As you desire it shall befall,
I'll settle thousands on you all,
And I shall be, despite my hoard,
The only bachelor on board.'

The boatswain of the *Mantelpiece*,
He blushed and spoke to CAPTAIN REECE.
'I beg your honour's leave,' he said,
'If you would wish to go and wed,

'I have a widowed mother who
Would be the very thing for you—
She long has loved you from afar,
She washes for you, CAPTAIN R.'

The captain saw the dame that day—
Addressed her in his playful way—
'And did it want a wedding ring?
It was a tempting ickle sing!

'Well, well, the chaplain I will seek,
We'll all be married this day week—
At yonder church upon the hill;
It is my duty, and I will!'

The sisters, cousins, aunts, and niece,
And widowed ma of CAPTAIN REECE,
Attended there as they were bid;
It was their duty, and they did.

(1869)

HENRY SAMBROOKE LEIGH

(1837–1883)

The Twins

IN form and feature, face and limb,
   I grew so like my brother,
That folks got taking me for him,
   And each for one another.
It puzzled all our kith and kin,
   It reach'd an awful pitch;
For one of us was born a twin,
   Yet not a soul knew which.

One day (to make the matter worse),
   Before our names were fix'd,
As we were being wash'd by nurse
   We got completely mix'd;
And thus, you see, by Fate's decree
   (Or rather nurse's whim),
My brother John got christen'd *me*,
   And I got christen'd *him*.

This fatal likeness even dogg'd
   My footsteps when at school,
And I was always getting flogg'd
   For John turn'd out a fool.
I put this question hopelessly
   To every one I knew—
What *would* you do, if you were me,
   To prove that you were *you*?

Our close resemblance turn'd the tide
   Of my domestic life;
For somehow my intended bride
   Became my brother's wife.
In short, year after year the same
   Absurd mistakes went on;
And when I died—the neighbours came
   And buried brother John!

(1869)

HARRY CHOLMONDELEY PENNELL
(1837–1915)

I've Lost My ——

PEELER, hast thou found my treasure,
   Hast thou seen my vanished fair?
Flora of the raven ringlets,
   Flora of the shining hair?

Tell me quick, and no palaver,
   For I am a man of heat—
Hast thou seen her, O Policeman!
   Hast thou marked her on thy beat?

Twigg'd, I say, her fairy figure
   In the wilderness of Bow?
Traced her Lilliputian footprints
   On the sands of Rotten Row?

Out alas! thou answerest nothing,
   And my senseless anger dies;
Who would look for 'speculation'
   In a boil'd potato's eyes?

Foggy Peeler! purblind Peeler!
   Wherefore walk'st thou in a dream?—
Ask a plethoric black beetle
   Why it walks into the cream!

Why the jolly gnats find pleasaunce
   In your drowsy orbs of sight,
Why besotted daddy long-legs
   Hum into the nearest light,

Ah, my Flora (graceless chit!) O
   Pearl of all thy peerless race!
Where shall fancy find one fit, O
   Fit to fill thy vacant place?
Who can be the graceful ditt-o
   Ditto to that form and face?

Hence, then, sentimental twaddle!
   Love, thy fetters I will fly—
Friendship is not worth a boddle,
   Lost, alas!   I've lost—MY SKYE.

(1861)

JOSEPH ASHBY STERRY
(1838–1917)

Spring's Delights

SPRING's Delights are now returning!
 Let the Lazy Minstrel sing;
While the ruddy logs are burning,
 Let his merry banjo ring!
Take no heed of pluvial patter,
 Waste no time in vain regrets;
Though our teeth are all a-chatter
 Like the clinking castanets!
Though it's freezing, sleeting, snowing,
 Though we're speechless from catarrh,
Though the east wind's wildly blowing,
 Let us warble, *Tra-la-la!*

Spring's Delights are now returning!
 Let us order new great-coats:
Never let us dream of spurning
 Woollen wraps around our throats.
Let us see the couch nocturnal
 Snugly swathed in eider-down:
Let not thoughts of weather vernal
 Tempt us to go out of Town.
Though the biting blast is cruel,
 Though our 'tonic's' not *sol-fa*,
Though we sadly sup on gruel,
 Let us warble, *Tra-la-la.*

Spring's Delights are now returning!
 Now the poet deftly weaves
Quaint conceits and rhymes concerning
 Croton oil and mustard leaves!
Let us, though we are a fixture,
 In our room compelled to stay—
Let us quaff the glad cough mixture,
 Gaily gargle time away!
Though we're racked with pains rheumatic,
 Though to sleep we've said ta-ta,
Let us, with a voice ecstatic,
 Wildly warble, *Tra-la-la!*

Spring's Delights are now returning!
  Doctors now are blithe and gay!
Heaps of money now they're earning,
  Calls they're making ev'ry day.
Ev'ry shepherd swain grows colder,
  As, in vain, he tries to sing;
Feels he now quite ten years older
  'Neath the blast of blighting Spring!
Though we're doubtful of the issue,
  Let us bravely shout Hurrah!
And in one superb *A-tishoo!*
  Sneeze and warble, *Tra-la-la!*

                                        (1882)

FRANCIS BRETT HARTE

(1839–1902)

That Heathen Chinee

WHICH I wish to remark—
  And my language is plain—
That for ways that are dark
  And for tricks that are vain,
The heathen Chinee is peculiar,
  Which the same I would rise to explain.

Ah Sin was his name;
  And I shall not deny
In regard to the same
  What that name might imply,
But his smile it was pensive and childlike,
  As I frequent remarked to Bill Nye.

It was August the third;
  And quite soft was the skies;
Which it might be inferred
  That Ah Sin was likewise;
Yet he played it that day upon William
  And me in a way I despise.

Which we had a small game,
  And Ah Sin took a hand:
It was Euchre. The same
  He did not understand;
But he smiled as he sat by the table,
  With the smile that was childlike and bland.

Yet the cards they were stocked
  In a way that I grieve,
And my feelings were shocked
  At the state of Nye's sleeve:
Which was stuffed full of aces and bowers,
  And the same with intent to deceive.

But the hands that were played
  By that heathen Chinee,
And the points that he made
  Were quite frightful to see—
Till at last he put down a right bower,
  Which the same Nye had dealt unto me.

Then I looked up at Nye,
  And he gazed upon me;
And he rose with a sigh,
  And said: 'Can this be?
We are ruined by Chinese cheap labour'—
  And he went for that heathen Chinee.

In the scene that ensued
  I did not take a hand,
But the floor it was strewed
  Like the leaves on the strand
With the cards that Ah Sin had been hiding,
  In the game 'he did not understand.'

In his sleeves, which were long,
  He had twenty-four packs—
Which was coming it strong,
  Yet I state but the facts;
And we found on his nails, which were taper,
  What is frequent in tapers—that's wax.

Which is why I remark,
  And my language is plain,
That for ways that are dark,
  And for tricks that are vain,
The heathen Chinee is peculiar—
  Which the same I am free to maintain.

                                        (1870)

Truthful James

Do I sleep? do I dream?
Do I wonder and doubt?
Are things what they seem?
Or is visions about?
Is our civilization a failure?
Or is the Caucasian played out?

Which expressions are strong;
Yet would feebly imply
Some account of a wrong—
Not to call it a lie—
As was worked off on William, my pardner,
And the same being W. Nye.

He came down to the Ford
On the very same day
Of that lottery drawed
By those sharps at the Bay;
And he says to me: 'Truthful, how goes it?'
I replied: 'It is far, far from gay;

'For the camp has gone wild
On this lottery game,
And has even beguiled
"Injin Dick" by the same.'
Which said Nye to me: 'Injins is pizen:
Do you know what his number is, James?'

I replied: '7, 2,
9, 8, 4, is his hand';
When he started, and drew
Out a list, which he scanned;
Then he softly went for his revolver
With language I cannot command.

Then I said: 'William Nye!'
But he turned upon me,
And the look in his eye
Was quite painful to see;
And he says: 'You mistake: this poor Injin
I protects from such sharps as you be!'

I was shocked and withdrew;
But I grieve to relate,
When he next met my view
Injin Dick was his mate,
And the two around town was a-lying
In a frightfully dissolute state.

Which the war-dance they had
Round a tree at the Bend
Was a sight that was sad;
And it seemed that the end
Would not justify the proceedings,
As I quiet remarked to a friend.

For that Injin he fled
The next day to his band;
And we found William spread
Very loose on the strand,
With a peaceful-like smile on his features,
And a dollar greenback in his hand;

Which, the same when rolled out,
We observed with surprise,
That the Injin, no doubt,
Had believed was the prize—
Them figures in red in the corner,
Which the number of notes specifies.

Was it guile, or a dream?
Is it Nye that I doubt?
Are things what they seem?
Or is visions about?
Is our civilization a failure?
Or is the Caucasian played out?

(1870)

HENRY AUSTIN DOBSON

(1840–1921)

Incognita

JUST for a space that I met her—
    Just for a day in the train!
It began when she feared it would wet her,
    That tiniest spurtle of rain:
So we tucked a great rug in the sashes,
    And carefully padded the pane;
And I sorrow in sackcloth and ashes,
    Longing to do it again!

Then it grew when she begged me to reach her
    A dressing-case under the seat;
She was 'really so tiny a creature,
    That she needed a stool for her feet!'
Which was promptly arranged to her order
    With a care that was even minute,
And a glimpse—of an open-work border,
    And a glance—of the fairyest boot.

Then it drooped, and revived at some hovels—
    'Were they houses for men or for pigs?'
Then it shifted to muscular novels,
    With a little digression on prigs:
She thought *Wives and Daughters* 'so jolly';
    'Had I read it?'   She knew when I had,
Like the rest, I should dote upon 'Molly';
    And 'poor Mrs Gaskell—how sad!'

'Like Browning?'   'But so-so.'   His proof lay
    Too deep for her frivolous mood,
That preferred your mere metrical *soufflé*
    To the stronger poetical food;
Yet at times he was good—'as a tonic';
    Was Tennyson writing just now?
And was this new poet Byronic
    And clever, and naughty, or how?

Then we trifled with concerts and croquet,
    Then she daintily dusted her face;
Then she sprinkled herself with 'Ess Bouquet,'
    Fished out from the foregoing case;
And we chattered of Gassier and Grisi,
    And voted Aunt Sally a bore;
Discussed if the tight rope were easy,
    Or Chopin much harder than Spohr.

And oh! the odd things that she quoted,
    With the prettiest possible look,
And the price of two buns that she noted
    In the prettiest possible book;
While her talk like a musical rillet
    Flashed on with the hours that flew;
And the carriage, her smile seemed to fill it
    With just enough summer—for Two.

Till at last in her corner, peeping
    From a nest of rugs and of furs,
With the white shut eyelids sleeping
    On those dangerous looks of hers,

She seemed like a snowdrop breaking,
　　Not wholly alive nor dead,
But with one blind impulse making
　　To the sounds of the spring overhead;

And I watched in the lamplight's swerving
　　The shade of the down-dropt lid,
And the lip-line's delicate curving,
　　Where a slumbering smile lay hid,
Till I longed that, rather than sever,
　　The train should shriek into space,
And carry us onward—for ever—
　　Me and that beautiful face.

But she suddenly woke in a fidget,
　　With fears she was 'nearly at home,'
And talk of a certain Aunt Bridget,
　　Whom I mentally wished—well, at Rome;
Got out at the very next station,
　　Looking back with a merry *Bon Soir*;
Adding, too, to my utter vexation,
　　A surplus, unkind *Au Revoir*.

So left me to muse on her graces,
　　To doze and to muse, till I dreamed
That we sailed through the sunniest places
　　In a glorified galley, it seemed;
But the cabin was made of a carriage,
　　And the ocean was eau-de-Cologne,
And we split on a rock labelled MARRIAGE,
　　And I woke—as cold as a stone.

And that's how I lost her—a jewel,
　　Incognita—one in a crowd,
Not prudent enough to be cruel,
　　Not worldly enough to be proud.
It was just a shut lid and its lashes,
　　Just a few hours in a train,
And I sorrow in sackcloth and ashes,
　　Longing to see her again.

(1866)

Rose-leaves

A KISS

ROSE kissed me to-day
　　Will she kiss me to-morrow?
Let it be as it may,
Rose kissed me to-day,

But the pleasure gives way
   To a savour of sorrow;--
Rose kissed me to-day,
   Will she kiss me to-morrow?

CIRCE

In the School of Coquettes
   Madam Rose is a scholar:
O, they fish with all nets
In the School of Coquettes!
When her brooch she forgets
   'Tis to show her new collar;
In the School of Coquettes
   Madam Rose is a scholar!

A TEAR

There's a tear in her eye—
   Such a clear little jewel!
What *can* make her cry?
There's a tear in her eye.
'Puck has killed a big fly,
   And it's *horribly* cruel';
There's a tear in her eye,
   Such a clear little jewel!

A GREEK GIFT

Here's a present for Rose,
   How pleased she is looking!
Is it verse?—is it prose?
Here's a present for Rose!
'*Plats*,' '*Entrées*,' and '*Rôts*'—
   Why, it's *Gouffé on Cooking*.
Here's a present for Rose,
   How *pleased* she is looking!

'URCEUS EXIT'

I intended an Ode,
   And it turned to a Sonnet.
It began *à la mode*,
I intended an Ode;
But Rose crossed the road
   In her latest new bonnet;
I intended an Ode;
   And it turned to a Sonnet.

(1874)

HENRY DUFF TRAILL

(1842–1900)

A Drawing-room Ballad

CAN you recall an ode to June
    Or lines to any river
In which you do not meet the 'moon,'
    And see 'the moonbeams quiver'?
I've heard such songs to many a tune
    But never yet—no niver—
Have I escaped that rhyme to 'June'
    Or missed that rhyme to 'river.'

At times the bard from his refrain
    A moment's respite snatches,
The while his over-cudgelled brain
    At some new jingle catches;
Yet long from the unlucky moon
    Himself he cannot sever;
But grasps once more that rhyme to 'June,
    And seeks a rhyme to 'river.'

Then let not indolence be blamed
    On him whose verses show it
By shunning 'burdens' (rightly named
    For reader and for poet);
For rhymes must fail him late or soon,
    Nor can he deal for ever
In words whose sound resembles 'June,'
    And assonents of 'river.'

When 'loon''s been used, and 'shoon' and 'spoon,'
    And 'stiver' sounded 'stīver,'
Think of a bard reduced to 'coon,'
    And left alone with 'liver'!
Ah, then, how blessèd were the boon!
    How doubly blest the giver,
Who gave him one rhyme more for 'June,'
    And one more rhyme for 'river'!

(1882)

After Dilettante Concetti

'WHY do you wear you hair like a man,
           Sister Helen?
This week is the third since you began.'
'I'm writing a ballad; be still if you can,
           Little brother.
             (*O Mother Carey, mother!*
What chickens are these between sea and heaven?)'

'But why does your figure appear so lean,
           Sister Helen?
And why do you dress in sage, sage green?'
'Children should never be heard, if seen,
           Little brother.
             (*O Mother Carey, mother!*
What fowls are a-wing in the stormy heaven!)'

'But why is your face so yellowy white,
           Sister Helen?
And why are your skirts so funnily tight?'
'Be quiet, you torment, or how can I write,
           Little Brother?
             (*O Mother Carey, mother!*
How gathers thy train to the sea from the heaven!)'

'And who's Mother Carey, and what is her train,
           Sister Helen?
And why do you call her again and again?'
'You troublesome boy, why that's the refrain,
           Little brother.
             (*O Mother Carey, mother!*
What work is toward in the startled heaven?)'

'And what's a refrain?   What a curious word,
           Sister Helen!
Is the ballad you're writing about a sea-bird?'
'Not at all; why should it be?   Don't be absurd,
           Little brother.
             (*O Mother Carey, mother!*
Thy brood flies lower as lowers the heaven.)'

[A big brother speaketh.]

'The refrain you've studied a meaning had,
           Sister Helen!
It gave strange force to a weird ballad,

But refrains have become a ridiculous 'fad,'
        Little brother.
    And *Mother Carey, mother,*
Has a bearing on nothing in earth or heaven.

'But the finical fashion has had its day,
        Sister Helen,
And let's try in the style of a different lay
To bid it adieu in poetical way,
        Little brother.
    So, Mother Carey, mother!
Collect your chickens and go to—heaven.'

        [A pause.   Then the big brother singeth, accom-
        panying himself in a plaintive wise on the triangle:]

'Look in my face.   My name is Used-to-was,
    I am also called Played-out and Done-to-death,
    And It-will-wash-no-more.   Awaketh
Slowly, but sure awakening it has,
The common-sense of man; and I alas!
    The ballad-burden trick, now known too well,
    Am turned to scorn, and grown contemptible—
A too transparent artifice to pass.

'What a cheap dodge I am!   The cats who dart
    Tin-kettled through the streets in wild surprise
    Assail judicious ears not otherwise;
And yet no critics praise the urchin's 'art,'
Who to the wretched creature's caudal part,
    Its foolish empty-jingling "burden" ties.'

                                        (1882)

CHARLES FOLLEN ADAMS

(1842–1918)

Prevalent Poetry

A WANDERING tribe called the Siouxs,
Wear moccasins, having no shiouxs.
    They are made of buckskin,
    With the fleshy side in,
Embroidered with beads of bright hyiouxs.

When out on the war-path the Siouxs
March single-file—never by tiouxs—
   And by 'blazing' the trees
   Can return at their ease,
And their way through the forest ne'er liouxs.

All new-fashioned boats he eschiouxs,
And uses the birch-bark caniouxs,
   These are handy and light,
   And, inverted at night,
Give shelter from storms and from dyiouxs.

The principal food of the Siouxs
Is Indian maize, which they briouxs
   And hominy make,
   Or mix in a cake
And eat it with pork, as they chiouxs.

     .   .   .

Now doesn't this spelling look cyiouxrious?
'Tis enough to make anyone fyiouxrious?
   So a word to the wise!
   Pray our language revise
With orthography not so injiouxrious.

                    (1881)

ANDREW LANG

(1844–1912)

A Psalm of Life

(AS EXHIBITED IN CHRISTMAS ANNUALS)

TELL me not, O Soul that slumbers,
   'Life is placid, Life is pale!'
'Tis not so in Christmas Numbers;
   There quite other views prevail.

Life is foaming, Life is frantic,
   Here the dagger, there the bowl;
'Stick at nothing that's romantic!'
   Says my Printer to my Soul.

Not to live as boys and girls would
   Is our men's and maidens' way;
But to act as if in Earlswood
   You might find them any day!

Write of fire, and flood, and battle,
　　Write of earls that gaily sin,
Write of governesses—that'll
　　Bring the sweet subscribers in!

Lives of Great Highwaymen show it,
　　How to make our tales sublime;
Bother sense and grammar!　Go it—
　　Give us something new in Crime!

Crimes that ne'er, perchance, another,
　　As he reached his volume's end,
Dreamed of—give us *these*, my brother.
　　Something fresh in guilt, my friend!

Let us then be up and raving,
　　Rave of ghosts, and sin, and fate;
These the gentle reader's craving,
　　And he does not like to wait!

(1885)

Brahma

(After EMERSON)

IF the wild bowler thinks he bowls,
　　Or if the batsman thinks he's bowled,
They know not, poor misguided souls,
　　They too shall perish unconsoled.
I am the batsman and the bat,
　　I am the bowler and the ball,
The umpire, the pavilion cat,
　　The roller, pitch, and stumps, and all.

(1888)

A New Shakespeare

RICHARD III

ACT I.　SCENE I.　*London: a Street*

Enter GLOSTER (reading the *Historical Review*).

GLOSTER.　I am a very personable man,
　　And did not cut my teeth ere I was born,
　　Still less may be described as 'half made up.'
　　My humpback is a myth: mine evil deeds
　　Were falsehoods of Archbishop Morton coined,
　　Paid for by Richmond, put in currency
　　By that detested caitiff, Thomas More.

Enter CLARENCE.

GLOSTER. Brother, good day! Thou canst not say *I* did it!
CLARENCE. There is a certain buzzing in my wits:
  The new historians distract my mind,
  Yet was I Clarence once, and bore a brain.
GLOSTER (*aside*). Wiser, perchance, if thou hadst brained a
  Boar!
  But, Hist! I am a moral character.
  I ask thee, who was guilty?
CLARENCE. I know not, but——
GLOSTER. But me no buts! That butt of Malmsey wine
  Is an exploded fable.
CLARENCE. Certainly.
  Yet, somehow, I was foully done to death
  Unhouseled, unanointed, unannealed.
GLOSTER. 'Twas Richmond, 'twas false, fleeting, perjured
  Richmond! [*Exit* CLARENCE.

SCENE II. *The Same*

To GLOSTER *enter* THE CORPSE *of* HENRY VI *and* LADY ANNE.

LADY ANNE. Rest you while I lament my Henry's corpse,
  While I adore my Henry's holy shade!
GLOSTER. *I* did not kill your husband; on the day
  Of our late King's deplorable demise
  I was not in the Tower—was out of town:
  At Sandwich—Mr Clements Markham proves—
  Was I: perchance pursued the devious ball,
  And in the Maiden bunker came to grief.
  Or if not so, I know not what I did,
  Or what foul fiend could take a man to Sandwich.
LADY ANNE. Never hung poison on a fouler toad!
GLOSTER. Nay, hear me swear a good mouth-filling oath
  That I can prove a perfect alibi.
  Listen, from this *Historical Review*,
  Put forth by Master Longman, in the Row,
  I'll prove me sackless of that monstrous deed!
LADY ANNE. A monstrous deal of sack!
GLOSTER.   Nay, mock me not!
  For Mr Clements Markham makes it plain
  That on the fatal day I was afar
  From Towers of Julius, London's lasting shame.
  'Tis true that Mr Samuel Gardiner
  Has put the matter in another light:
  A question 'tis of dates, but what are they?
  Myself am strong on Clements Markham's side;
  (*aside*) Yet Mrs Markham tells another tale!

LADY ANNE. 'Samivel, a halibi.'   This likes me well!
GLOSTER. Then, then we may consider ourselves engaged?
LADY ANNE. Perdition catch my soul, but I do love thee!

                                           [*Exit* LADY ANNE *and* CORPSE.

SCENE III

To GLOSTER *enter* KING EDWARD, *led in sick* [*sic*].

KING EDWARD. Alas! 'twas aye my lamentable custom
    To make the cold-baked meats to furnish forth
    The wedding breakfast!   Widows were my bane.
    Still fast on one, I wooed another widow,
    And all the while was wedded to Another.
    None knew but the archbishop: thus my sons,
    These thrice unhappy children in the Tower,
    Are, to speak plainly, illegitimate.
    Thou wilt not slay them, Gloster?
GLOSTER.   Fear me not!
    My title, the *Historical Review*
    Assures me, is writ plain: there is no need
    That *I* should smother children in the Tower.
    'Twas Richmond did it!   Mr Clements Markham,
    In spite of the Croyland Continuator
    Has made this view extremely plausible,
    (*aside*) But *Mrs* Markham tells another tale!
KING EDWARD. Bless thee: but I feel poorly and would go.

                              [KING EDWARD *is led out sick.*

SCENE IV

To GLOSTER *enter* HASTINGS.

HASTINGS. Come, lead me to the block!   'Tis falsely said
    That, ere he tried me, Richard had my head!
GLOSTER. Exactly!   The *Historical Review*
    And Mr Clements Markham vouch for it.
    Thou, Hastings, hadst due trial of thy peers;
    And so, farewell, a plunger wert thou ever,
    Yet could I better spare a better man!

                            [HASTINGS *is led to the block.*

SCENE V

To GLOSTER *enter* DIGHTON *and* FORREST.

DIGHTON. It is a very palpable relief
    To learn, my Forrest, that we never smothered
    (At all events, not in King Richard's time),
    The most replenished, sweet work of nature,
    These everlasting babes within the Tower!

FORREST. Nay; it was Henry VII who bade us smother!
GLOSTER. What! wed a Princess and work off her brother!

[*Exeunt* DIGHTON *and* FORREST.

SCENE VI

To GLOSTER *enter* GHOSTS.

GHOST OF PRINCE EDWARD.

Let me not sit upon thy soul to-morrow.
I do misdoubt me 'twas another's hand
That stabbed me in the field by Tewkesbury!

GHOST OF HENRY VI.

When I was mortal, my anointed body
By someone was punched full of deadly holes;
But *who* that puncher is who punched with care
Is, bless us all! a very different thing.

GHOSTS *of* RIVERS, VAUGHAN, GREY, *and a Number* *of* OTHER GHOSTS.

We come to offer our apologies,
And to regret that we were much misled
By rumour, painted full of fiery tongues.
'Tis true there was a lot of killing done,
And massacre made merry round the throne;
But liars were the Tudor chroniclers,
Especially the lewd Archbishop Morton.
GLOSTER. It was not I who did the thing ye wot of?
GHOSTS. Apparently it was not!   Fare ye well!

[*Exeunt* GHOSTS.

GLOSTER. Richard's himself again!   Now to the field
A horse, a horse, my kingdom for a horse!
For there's no way of getting over it,
That, after doing prodigies of valour,
Myself was foully slain on Bosworth Field,
Unless, indeed, 'tis I was Perkin Warbeck!
A view not broached by Mr Clements Markham,
Yet tenable, at least, in magazines,
And among modern speculations.
A horse, a horse, my kingdom for a horse!

[*Exit fighting.*

CURTAIN

(1891)

GEORGE THOMAS LANIGAN

(1845–1886)

A Threnody on the Ahkoond of Swat

WHAT, what, what,
What's the news from Swat?
    Sad news,
    Bad news,
Comes by the cable led
Through the Indian Ocean's bed,
Through the Persian Gulf, the Red
Sea and the Med—
Iterranean—he's dead;
The Ahkoond is dead!

For the Ahkoond I mourn,
    Who wouldn't?
He strove to disregard the message stern,
    But he Ahkoodn't.
Dead, dead, dead,
    (Sorrow Swats!)
Swats wha hae wi' Ahkoond bled,
Swats whom he hath often led
Onward to a gory bed,
    Or to victory,
    As the case might be,
        Sorrow Swats!

Tears shed,
    Shed tears like water,
Your great Ahkoond is dead!
    That Swats the matter!

Mourn, city of Swat!
Your great Ahkoond is not,
But laid mid worms to rot.
His mortal part alone, his soul was caught
    (Because he was a good Ahkoond)
    Up to the bosom of Mahound.
Though earthy walls his frame surround
(Forever hallowed be the ground!)

And sceptics mock the lowly mound
And say: 'He's now of no Ahkoond!'
  His soul is in the skies—
The azure skies that bend above his loved
  Metropolis of Swat.
He sees with larger, other eyes
Athwart all earthly mysteries—
  He knows what's Swat.

Let Swat bury the great Ahkoond
    With a noise of mourning and lamentation!
Let Swat bury the great Ahkoond
With the noise of the mourning of the
  Swattish nation!

  Fallen is at length
  Its tower of strength,
Its sun is dimmed ere it had nooned;
Dead lies the great Ahkoond,
  The great Ahkoond of Swat
  Is not!

                        (1873)

EDWARD NOLAN

(1846–1870)

'Oxford is a Stage'

OXFORD is a stage,
And all the men in residence are players:
They have their exeats and examinations;
And one man in his time plays many parts,
His acts being seven ages.   At first the Freshman,
Stumbling and stuttering in his tutor's rooms.
And then the aspiring Classman, with white tie
And shy desponding face, creeping along
Unwilling to the Schools.   Then, at the Union,
Spouting like fury, with some woeful twaddle
Upon the 'Crisis.'   Then a billiard-player,
Full of strange oaths, a keen and cunning card,
Clever in cannons, sudden and quick in hazards,
Seeking a billiard reputation

Even in the pocket's mouth.   And then the Fellow,
His fair round forehead with hard furrows lined,
With weakened eyes and beard of doubtful growth,
Crammed with old lore of useless application,
And so he plays his part.   The sixth age shifts
Into the lean and study-worn Professor,
With spectacles on nose and class at side;
His youthful nose has grown a world too large
For his shrunk face; and his big manly voice,
Turning again towards childish treble, pipes
And whistles in his sound.   Last scene of all,
That ends this strange eventful history,
Is utter donnishness and mere nonentity,
Without respect, or tact, or taste, or anything.

(1868)

'MAX ADELER'
(CHARLES HEBER CLARK)
(1847–1915)

Out of the Hurly-Burly

I

THE death-angel smote Alexander McGlue,
    And gave him protracted repose;
He wore a checked shirt and a Number Nine shoe,
    And he had a pink wart on his nose.
No doubt he is happier dwelling in space
    Over there on the evergreen shore.
His friends are informed that his funeral takes place
    Precisely at quarter past four.

II

Willie had a purple monkey climbing up a yellow stick
And when he sucked the paint all off it made him deathly sick;
And in his latest hours he clasped that monkey in his hand,
And bade good-bye to earth and went into a better land.

Oh! no more he'll shoot his sister with his little wooden gun;
And no more he'll twist the pussy's tail and make her yowl, for fun.
The pussy's tail now stands out straight; the gun is laid aside;
The monkey doesn't jump around since little Willie died.

III

Four doctors tackled Johnny Smith—
    They blistered and they bled him;
With squills and antibilious pills
    And ipecac. they fed him.
They stirred him up with calomel,
    And tried to move his liver;
But all in vain—his little soul
    Was wafted o'er The River.

IV

We have lost our little Hanner in a very painful manner,
    And we often ask, How can her harsh sufferings be borne?
When her death was first reported, her aunt got up and snorted
    With the grief that she supported, for it made her feel forlorn.

She was such a little seraph that her father, who is sheriff,
    Really doesn't seem to care if he ne'er smiles in life again.
She has gone, we hope, to heaven, at the early age of seven
    (Funeral starts off at eleven), where she'll never more have
    pain.

V

Oh! bury Bartholomew out in the woods,
    In a beautiful hole in the ground,
Where the bumble-bees buzz and the woodpeckers sing,
    And the straddle-bugs fumble around;
So that, in winter, when the snow and the slush
    Have covered his last little bed,
His brother Artemas can go out with Jane
    And visit the place with his sled.

VI

Mrs McFadden has gone from this life;
    She has left all its sorrows and cares;
She caught the rheumatics in both of her legs
    With scrubbing the cellar and stairs.
They put mustard-plasters upon her in vain;
    They bathed her with whisky and rum;
But Thursday her spirit departed, and left
    Her body entirely numb.

VII

Little Alexander's dead;
 Jam him in a coffin;
Don't have as good a chance
 For a fun'ral often.

Rush his body right around
 To the cemetery;
Drop him in the sepulchre
 With his Uncle Jerry.

VIII

Stranger, pause and drop a tear,
For Susan Sparks lies buried here;
Mingled, in some perplexing manner,
With Jane, Maria, and portions of Hannah.

(1878)

WILLIAM ERNEST HENLEY

(1849–1903)

Culture in the Slums

(INSCRIBED TO AN INTENSE POET)

I. RONDEAU

'O CRIKEY, Bill!' she ses to me, she ses.
 'Look sharp,' ses she, 'with them there sossiges.
Yea; sharp with them there bags of mysteree!
For lo!' she ses, 'for lo! old pal,' ses she,
 'I'm blooming peckish, neither more nor less.'

Was it not prime—I leave you all to guess
How prime!—to have a jude in love's distress
 Come spooning round, and murmuring balmilee,
     'O crikey, Bill!'

For in such rorty wise doth Love express
His blooming views, and asks for your address,
 And makes it right, and does the gay and free.
 I kissed her—I did so! And her and me
Was pals. And if that ain't good business,
     O crikey, Bill!

II. VILLANELLE

Now ain't they utterly too-too
    (She ses, my Missus mine, ses she),
Them flymy little bits of Blue.

Joe, just you kool 'em—nice and skew
    Upon our old meogginee,
Now ain't they utterly too-too?

They're better than a pot'n' a screw,
    They're equal to a Sunday spree,
Them flymy little bits of Blue!

Suppose I put 'em up the flue,
    And booze the profits, Joe?   Not me.
Now ain't they utterly too-too?

I do the 'Igh Art fake, I do.
    Joe, I'm consummate; and I *see*
Them flymy little bits of Blue.

Which, Joe, is why I ses te you—
    Aesthetic-like, and limp, and free—
Now *ain't* they utterly too-too,
Them flymy little bits of Blue?

III. BALLADE

I often does a quiet read
    At Booty Shelly's poetry;
I thinks that Swinburne at a screed
    Is really almost too-too fly;
    At Signor Vagna's harmony
I likes a merry little flutter;
    I've had at Pater many a shy;
In fact, my form's the Bloomin' Utter.

My mark's a tidy little feed,
    And 'Enery Irving's gallery,
To see old 'Amlick do a bleed,
    And Ellen Terry on the die.
    Or Franky's ghostes at hi-spy,
And parties carried on a shutter.
    Them vulgar Coupeaus is my eye!
In fact, my form's the Bloomin' Utter.

The Grosvenor's nuts—it is, indeed!
    I goes for 'Olman 'Unt like pie.
It's equal to a friendly lead
    To see B. Jones's judes go by.
    Stanhope he makes me fit to cry.
Whistler he makes me melt like butter.
    Strudwick he makes me flash my cly—
In fact, my form's the Bloomin' Utter.

ENVOY

I'm on for any Art that's 'Igh;
    I talks as quite as I can splutter;
    I keeps a Dado on the sly;
In fact, my form's the Bloomin' Utter!

                                    (1887)

Villon's Straight Tip to all Cross Coves

SUPPOSE you screeve? or go cheap-jack?
    Or fake the broads? or fig a nag?
Or thimble-rig? or knap a yack?
    Or pitch a snide? or smash a rag?
    Suppose you duff? or nose and lag?
Or get the straight, and land your pot?
    How do you melt the multy swag?
Booze and the blowens cop the lot.

Fiddle, or fence, or mace, or mack;
    Or moskeneer, or flash the drag;
Dead-lurk a crib, or do a crack;
    Pad with a slang, or chuck a fag;
    Bonnet, or tout, or mump and gag;
Rattle the tats, or mark the spot;
    You can not bank a single stag;
Booze and the blowens cop the lot.

Suppose you try a different tack,
    And on the square you flash your flag?
At penny-a-lining make your whack,
    Or with the mummers mug and gag?
    For nix, for nix the dibbs you bag!
At any graft, no matter what,
    Your merry goblins soon stravag:
Booze and the blowens cop the lot.

THE MORAL

It's up the spout and Charley Wag
With wipes and tickers and what not.
Until the squeezer nips your scrag,
Booze and the blowens cop the lot.

(1887)

Villon's Good-night

YOU bible-sharps that thump on tubs,
You lurkers on the abram sham,
You spunges miking round the pubs,
You flymy titters fond of flam,
You judes that clobber for the stramm,
You ponces good at talking tall,
With fawneys on your dexter famm—
A mot's good-night to one and all!

Likewise you molls that flash your bubs
For swells to spot and stand you sam,
You bloody bonnets, pugs, and subs,
You swatchel coves that pitch and slam,
You mugsmen bold that work the cram,
You flats and joskins great and small,
Gay grass-widows and lawful jam—
A mot's good-night to one and all!

For you, you coppers, narks, and dubs,
Who pinched me when upon the snam,
And gave me mumps and mulligrubs
With skilly and swill that made me clam,
At you I merely lift my gam—
I drink your health against the wall!
That is the sort of man I am.
A mot's good-night to one and all!

THE FAREWELL

Paste 'em, and larrup 'em, and lamm!
Give Kennedy and make 'em crawl!
I do not care one little damn.
A mot's good-night to one and all!

(1888)

EUGENE FIELD

(1850–1895)

The Duel

THE gingham dog and the calico cat
Side by side on the table sat;
'Twas half past twelve, and (what do you think!)
Nor one nor t'other had slept a wink!
　　The old Dutch clock and the Chinese plate
　　Appeared to know as sure as fate
There was going to be a terrible spat.
　　(*I wasn't there; I simply state*
　　What was told to me by the Chinese plate!)

The gingham dog went 'Bow-wow-wow!'
And the calico cat replied 'Mee-ow!'
The air was littered, an hour or so,
With bits of gingham and calico,
　　While the old Dutch clock in the chimney-place
　　Up with its hands before its face,
For it always dreaded a family row!
　　(*Now mind: I'm only telling you*
　　What the old Dutch clock declares is true!)

The Chinese plate looked very blue,
And wailed: 'Oh, dear! what shall we do?'
But the gingham dog and the calico cat
Wallowed this way and tumbled that,
　　Employing every tooth and claw
　　In the awfullest way you ever saw—
And, oh! how the gingham and calico flew!
　　(*Don't fancy I exaggerate!*
　　I got my news from the Chinese plate!)

Next morning, where the two had sat,
They found no trace of dog or cat;
And some folks think unto this day
That burglars stole that pair away!
　　But the truth about the cat and pup
　　Is this: they ate each other up!
Now what do you really think of that!
　　(*The old Dutch clock it told me so,*
　　And that is how I came to know.)

(1894)

WARHAM ST LEGER
(1850–c.1915)

To My Hairdresser
(NOT TO MAKE CONVERSATION)

YOU tell me that the day is fine,
  You say my hair is getting thin,
Anon you proffer Smearoline,
  Or comment on my tender skin;
Good friend, for goodness' sake forbear,
I prithee only cut my hair.

For think—a shy, retiring man,
  I shun the toilet's public rite,
Until my Cousins—Cousins can—
  Reproach me for a Perfect Fright,
And must I bear, too shy to snub,
The babble of your Toilet Club?

I know, for every day for years
  I've scanned the glass with careful eye,
Whether the heaven clouds or clears,
  Whether the roads are wet or dry;
Indeed, indeed, I do not care
Whether you think it foul or fair.

And why observe, with honied zest,
  What men by many phrases call,
That phase which must be dubb'd at best
  Unduly intellectual?
What though my loftier temples shine,
That is no business of thine.

Think you, when, in your wrapper swathed,
  I cower beneath the harrowing comb,
Or crouch, in creaming lather bathed,
  Beneath the hose's numbing foam,
Or bear, while tears unbidden gush,
The rigours of your softest brush—

Think you, at such a time as this,
  I care to hear, with nerves unstrung,
The dirge of bygone days of bliss
  Trip lightly from a stranger's tongue?
What if your victim stood at bay,
And told you *you* were bald or grey?

The head you handle like a block,
  And brand with slighting comments cool,
Has bravely borne the battle's shock,
  And starr'd the grey old walls at school;
Has sprained a bishop's reverend wrist,
And badly bruised a judge's fist.

They were not judge and bishop then,
  But only chubby, scrubby boys;
And now they're grave and reverend men.
  I value those remember'd joys,
And grieve that evil should be said
About my own, my only head.

Your politics are nought to me;
  I'll keep my views about the weather:
I only wish we could agree
  That I am neither wood nor leather.
Be gentle; 'tis the nobler plan,
And stint your chatter, if you can.

                                        (1888)

A False Gallop of Analogies

'THE CHAVENDER, OR CHUB'—IZAAK WALTON

THERE is a fine stuffed chavender,
  A chavender or chub,
That decks the rural pavender,
  The pavender or pub,
Wherein I eat my gravender,
  My gravender or grub.

How good the honest gravender!
  How snug the rustic pavender!
From sheets as sweet as lavender,
  As lavender, or lub,
I jump into my tavender,
  My tavender, or tub.

Alas! for town and clavender,
　For business and club!
They call me from my pavender
To-night; ay, there's the ravender,
　Ay, there comes in the rub!
To leave each blooming shravender,
　Each spring-bedizened shrub,
And meet the horsy savender,
　The very forward sub,
At dinner at the clavender,
And then at billiards dravender,
　At billiards roundly drub
The self-sufficient cavender,
　The not ill-meaning cub,
Who me a bear will davender,
　A bear unfairly dub,
Because I sometimes snavender,
　Not too severely snub
His setting right the clavender,
　His teaching all the club!

Farewell to peaceful pavender,
　My river-dreaming pub,
To bed as sweet as lavender,
To homely, wholesome gravender,
And you, inspiring chavender,
　Stuff'd, chavender, or chub.

(1894)

ARTHUR CLEMENT HILTON

(1851–1877)

The Vulture and the Husbandman

THE rain was raining cheerfully
　As if it had been May;
The Senate-House appeared inside
　Unusually gay;
And this was strange, because it was
　A Viva-voce day.

The men were sitting sulkily,
　　Their paper work was done;
They wanted much to go away
　　To ride or row or run;
'It's very rude,' they said, 'to keep
　　Us here, and spoil our fun.'

The papers they had finished lay
　　In piles of blue and white.
They answered everything they could,
　　And wrote with all their might,
But, though they wrote it all by rote,
　　They did not write it right.

The Vulture and the Husbandman
　　Beside these piles did stand,
They wept like anything to see
　　The work they had in hand,
'If this were only finished up,'
　　Said they: 'it would be grand!'

'If seven D's or seven C's
　　We give to all the crowd,
Do you suppose,' the Vulture said,
　　'That we could get them ploughed?'
'I think so,' said the Husbandman,
　　'But pray don't talk so loud.'

'O undergraduates, come up,'
　　The Vulture did beseech,
'And let us see if you can learn
　　As well as we can teach;
We cannot do with more than two
　　To have a word with each.'

Two Undergraduates came up,
　　And slowly took a seat,
They knit their brows, and bit their thumbs,
　　As if they found them sweet,
And this was odd, because you know
　　Thumbs are not good to eat.

'The time has come,' the Vulture said,
　　'To talk of many things,
Of Accidence and Adjectives,
　　And names of Jewish kings,
How many notes a sackbut has,
　　And whether shawms have strings.'

'Please, sir,' the Undergraduates said,
  Turning a little blue,
'We did not know that was the sort
  Of thing we had to do.'
'We thank you much,' the Vulture said,
  'Send up another two.'

Two more came up, and then two more;
  And more, and more, and more;
And some looked upwards at the roof,
  Some down upon the floor,
But none were any wiser than
  The pair that went before.

'I weep for you,' the Vulture said,
  'I deeply sympathize!'
With sobs and tears he gave them all
  D's of the largest size,
While at the Husbandman he winked
  One of his streaming eyes.

'I think,' observed the Husbandman,
  'We're getting on too quick.
Are we not putting down the D's
  A little bit too thick?'
The Vulture said with much disgust
  'Their answers make me sick.'

'Now, Undergraduates,' he cried,
  'Our fun is nearly done,
Will anybody else come up?'
  But answer came there none;
And this was scarcely odd, because
  They'd ploughed them every one!

                                    (1872)

The Heathen Pass-ee

WHICH I wish to remark,
  And my language is plain,
That for plots that are dark
  And not always in vain,
The heathen Pass-ee is peculiar,
  And the same I would rise to explain.

I would also premise
  That the term of Pass-ee
Most fitly applies,
  As you probably see,
To one whose vocation is passing
  The 'ordinary B.A. degree.'

Tom Crib was his name,
  And I shall not deny
In regard to the same
  What that name might imply.
But his face it was trustful and childlike,
  And he had the most innocent eye.

Upon April the First
  The Little-Go fell,
And that was the worst
  Of the gentleman's sell,
For he fooled the Examining Body
  In a way I'm reluctant to tell.

The candidates came
  And Tom Crib soon appeared;
It was Euclid.   The same
  Was 'the subject he feared,'
But he smiled as he sat by the table
  With a smile that was wary and weird.

Yet he did what he could,
  And the papers he showed
Were remarkably good,
  And his countenance glowed
With pride when I met him soon after
  As he walked down the Trumpington Road.

We did not find him out,
  Which I bitterly grieve,
For I've not the least doubt
  That he'd placed up his sleeve
Mr Todhunter's excellent Euclid,
  The same with intent to deceive.

But I shall not forget
  How the next day at two
A stiff paper was set
  By Examiner U . . .
On Euripides' tragedy, *Bacchae*.
  A subject Tom 'partially knew.'

But the knowledge displayed
   By that heathen Pass-ee,
And the answers he made
   Were quite frightful to see,
For he rapidly floored the whole paper
   By about twenty minutes to three.

Then I looked up at U . . .
   And he gazed upon me.
I observed: 'This won't do.'
   He replied: 'Goodness me!
We are fooled by this artful young person,'
   And he sent for that heathen Pass-ee.

The scene that ensued
   Was disgraceful to view,
For the floor it was strewed
   With a tolerable few
Of the 'tips' that Tom Crib had been hiding
   For the 'subject he partially knew.'

On the cuff of his shirt
   He had managed to get
What we hoped had been dirt,
   But which proved, I regret,
To be notes on the rise of the drama,
   A question invariably set.

In his various coats
   We proceeded to seek,
Where we found sundry notes
   And—with sorrow I speak—
One of Bohn's publications, so useful
   To the student of Latin or Greek.

In the crown of his cap
   Were the Furies and Fates,
And a delicate map
   Of the Dorian States,
And we found in his palms which were hollow,
   What are frequent in palms—that is dates.

Which is why I remark,
   And my language is plain,
That for plots that are dark
   And not always in vain,
The heathen Pass-ee is peculiar,
   Which the same I am free to maintain.

(1872)

Octopus

STRANGE beauty, eight-limbed and eight-handed
    Whence camest to dazzle our eyes?
With thy bosom bespangled and banded
    With the hues of the seas and the skies;
Is thy home European or Asian,
    O mystical monster marine?
Part molluscous and partly crustacean,
    Betwixt and between.

Wast thou born to the sound of sea-trumpets?
    Hast thou eaten and drunk to excess
Of the sponges—thy muffins and crumpets,
    Of the seaweed—thy mustard and cress?
Wast thou nurtured in caverns of coral,
    Remote from reproof or restraint?
Art thou innocent, art thou immoral,
    Sinburnian or Saint?

Lithe limbs, curling free, as a creeper
    That creeps in a desolate place,
To enrol and envelop the sleeper
    In a silent and stealthy embrace,
Cruel beak craning forward to bite us,
    Our juices to drain and to drink,
Or to whelm us in waves of Cocytus,
    Indelible ink!

O breast, that 'twere rapture to writhe on!
    O arms 'twere delicious to feel
Clinging close with the crush of the Python,
    When she maketh her murderous meal!
In thy eight-fold embraces enfolden,
    Let our empty existence escape;
Give us death that is glorious and golden,
    Crushed all out of shape!

Ah! thy red lips, lascivious and luscious,
    With death in their amorous kiss!
Cling round us, and clasp us, and crush us,
    With bitings of agonized bliss;
We are sick with the poison of pleasure,
    Dispense us the potion of pain;
Ope thy mouth to its uttermost measure
    And bite us again!

                                                    (1872)

WILLIAM PERCY FRENCH

(1854–1920)

Fighting McGuire

Now, Gibbon has told the story of old,
  Of the Fall of the Roman Empire,
But I would recall the rise an' the fall
  Of a man of the name of McGuire.
He came to our town as a man of renown,
  And peace was, he said, his desire,
Still he'd frequently state what would be the sad fate
  Of the man who molested McGuire.

Well, we all were afraid of this quarrelsome blade,
  An' we told him to draw near the fire,
An' laughed at his jest, tho' it wasn't the best,
  An' swore there's no man like McGuire.
An' when he came up with the neighbours to sup,
  His friendliness all would admire,
An' he'd have the best bed—for we'd sleep in the shed
  For fear of insulting McGuire.

But Macgilligan's Dan—who's a rale fightin' man,
  Said: 'Of all this tall talkin' I tire,
I'll step in an' see whyever should he
  Be called always Fightin' McGuire.
I'll step in and say, in a casual way,
  That I think he's a thief an' a liar,
Then I'll hit him a clout, and unless I misdoubt,
  That's a way of insulting McGuire.'

Then onward he strode to McGuire's abode,
  His glorious eye shootin' fire,
An' we thought as he passed we have all looked our last
  On the man who insulted McGuire;
Then we listened with grief while we heard him called thief,
  An' abused as a rogue an' a liar,
Oh! we all held our breath, for we knew it was death
  To give any chat to McGuire.

Well, the row wasn't long, but 'twas hot an' 'twas strong,
    An' the noise it grew higher an' higher,
Then it stopt!—an' we said: 'Oh, begorra, he's dead!
    He's been kilt out an' out be McGuire!'
Then out like a thrush from a hawthorn bush
    Came something in tattered attire,
And after it fled the man we thought dead—
    The man who maltreated McGuire.

'Twas Macgilligan's son, the victory won,
    An' we crowded around to admire
The bowld-hearted boy who was first to destroy
    The Yoke of the Tyrant McGuire.
An' altho' it's not true, we all said that we knew
    From the first he was only a liar,
An' we'd all had a mind to attack—from behind—
    That cowardly scoundrel—McGuire.

(1925)

Goosey Goosey Gander—By Various Authors

KIPLING'S VERSION

AND this is the song that the white woman sings,
    When her baby begins to howl;
The song of the goose and its wanderings,
    The song of the fate-led fowl.

The song of the chamber of her whom I loved,
    The song of the chamber where—
I met an old reprobate, scented and gloved,
    And hurled him down the stair.

And wherever the Saxon speech is heard,
    By the pig or the polar bear,
We follow the feet of that wandering bird
    As they wobble from stair to stair.

SWINBURNE'S VERSION

Oh whither, oh why, and oh wherefore
    Great goose thou art gosling no more,
With none to caress thee nor care for,
    Wilt wander from floor to floor?

Is it upstairs thy Gandership's goal is,
   Or dost thou descend from above?
To where in her Holy of Holies
   Low lieth my love.

Where I met with the man who is hairless
   And holding his left leg in thrall,
Propelled him, all pallid and prayerless,
   From attic to hall.

MACAULAY'S VERSION

'Twas Goosey Goosey Gander
Had wandered far away,
From the green steeps
Where Anio leaps
In clouds of silver spray.
This week the stately gander sails
Untended on the tide,
This week the yellow gosling finds
No mother by its side.
This week the large-eyed frog may leap
All careless from the foam,
For Goosey Goosey Gander
Has wandered off to Rome.

But in my lady's chamber
Is terror and affright,
For news they bring
Of a fearsome thing
That wanders through the night.
Then spake the boy in buttons
Give me the knife and fork,
And I will assail
The spectre pale,
That wanders through the dark.
The knife and fork they bring him,
He rushes forth to slay,
One wild death cry
And giblet pie
Is cheap in Rome to-day.

LONGFELLOW'S VERSION

If you ask me whence the story
Whence the tale and the tradition,
Whence the tale of Goosey Gander,
I would answer 'ask a p'liceman,'

Ask the blue bird the policeman
Whither wanders Goosey Gander?
From its home in Nursery Rhymeland,
Till it reach my lady's chamber,
Where it disappears abruptly
And for ever from my story.
For a man becomes the hero,
Who, renouncing his devotions,
Is subjected by the author
To the most outrageous treatment.
—And I could go on for ever
In this very simple metre,
But the reader mightn't like it,
So perhaps I'd better drop it.

(1925)

HENRY CUYLER BUNNER

(1855–1896)

Home, Sweet Home, with Variations

I

As SWINBURNE *might have wrapped it up:*

As sea-foam blown of the winds, as blossom of brine that is
     drifted
  Hither and yon on the barren breast of the breeze,
Though we wander on gusts of a god's breath shaken and shifted,
  The salt of us stings and is sore for the sobbing seas.
For home's sake hungry at heart, we sicken in pillared porches,
  Of bliss made sick for a life that is barren of bliss,
For the place whereon is a light out of heaven that sears not nor
     scorches,
  Nor elsewhere than this.

For here we know shall no gold thing glisten,
  No bright thing burn, and no sweet thing shine;
Nor love lower never an ear to listen
  To words that work in the heart like wine.
    What time we are set from our land apart,
    For pain of passion and hunger of heart,
Though we walk with exiles fame faints to christen,
  Or sing at the Cytherean's shrine.

II

As BRET HARTE *might have woven it into a
touching tale of a Western Gentleman:*

Stranger, you freeze to this: there ain't no kinder gin-palace,
Nor no variety-show lays over a man's own rancho.
May be it haint no style, but the queen in the Tower o' London
Aint got naathin' I'd swop for that house over thar on the hillside.
Thar is my ole gal, 'n' the kids, 'n' the rest o' my live-stock;
Thar my Remington hangs, and thar there's a griddle-cake
    br'ilin'—
Fer the two of us, pard—and thar, I allow, the heavens
Smile more friendly-like than on any other locality.

Stranger, nowhere else I don't take no satisfaction.
Gimme my ranch, 'n' them friendly old Shanghai chickens—
I brung the original pair f'm the States in eighteen-'n'-fifty—
Gimme them, and the feelin' of solid domestic comfort.

III

As AUSTIN DOBSON *might have translated it from*
HORACE, *if it had ever occurred to* HORACE
to write it:

RONDEAU

At home alone, O Nomades,
Although Maecenas' marble frieze
   Stand not between you and the sky,
   Nor Persian luxury supply
Its rosy surfeit, find ye ease.

Tempt not the far Aegean breeze;
With home-made wine and books that please,
   To duns and bores the door deny
          At home, alone.

Strange joys may lure.   Your deities
Smile here alone.   Oh, give me these:
   Low eaves, where birds familiar fly,
   And peace of mind, and, fluttering by,
My Lydia's graceful draperies.
          At home *alone.*

IV

As it might have been constructed in 1744, OLIVER
GOLDSMITH, *at 19, writing the first stanza, and*
ALEXANDER POPE, *at 52, the second:*

Home! at the word, what blissful visions rise;
Lift us from earth, and draw toward the skies!
'Mid mirag'd towers, or meretricious joys
Although we roam, one thought the mind employs:
Or lowly hut, good friend, or loftiest dome,
Earth knows no spot so holy as our Home.
There, where affection warms the father's breast,
There is the spot of heav'n most surely blest.
Howe'er we search, though wandering with the wind
Through frigid Zembla, or the heats of Ind,
Not elsewhere may we seek, nor elsewhere know,
The light of heav'n upon our dark below.

When from our dearest hope and haven reft,
Delight nor dazzles, nor is luxury left,
We long, obedient to our nature's law,
To see again our hovel thatched with straw:
See birds that know our avenaceous store
Stoop to our hand, and thence repleted soar:
But, of all hopes the wanderer's soul that share,
His pristine peace of mind's his final prayer.

V

As WALT WHITMAN *might have written all around it:*

You over there, young man with the guide-book, red-bound,
covered flexibly with red linen,
Come here, I want to talk with you; I, Walt, the Manhattanese,
citizen of these States, call you.
Yes, and the courier, too, smirking, smug-mouthed, with oil'd
hair; a garlicky look about him generally; him, too, I take in,
just as I would a coyote, or a king, or a toadstool, or a ham-
sandwich, or anything or anybody else in the world.
Where are you going?
You want to see Paris, to eat truffles, to have a good time; in
Vienna, London, Florence, Monaco, to have a good time; you
want to see Venice.
Come with me. I will give you a good time; I will give you all
the Venice you want, and most of the Paris.
I, Walt, I call to you! I am all on deck! Come and loafe with me!
Let me tote you around by your elbow and show you things.
You listen to my ophicleide!
Home!

Home I celebrate. I elevate my fog-whistle, inspir'd by the
  thought of home.
Come in!—take a front seat; the jostle of the crowd not minding;
  there is room enough for all of you.
This is my exhibition—it is the greatest show on earth—there is
  no charge for admission.
All you have to pay me is to take in my romanza.

                                                    (1881)

ALFRED DENIS GODLEY

(1856–1925)

Lines on a Mysterious Occurrence

I WISH I knew geography—for that would tell me why
'Twixt New South Wales and Paddington you needs must pass
  the High!
Of course I know the fact is so: 'tis singular, but then
Veracity is still the mark of literary men.

All in the High a Yankee man I happened for to find:
He'd come from the Antipodes, and left his purse behind:
And here by his embarrassments compelled he was to stay.
('Twixt New South Wales and London town 'tis all upon the
  way.)

His simple tale affected me: 'twas more than I could bear:
I brought him to my humble cot and entertained him there.
And 'Books!' he cried, while gazing on my well-assorted shelf,
'I've written some immortal works—anonymous—myself!

'Full well I know the authors of those venerable tomes—
Yes, there's Nathaniel Hawthorne, and there is Wendell
  Holmes!
My literary relatives I number by the score:
Mark Twain's my cousin twice removed, by far Missouri's
  shore.'

He spoke of many famous men, and all by Christian names—
Yes, Howells he called William D., and Russell Lowell, James:
His kinsmen and acquaintances were all in Culture's van;
I do not think I ever met a more related man.

'But what's the use of all that crowd,' the Transatlantic said,
'When I am bound to catch the cars, and ain't got nary red?
Stranger, I guess with Caius C. Maecenas you'll be known
If you will just oblige me with a temporary loan.'

I can't resist celebrity—I lent him shillings ten,
That impecunious relative of literary men:
And when he comes to pay it back, no doubt he'll tell me why
From New South Wales to Paddington the shortest way's the
    High.

(1892)

Football and Rowing—An Eclogue

MELIBOEUS.   CORYDON

MEL. Nay, tempt me not, my Corydon; I tell you once again
    That football is a game beneath the dignity of men.
    Time was, I chased the bounding ball athwart the meadows
        green—
    Before I read what critics said, within the *Magazine*.
    Degrading sport! at which, indeed, I used to shine at school;
    Alas! I knew no better then, and was, in fact, a fool;
    Of all the spectacles on earth, I know no sight that's sadder
    Than thirty men pursuing of a mere inflated bladder.
    Were I to play at games like this, when nearly in my twenties,
    'Twould argue me behind my age, and *parum compos mentis*.
    'Tis 'semi-gladiatorial' too—a thing which I abhor—
    At least that's what the papers say, and likewise Dr Warre—
    And so I've donned my boating-coat, and down to row I'm
        going,
    For oarsmen swear (they often do) there's no such sport as
        rowing.
CORYD. Ah, hapless youth!   Why, don't you know what count-
        less ills await
    The man who strives to figure in a Torpid or an Eight?
    Learn, then, that such (you'll find it all in last week's *Magazine*)
    Of individuality have less than a machine;
    'Two' looks at stroke, and bow at 'Three,' and imitates him
        stiffly,
    And once embarked, you can't get out between the Barge and
        Iffley.
    The chops and steaks on which you dine are (like your person)
        raw;
    You can't devote your mind to Greats, or History, or Law—
    For when they're rowing in an Eight, I'm told that gentlemen
    Are comatose at half past eight, and sent to bed at ten!
MEL. Alas!   'Tis clear, such sports as these can ne'er have been
        designed
    To satisfy a person of a cultivated mind.
    Since both alike a mark present for journalistic sneers,
    Rowing and football I'll forswear, and join the Volunteers!

(1892)

Eureka!

IF you ask for the cause of our national flaws, and the reason
we're blamed for our vices—
We are too much controlled by Academies old on the banks of
the Cam and the Isis;
'Tis the methods of cram by the Isis and Cam that provide an
excuse for the mocker,
With the languages dead that they put in your head and their
rooted aversion to Soccer!

What's the good to the State of your pedants who prate of the
meaning of classical poets?
Of your comments and notes on your Mommsens and Grotes
and perusing of Platos and Jowetts?
You might really as well be unable to spell or immersed in a
sixpenny shocker
As employing the day in this frivolous way—when you ought to
be playing at Soccer.

When my optic I cast o'er the deeds of the past and the things
that historians have written,
I reflect with distrust (as the critical must) on the mythical
glories of Britain:
She had capable men with the sword and the pen, and financiers
with riches to stock her:
And I freely admit there was Gladstone and Pitt—but they were
not exponents of Soccer.

For the Man who is born to release us from scorn, and to lighten
our hapless condition—
He is sadly to seek in his Latin and Greek, and he is not a skilful
logician:
He has views in the Schools on Arithmetic's rules which are
hardly according to Cocker—
But I think you will grant he's the man that we want—for he's
simply a demon at Soccer.

Then behave as you're told, O Academies old, and reform all
your ancient foundations,
And reflect (as I've shown) that athletics alone are the way to
regenerate nations:
For whatever the blows we receive from our foes, we've a shot
that remains in the locker,
And our efforts success will assuredly bless if we only are
faithful to Soccer!

(1902)

The College Cat

WITHIN those halls where student zeal
　　Hangs every morn on learning's lips,
Intent to make its daily meal
　　Of Tips,

While drones the conscientious Don
　　Of Latin Prose, of Human Will,
Of Aristotle and of John
　　Stuart Mill,

We mouth with stern didactic air:
　　We prate of this, we rant of that:
While slumbers on his favourite chair
　　The Cat!

For what is Mill, and what is Prose,
　　Compared with warmth, and sleep, and food,
—All which collectively compose
　　The Good?

Although thy unreceptive pose
　　In presence of eternal Truth
No virtuous example shows
　　To youth,

Sleep on, O Cat! serenely through
　　My hurricanes of hoarded lore,
Nor seek with agitated mew
　　The door:

Thy calm repose I would not mar,
　　Nor chase thee forth in angry flight
Protesting loud (though some there are
　　Who might),

Because to my reflective mind
　　Thou dost from generations gone
Recall a wholly different kind
　　Of Don,

Who took his glass, his social cup,
　　And having quaffed it, mostly sat
Curled (metaphorically) up
　　Like that!

Far from those scenes of daily strife
   And seldom necessary fuss
Wherein consists the most of life
   For us,

When Movements moved, they let them move:
   When Problems raged, they let them rage:
And quite ignored the Spirit of
   The Age.

Of such thou wert the proper mate,
   O peaceful-minded quadruped!
But liv'st with fellows up to date
   Instead—

With men who spend their vital span
   In petty stress and futile storm,
And for a recreation plan
   Reform:

Whom pupils ne'er in quiet leave,
   But throng their rooms in countless hordes:
Who sit from morn to dewy eve
   On Boards:

Who skim but erudition's cream,
   And con by night and cram by day
Such subjects as the likeliest seem
   To pay!

But thou, from cares like these exempt,
   Our follies dost serenely scan,
Professing thus thy just contempt
   For Man:

For well thou knowest, that wished-for goal
   Which still to win we vainly pine,
That calm tranquillity of soul
   Is thine!

                       (1902)

RUDOLF CHAMBERS LEHMANN

(1856–1929)

A Plea for a Plural

YOU, who in sultry weather
    To Scotland take your way,
To roam the purple heather
    And bring the grouse to bay,
Oh, sportsmen intramooral,
    Declare, I beg, to me,
If grouse possessed a plural,
    What would that plural be?

What fairness is there in it
    If other, meaner birds,
Lark, sparrow, swallow, linnet,
    Have, all, their plural words?
One grouse we know and cherish;
    It shows but little νοῦς,
When ten or twenty perish,
    To group them all as grouse.

No matter what intention
    Inspires them, I accuse
Of poorness of invention
    These paltry single views.
If men may dwell in houses,
    Why deem it a disgrace
To speak of grouse as 'grouses'
    Whenever there's a brace?

This word I note with pain, Sir,
    Is hardly to your mind;
You bid me try again, Sir,
    Some better term to find.
Well, 'grouses' I abandon;
    Since mouse gives birth to mice,
I'll take my final stand on
    The missing word as 'grice.'

With this new word provided,
  Go, let your sport be good.
Shoot, shoot as oft as I did,
  But hit—I rarely could.
Yet count not ere you grass them
  Your grice as in the house.
How oft your pellets pass them
  Is singular—like grouse.

(1900)

'F. ANSTEY'
(THOMAS ANSTEY GUTHRIE)
(1856–1934)

Mr Punch's Young Reciter

Example No. I: BURGLAR BILL

Style: *The 'Sympathetic Artless.'*

The compiler would not be acting fairly by the young Reciter if, in recommending the following poem as a subject for earnest study, he did not caution him—or her—not to be betrayed by the apparent simplicity of this exercise into the grave error of underestimating its real difficulty. It is true that it is an illustration of pathos of an elementary order, but, for all that, this piece bristles with as many points as a porcupine, and consequently requires the most cautious and careful handling.

Upon the whole, it is perhaps better suited to students of the softer sex.

Announce the title with a suggestion of shy innocence—in this way:

BURGLAR [*now open both eyes very wide*] BILL.

Then go on in a hushed voice, and with an air of wonder at the world's iniquity.

I

Through a window in the attic,
  Brawny Burglar Bill has crept;
Seeking stealthily a chamber
  Where the jewellery is kept.

Pronounce either 'jewelry' or 'joolery,' according to taste.

II

He is furnished with a 'jemmy,'
　　Centre-bit, and carpet-bag,
For the latter 'comes in handy,'
　　So he says, 'to stow the swag.'

'Jemmy,' 'centre-bit,' 'carpet-bag' are important words—put good colouring into them.

III

Here, upon the second landing,
　　He, secure, may work his will;
Down below's a dinner party.
　　Up above—the house is still.

Here start and extend first finger, remembering to make it waggle slightly, as from fear.

IV

Suddenly—in spell-bound horror,
　　All his satisfaction ends—
For a little white-robed figure
　　By the banister descends!

This last line requires care in the delivery, or it may be imagined that the little figure is sliding DOWN *the banisters, which would simply ruin the effect.   Note the bold but classic use of the singular in 'banister,' which is more pleasing to a nice ear than the plural.*

V

Bill has reached for his revolver,
　　　　　　　　　　　[Business here with your fan.
　　Yet—he hesitates to fire . . .
Child is it? [*in a dread whisper*] or—apparition,
　　That provokes him to perspire?

VI

Can it be his guardian angel,
　　Sent to stay his hand from crime?
　　　　　　　　　　　[In a tone of awe.
He could wish she had selected
　　Some more seasonable time!
　　　　　　　　　　　[Touch of peevish discontent here.

VII

'Go away!' he whimpers hoarsely,
   'Burglars hev their bread ter earn.
I don't need no Gordian angel
   Givin' of me sech a *turn!*'
     [*Shudder here, and retreat, shielding eyes with hand.*
Now change your manner to a naïve surprise; this, in spite of any-
thing we may have said previously, is in this particular instance
NOT *best indicated by a shrill falsetto.*

VIII

But the blue eyes open wider,
   Ruby lips reveal their pearl;
     [*This must not be taken to refer to the Burglar.*
'I is not a Garden anzel,
   Only—dust a yickle dirl!
  [*Be particularly artless here and through next stanza.*

IX

'On the thtairs to thit I'm doin'
   Till the tarts and dellies tum;
Partinthon (our Butler) alwayth
   Thaves for Baby Bella thome!

X

'Poor man, 'oo is yookin' 'ungwy—
   Leave 'oo burgling fings up dere;
Tum viz me and share the sweeties,
   Thitting on the bottom thtair!'
In rendering the above the young Reciter should strive to be idiomatic
without ever becoming idiotic—which is not so easy as might be
imagined.

XI

'Reely, Miss, you must excoose me!'
   Says the Burglar with a jerk:
Indicate embarrassment here by smoothing down the folds of your
gown, and swaying awkwardly.
   'Dooty calls, and time is pressing;
     I must set about my work!'
       [*This with a gruff conscientiousness.*

XII

Now assume your wide-eyed innocence again.
   'Is 'oo work to bweak in houses?
   Nana *told* me so, I'm sure!
Will 'oo see if 'oo can manage
   To bweak in my *doll's-house* door?

XIII

'I tan *never* det it undone,
  So my dollies tan't det out;
They don't *yike* the fwont to open
  Evewy time they'd walk about!

XIV

'Twy, and—if 'oo does it nithely—
  When I'm thent upthtairs to thleep,
                    [*Don't overdo the lisp.*
I will bwing 'oo up thome doodies,
  'Oo thall have them all—to keep!'

XV

Pause here; then, with intense feeling and sympathy:
  Off the little 'angel' flutters;
                    [*Delicate stress on 'angel.'*
  But the Burglar—wipes his brow.
  He is wholly unaccustomed
    To a kindly greeting now!
                    [*Tremble in voice here.*

XVI

Never with a smile of welcome
  Has he seen his entrance met!
Nobody—except the policeman—[*bitterly*]
  Ever wanted *him* as yet!

XVII

Many a stately home he's entered,
  But, with unobtrusive tact,
He has ne'er, in paying visits,
  Called attention to the fact.

XVIII

Gain he counts it, on departing,
  Should he have avoided strife.
In tone of passionate lament—
  Ah, my Brothers, but the Burglar's
    Is a sad, a lonely life!

XIX

All forgotten now the jewels,
  Once the purpose of his 'job';
Down he sinks upon the door-mat,
  With a deep and choking sob.

XX

Then, the infant's plea recalling,
  Seeks the nursery above;
Looking for the Lilliputian
  Crib he is to crack—for *love*!
        [It is more usually done for MONEY.

XXI

In the corner stands the dolls'-house
  Gaily painted green and red;
        [Colouring again here.
And its door declines to open,
  Even as the child has said!

XXII

Forth come centre-bit and jemmy: *[Briskly.*
  All his implements are plied;
        [Enthusiastically—
Never has he burgled better!
  As he feels, with honest pride.

XXIII

Deftly is the task accomplished,
  For the door will open well;
When—a childish voice behind him
  Breaks the silence—like a bell.

XXIV

'Sank 'oo, Misser Burglar, sank 'oo!
  And, betause 'oo's been so nice,
See what I have dot—a tartlet!
  Gweat big gweedies ate the ice.'
        [Resentful accent on ' ate.'

XXV

'Pappa says he wants to see 'oo,
  Partinthon is tummin too—
Tan't 'oo wait?'
[This with guileless surprise—then change to a husky emotion.
      —'Well, *not* this evenin',
  So, my little dear [*brusquely*], adoo!'

XXVI

*You are now to produce your greatest effect; the audience should be
made actually to* SEE *the poor hunted victim of social prejudice
escaping, consoled in the very act of flight by memories of this*

last adventure—the one bright and cheering episode, possibly, in his entire professional career.

Fast he speeds across the housetops!—
[*Rapid delivery for this.*

[*Very gently.*]   But his bosom throbs with bliss,
For upon his rough lips linger
Traces of a baby's kiss.

Most delicate treatment will be necessary in the last couplet—or the audience may understand it in a painfully literal sense.

.   .   .   .   .

You have nothing before you now but the finale.   Make the contrast as marked as possible.

XXVII

Dreamily on downy pillow
[*Soft musical intonation for this.*
Baby Bella murmurs sweet:
[*Smile here with sleepy tenderness.*
'Burglar—tum adain, and thee me . . .
I will dive 'oo cakes to eat!'

That is one side of the medal—now for the other.

XXVIII

Harsh but emotional.

In a garret, worn and weary,
Burglar Bill has sunk to rest,
Clasping tenderly a damson—
Tartlet to his burly breast.

Dwell lovingly upon the word 'tartlet'—which you should press home upon every one of your hearers, remembering to fold your hands lightly over your heart as you conclude.   If you do not find that several susceptible and eligible bachelors have been knocked completely out of time by this little recitation, you will have made less progress in your Art than may be confidently anticipated.

(1887)

Example No. II: THE CONSCIENCE-CURST!

Style: *The 'Melodramatic Weird.'*

It is the dearest wish of most young amateur reciters to succeed—though but for one moment—in curdling a horrified audience.   This desire, if restrained within moderate bounds, is by no means deserving of discouragement.   There is no reason whatever why audiences should not be curdled—provided they do not personally object to this form of dissipation. The only danger is that he who goes forth to curdle may excite nothing more than a mild amusement, which, to all intents and purposes, amounts practically to a failure in Art. However, the student may dismiss any gloomy anticipations of this kind in the case of the present piece, on condition, of course, that the accompanying directions are implicitly followed in public, for, unless the pupil is willing to submit to our method, we cannot guarantee him even a moderate degree of success.

As before, you should devote special attention to your title, which may be announced after this fashion. Stalk into the middle of the room or platform, with one hand in your bosom, and your eyes staring as in a trace. Then, in a hollow voice, hurl the name of the poem at the nearest old lady:

THE CONSCIENCE-CURST!

And, if you do it properly, she will jump like anything.

I

The night-owl shrieked: a gibbous moon peered pallid o'er the
    yew;
The clammy tombstones each distilled a dank unwholesome dew;
        [*Shudder here with your shoulders.*
As through the sleeping village passed a wight of aspect weird,
Whose haggard face was half obscured by a long neglected beard.
In order that the audience should grasp this idea, you should pass
    your hand lightly over your chin.

II

His tinted spectacles gave back the gleaming of the moon,
He wore a pair of overcoats, although the time was June.
Give a dark significance to this piece of apparent eccentricity.

Two slippers wrought in faded wools hid his ungainly feet,
And he danced a grisly polka-step all down the silent street.
You might just indicate this, if you think you can do so in a suffi-
    ciently ghastly and impressive manner; otherwise—don't.

III

Then by the village green, he gave a conscience-stricken jump,
As guiltily he gazed upon the Presentation Pump!
Start here, as if you had just observed a centipede upon the carpet.

'How like,' he muttered with a groan, 'my uncle as he slept!'
Then raised its handle reverently—but found it cold, and wept.
In last line bend slightly forward with extended hand, then allow

*your arm to drop lifelessly to your side, and bow your head
twice, very solemnly. We have seen this most effective in
other pieces.*

IV

The rural Policeman [*raise voice at 'Policeman,' with a confi-
dential look at audience*] on his round perceived the Stranger
grim;
'I'd better step across,' he thought, 'an' hev a talk with him.
                          [*Country accent for this.*
It doan't sim nateral nohow as pumps should prompt such grief,
'Ere, what be you about?' said he. [*Pause; then in a hollow
voice—*] 'Confession brings relief!'

V

The Stranger answered, with a smile that froze his hearer's
blood,   [*Try to do this smile yourself.*
Then down he sank upon the stones with a dull and heavy thud,
The hearse-plume nodding in his hat as he inclined his head,
'Full long,' he wailed, 'upon this heart the worm hath ban-
queted!'

VI

(A drifting scud had veiled the moon, and sicklier she shone
As he began:) 'You never knew, methinks, my Uncle John?
A better, aye, a bulkier man this earth has hardly seen—
He was the first that ever burst a "Try-your-weight" machine!
                  [*A melancholy pride as you mention this.*

VII

'And I [*with a smile full of misery*], Ah, me! a careless lad, I
sported at his side,
That was before a kinsman's gore these felon hands had dyed!
                      [*Look disparagingly at your hands.*
Before the stain was on my brow, that sickens as it shames!
                                  [*Gesture of loathing.*
Ere yet my knife had let the life from gentle Uncle James!

VIII

'His blameless days were spent within the neighbourhood of
York;
A dentist (so at least 'twas noised), a connoisseur in pork.
                          [*Tender stress on last word.*
Ah! could I have predicted then that *I* should deal a blow
Upon the highly polished head of generous Uncle Joe!

IX

'Now Uncle Joseph sold ("purvey," I think, he termed it) meat,
His veins with vital fluid were abnormally replete!
*Close your eyes, and shiver here, as if at some unpleasing reminis-
cence.*

Who would have thought so old a man——? . . . [*with a dazed
abruptness*] Enough!—Within the tank
I flung the still unconscious corse of my favourite Uncle—Frank!
*Here you should strike the attitude of a man who is hurling a
favourite uncle to his doom.*

X

'My Uncle Francis was a man to know, was to esteem.
At times I hear him coughing yet—ah! only in a dream!
Is that a step behind the pump?   [*Nervous movement.*
    Nay, craven heart, be still!
                    [*Hand clutching side, cowering attitude.*
Till I have told how, for his gold—[*bitter emphasis on 'gold,'
as if it had turned out, on the whole, less than you were given to
expect*]—I struck down Uncle Bill!'

XI

*A slight pause here. Some amateurs would pull down their cuffs
at this point; but we cannot recommend this method of fixing an
audience's attention: it is a little inartistic.*

A stolid but attentive eye on him the Policeman fixed:
'It seems to me as how,' said he, 'you've got your uncles mixed!'
A ray of recollection seemed the Stranger's brain to strike;
                    [*Both hands to forehead.*
'Perchance!' he owned; 'they were,' he moaned, 'so won-
drously alike!

*Here you should allow your eyes to wander wildly round the room
before beginning the next line, which should be given with a
pathetic effort to be calm and collected.*

XII

'But let me recapitulate my catalogue of crime!—
Old Uncle Robert——'   [*Complete alteration of manner here.*
Hastily alleging, 'Want of time,'
The hearer fled.   'My gloomy tale the rustic soul alarms,'
The Stranger mused. . . .   That night he slept—within the
    Railway Arms!

    The last line is full of the deepest suggestion, so do not slur
over its full significance. Owing to a certain strain of mysticism

in some of the lines, you may find that your audience does not
quite understand this recitation on a first hearing; but of course
if you detect any symptoms of this, you can always offer, like
Mrs Leo Hunter, to recite it again.

(1887)

CHARLES LARCOM GRAVES

(1856–1944)

Horace, Book V, Ode III [1]

HOW unhappy (though unmarried) is an uncle who, bereft
Of the solace of the wine-cup, is continually left
   At the mercy of an energetic niece.
Neobule is unfailing in attendance at the Games,
Imperturbably regardless of the Muses or their claims
   And relentless in denying me release.
Her equipment is amphibious: she can swim a mile or more;
Her appearance in the saddle I both envy and adore;
   She's the super-Atalanta of the young.
She declines to ply her needle, and she never reads a book,
But she withers me completely with a single scorching look,
   And she cows me with the lashing of her tongue.

(1920)

An Old Song Resung

WHO, long before she left her teens,
Gaily deriding gloomy Deans,
Addressed her parents as 'old beans'?—
   My daughter.

Who, substituting 'must' for 'mayn't,'
Resentful of the least restraint,
Plasters her cheeks and lips with paint?—
   My daughter.

Who smokes some thirty cigarettes
Per day; who keeps two marmosets
And other disconcerting pets?—
   My daughter.

[1] See also page 239.

Who takes the tickets for the play
From which, although I have to pay,
I find it best to keep away?—
    My daughter.

Who on Victorian fiction looks
With deep disdain, but swallows books
That deal in sheiks and vamps and crooks?—
    My daughter.

Who runs, on self-expression bent,
A separate establishment
(We pay all charges, rates and rent)?—
    My daughter.

Who, in accordance with the fashion,
Of 'pals' secures a liberal ration,
Yet fails to stir the tender passion?—
    My daughter.

Who comes to see me when a bill
Is urgent, or to loot my till—
But sometimes comes if I am ill?—
    My daughter.

So, since she's young enough to mend,
And *does* regard me as a friend,
I hope to win her in the end—
    My daughter.

        (1925)

JAMES KENNETH STEPHEN

(1859–1892)

To R. K.

WILL there never come a season
Which shall rid us from the curse
Of a prose which knows no reason
And an unmelodious verse:
When the world shall cease to wonder
At the genius of an Ass,
And a boy's eccentric blunder
Shall not bring success to pass:

When mankind shall be delivered
From the clash of magazines,
And the inkstand shall be shivered
Into countless smithereens:
When there stands a muzzled stripling,
Mute, beside a muzzled bore:
When the Rudyards cease from Kipling
And the Haggards Ride no more.

(1891)

The Old School List

IN a wild moraine of forgotten books,
    On the glacier of years gone by,
As I plied my rake for order's sake,
    There was one that caught my eye;
And I sat by the shelf till I lost myself,
    And roamed in a crowded mist,
And heard lost voices and saw lost looks,
    As I pored on an old school List.

What a jumble of names! there were some that I knew,
    As a brother is known: to-day
Gone I know not where, nay I hardly care,
    For their places are full: and, they—
What climes they have ranged: how much they're changed!
    Time, place, and pursuits assist
In transforming them: stay where you are: adieu!
    You are all in the old school List.

There are some who did nothing at school, much since:
    And others much then, since naught:
They are middle-aged men, grown bald since then:
    Some have travelled, and some have fought:
And some have written, and some are bitten
    With strange new faiths: desist
From tracking them: broker or priest or prince,
    They are all in the old school List.

There's a grave grey lawyer in King's Bench Walk,
    Whose clients are passing few:
He seldom speaks: in those lonely weeks,
    What on earth can he find to do?
Well, he stroked the eight—what a splendid fate!—
    And the Newcastle barely missed:
'A future Lord Chancellor!' so we'd talk
    In the days of the old school List.

There were several duffers and several bores,
   Whose faces I've half forgot,
Whom I lived among, when the world was young,
   And who talked 'no end of rot':
Are they now little clerks who stroll in the parks
   Or scribble with grimy fist,
Or rich little peers who hire Scotch moors?
   Well—they're all in the old school List.

There were some who were certain to prosper and thrive,
   And certain to do no more,
Who were 'capital chaps,' and, tho' moderate *saps*,
   Would never stay in *after four*:
Now day after day they are packed away,
   After being connubially kissed,
To work in the city from ten to five:
   There they are in the old school List.

There were two good fellows I used to know,
   —How distant it all appears!
We played together in football weather,
   And messed together for years:
Now one of them's wed, and the other's dead
   So long that he's hardly missed
Save by us, who messed with him years ago:
   But we're all in the old school List.

(1891)

The Splinter

ONE stormy day in winter,
   When all the world was snow,
I chanced upon a splinter,
   Which ran into my toe.
The world went round:
The stubborn ground
   Defied the deadliest dinter:
They brought me tea,
And muffins three:
My little maid
Fetched marmalade:
My grace I said,
And breakfasted:
But all that morn in winter
I thought about the splinter.

At ten o'clock
The postman's knock:
A friend was dead:
Another wed:
Two invitations:
Five objurgations:
A screed from my solicitor:
They brought *The Times*:
A list of crimes:
A deadly fight
'Twixt black and white:
A note from 'B'
On Mr G.,
And other things
From cats to kings,
Known to that grand Inquisitor:—
But all that morn in winter
I thought about the splinter.

But, oh; at last
A lady passed
   Beside my chamber casement,
With modest guise
And downcast eyes
   And fair beyond amazement:
She passed away
Like some bright fay
   Too fair for earthly regions,
So sweet a sight
Would put to flight
   The fiend and all his legions!
And I, that noon in winter,
Forgot the cruel splinter.

(1891)

Two Epigrams

SENEX TO MATT. PRIOR

AH! Matt.: old age has brought to me
Thy wisdom, less thy certainty:
The world's a jest, and joy's a trinket:
I knew that once: but now—I think it.

CYNICUS TO W. SHAKSPERE

YOU wrote a line too much, my sage,
   Of seers the first, and first of sayers;
For only half the world's a stage,
   And only all the women players.

(1891)

A Sonnet on Wordsworth

TWO voices are there: one is of the deep;
It learns the storm-cloud's thunderous melody,
Now roars, now murmurs with the changing sea,
Now bird-like pipes, now closes soft in sleep:
And one is of an old half-witted sheep
Which bleats articulate monotony,
And indicates that two and one are three,
That grass is green, lakes damp, and mountains steep:
And, Wordsworth, both are thine: at certain times
Forth from the heart of thy melodious rhymes,
The form and pressure of high thoughts will burst:
At other times—good Lord!   I 'd rather be
Quite unacquainted with the A B C.
Than write such hopeless rubbish as thy worst.

(1891)

The Last Ride Together

(FROM HER POINT OF VIEW)

WHEN I had firmly answered 'No,'
And he allowed that that was so,
I really thought I should be free
For good and all from Mr B.,
    And that he would soberly acquiesce:
I said that it would be discreet
That for a while we should not meet;
I promised I would always feel
A kindly interest in his weal;
I thanked him for his amorous zeal;
    In short, I said all I could but 'yes.'

I said what I 'm accustomed to;
I acted as I always do;
I promised he should find in me
A friend—a sister, if that might be:
    But he was still dissatisfied:
He certainly was most polite;
He said exactly what was right,
He acted very properly,
Except indeed for this, that he
Insisted on inviting me
    To come with him for 'one more last ride.'

A little while in doubt I stood:
A ride, no doubt, would do me good:
I had a habit and a hat
Extremely well worth looking at:
    The weather was distinctly fine:
My horse too wanted exercise,
And time, when one is riding, flies:
Besides it really seemed, you see,
The only way of ridding me
Of pertinacious Mr B.:
    So my head I graciously incline.

I won't say much of what happened next:
I own I was extremely vexed:
Indeed I should have been aghast
If any one had seen what passed:
    But nobody need ever know
That, as I leaned forward to stir the fire,
He advanced before I could well retire,
And I suddenly felt, to my great alarm,
The grasp of a warm unlicensed arm,
An embrace in which I found no charm;
    I was awfully glad when he let me go.

Then we began to ride: my steed
Was rather fresh, too fresh indeed,
And at first I thought of little, save
The way to escape an early grave,
    As the dust rose up on either side.
My stern companion jogged along
On a brown old cob both broad and strong:
He looked as he does when he's writing verse,
Or endeavouring not to swear and curse,
Or wondering where he has left his purse:
    Indeed it was a sombre ride.

I spoke of the weather to Mr B.:
But he neither listened nor spoke to me:
I praised his horse, and I smiled the smile
Which was wont to move him once on a while;
    I said I was wearing his favourite flowers:
But I wasted my words on the desert air,
For he rode with a fixed and gloomy stare:
I wonder what he was thinking about:
As I don't read verse, I sha'n't find out:
It was something subtle and deep, no doubt,
    A theme to detain a man for hours.

Ah! there was the corner where Mr S.
So nearly induced me to whisper 'yes':
And here it was that the next but one
Proposed on horseback, or would have done,
    Had his horse not most opportunely shied;
Which perhaps was due to the unseen flick
He received from my whip: 'twas a scurvy trick,
But I never could do with that young man:
I hope his present young woman can.
Well, I must say, never, since time began,
    Did I go for a duller or longer ride.

He never smiles and he never speaks:
He might go on like this for weeks:
He rolls a slightly frenzied eye
Towards the blue and burning sky,
    And the cob bounds on with tireless stride.
If we aren't at home for lunch at two
I don't know what papa will do;
But I know full well he will say to me
'I never approved of Mr B.:
It's the very devil that you and he
    Ride, ride together, for ever ride.'

                          (1891)

ALFRED EDWARD HOUSMAN

(1859–1936)

Fragment of a Greek Tragedy

ALCMAEN.   CHORUS.

CHO. O suitably-attired-in-leather-boots
  Head of a traveller, wherefore seeking whom
  Whence by what way how purposed art thou come
  To this well-nightingaled vicinity?
  My object in inquiring is to know.
  But if you happen to be deaf and dumb
  And do not understand a word I say
  Then wave your hand, to signify as much.

ALC. I journeyed hither a Boeotian road.
CHO. Sailing on horseback, or with feet for oars?
ALC. Plying with speed my partnership of legs.
CHO. Beneath a shining or a rainy Zeus?
ALC. Mud's sister, not himself, adorns my shoes.
CHO. To learn your name would not displease me much.
ALC. Not all that men desire do they obtain.
CHO. Might I then hear at what your presence shoots?
ALC. A shepherd's questioned mouth informed me that——
CHO. What? for I know not yet what you will say——
ALC. Nor will you ever, if you interrupt.
CHO. Proceed, and I will hold my speechless tongue.
ALC. —This house was Eriphyla's, no one's else.
CHO. Nor did he shame his throat with hateful lies.
ALC. May I then enter, passing through the door?
CHO. Go, chase into the house a lucky foot.
 And, O my son, be, on the one hand, good,
 And do not, on the other hand, be bad;
 For that is very much the safest plan.
ALC. I go into the house with heels and speed.

CHORUS

 In speculation   *Strophe*
I would not willingly acquire a name
  For ill-digested thought;
  But after pondering much
To this conclusion I at last have come:
  Life is uncertain.
  This truth I have written deep
  In my reflective midriff
  On tablets not of wax,
Nor with a pen did I inscribe it there,
For many reasons: *Life, I say, is not*
  A stranger to uncertainty.
Not from the flight of omen-yelling fowls
  This fact did I discover.
Nor did the Delphic tripod bark it out,
  Nor yet Dodona.
Its native ingenuity sufficed
  My self-taught diaphragm.

 Why should I mention   *Antistrophe*
The Inachean daughter, loved of Zeus?
  Her whom of old the gods,
  More provident than kind,
Provided with four hoofs, two horns, one tail,

A gift not asked for
And sent her forth to learn
The unfamiliar science
Of how to chew the cud.
She therefore, all about the Argive fields,
Went cropping pale green grass and nettle-tops,
Nor did they disagree with her.
But yet, howe'er nutritious, such repasts
I do not hanker after:
Never may Cypris for her seat select
My dappled liver!
Why should I mention Io?   Why indeed?
I have no notion why.

But now does my boding heart,   *Epode*
Unhired, unaccompanied, sing
A strain not meet for the dance.
Yea even the palace appears
To my yoke of circular eyes
(The right, nor omit I the left)
Like a slaughterhouse, so to speak,
Garnished with woolly deaths
And many shipwrecks of cows.
I therefore in a Cissian strain lament;
And to the rapid,
Loud, linen-tattering thumps upon my chest
Resounds in concert
The battering of my unlucky head.

ERIPHYLA [*within*]. O, I am smitten with a hatchet's jaw;
  And that in deed and not in word alone.
CHO. I thought I heard a sound within the house
  Unlike the voice of one that jumps for joy.
ERI. He splits my skull, not in a friendly way,
  One more: he purposes to kill me dead.
CHO. I would not be reputed rash, but yet
  I doubt if all be gay within the house.
ERI. O! O! another stroke! that makes the third.
  He stabs me to the heart against my wish.
CHO. If that be so, thy state of health is poor;
  But thine arithmetic is quite correct.

                                                   (1883; 1901)

DUGALD SUTHERLAND MacCOLL

(1859–1948)

Ballade of Andrew Lang

YOU ask me, Fresher, who it is
   Who rhymes, researches, and reviews,
Who sometimes writes like Genesis,
   And sometimes for the *Daily News*:
   Who jests in words that angels use,
      And is most solemn with most slang:
   Who's who—who's which—and which is whose?
      Who can it be but Andrew Lang?

Quips, Quirks are his, and Quiddities,
   The epic and the teacup Muse,
Bookbindings, Aborigines,
   Ballades that banish all the Blues,
   Young Married Life among Yahoos,
      An Iliad, an Orang-outang,
   Triolets, Totems, and Tattoos—
      Who can it be but Andrew Lang?

Ah Ballade makers! tell me this,
   When did the hardest rhymes refuse
The guile that filled that book of his
   With multiplying Xs and IIs?
   You see me shuffle in his shoes,
      You hear me stammer where he sang,
   Who cannot charm you as I choose,
      Who cannot be an Andrew Lang.

ENVOY

Fresher! he dwelt with Torpid Crews,
   And once, like you, he knew the pang
Of Mods, of Greats, of Weekly Dues,
   And yet he is an Andrew Lang!

(1883)

GELETT BURGESS
(1860–1951)

Nonsense Quatrains

I NEVER saw a Purple Cow,
  I never hope to see one;
But I can tell you, anyhow,
  I'd rather see than be one!

· · ·

MANY people seem to think
Plaster o' Paris good to drink;
Though conductive unto quiet,
I prefer Another Diet.

· · ·

THE proper way to leave a room
Is not to plunge it into gloom;
Just make a Joke before you go,
And then escape before they know.

· · ·

I SENT my Collie to the wash—
They starched and ironed her, by Gosh!
And then they charged me half a dollar
For laundrying the Collie's collar!

· · ·

AH, yes! I wrote the 'Purple Cow'—
  I'm sorry, now, I wrote it!
But I can tell you anyhow,
  I'll kill you if you quote it!

(1895–7)

Psycholophon

TWINE then the rays
  Round her soft Theban tissues!
All will be as she says
  When the dead Past reissues.

Matters not what nor where,
  Hark, to the moon's dim cluster!
How was her heavy hair
  Lithe as a feather duster!

Matters not when nor whence;
    Flittertigibbet!
Sounds make the song, not sense,
    Thus I inhibit!

                      (1914)

Abstrosophy

IF echoes from the fitful past
    Could rise to mental view,
Would all their fancied radiance last
Or would some odours from the blast,
    Untouched by time, accrue?

Is present pain a future bliss,
    Or is it something worse?
For instance, take a case like this:
Is fancied kick a real kiss,
    Or rather the reverse?

Is plentitude of passion palled
    By poverty of scorn?
Does Fiction mend where Fact has mauled?
Has Death its wisest victims called
    When idiots are born?

                      (1914)

OWEN SEAMAN

(1861–1936)

The Battle of the Bays

I. A SONG OF RENUNCIATION
(After A. C. S.)

IN the days of my season of salad,
    When the down was as dew on my cheek,
And for French I was bred on the ballad,
    For Greek on the writers of Greek,
Then I sang of the rose that is ruddy,
    Of 'pleasure that winces and stings,'
Of white women and wine that is bloody,
    And similar things.

Of Delight that is dear as Desi-er,
   And Desire that is dear as Delight;
Of the fangs of the flame that is fi-er,
   Of the bruises of kisses that bite;
Of embraces that clasp and that sever,
   Of blushes that flutter and flee
Round the limbs of Dolores, whoever
   Dolores may be.

I sang of false faith that is fleeting
   As froth of the swallowing seas,
Time's curse that is fatal as Keating
   Is fatal to amorous fleas;
Of the wanness of woe that is whelp of
   The lust that is blind as a bat—
By the help of my Muse and the help of
   The relative THAT.

Panatheist, bruiser, and breaker
   Of kings and the creatures of kings,
I shouted on Freedom to shake her
   Feet loose of the fetter that clings;
Far rolling my ravenous red eye
   And lifting a mutinous lid,
To all monarchs and matrons I said I
   Would shock them—and did.

Thee I sang, and thy loves, O Thalassian,
   O 'noble and nude and antique!'
Unashamed in the 'fearless old fashion'
   Ere washing was done by the week;
When the 'roses and rapture' that girt you
   Were visions of delicate vice,
And the 'lilies and languors of virtue'
   Not nearly so nice.

O delights of the time of my teething,
   Félise, Fragoletta, Yolande!
Foam-yeast of a youth in its seething
   On blasted and blithering sand!
Snake-crowned on your tresses and belted
   With blossoms that coil and decay,
Ye are gone; ye are lost; ye are melted
   Like ices in May.

Hushed now is the bibulous bubble
   Of 'lithe and lascivious' throats;
Long stript and extinct is the stubble
   Of hoary and harvested oats;

From the sweets that are sour as the sorrel's
    The bees have abortively swarmed;
And Algernon's earlier morals
    Are fairly reformed.

I have written a loyal Armada,
    And posed in a Jubilee pose;
I have babbled of babies and played a
    New tune on the turn of their toes;
Washed white from the stain of Astarte,
    My books any virgin may buy;
And I hear I am praised by a party
    Called Something Mackay!

When erased are the records, and rotten
    The meshes of memory's net;
When the grace that forgives has forgotten
    The things that are good to forget;
When the trill of my juvenile trumpet
    Is dead and its echoes are dead;
Then the laurel shall lie on the crumpet
    And crown of my head!

                                  (1896)

II. THE RHYME OF THE KIPPERLING
(After R. K.)

Away by the haunts of the Yang-tse-boo,
    Where the Yuletide runs cold gin,
And the rollicking sign of the *Lord Knows Who*
    Sees mariners drink like sin;
Where the *Jolly Roger* tips his quart
    To the luck of the *Union Jack*;
And some are screwed on the foreign port,
    And some on the starboard tack;—
Ever they tell the tale anew
    Of the chase for the kipperling swag;
How the smack *Tommy This* and the smack *Tommy That*
They broached each other like a whisky-vat,
    And the *Fuzzy-wuz* took the bag.

Now this is the law of the herring fleet that harries the northern
    main,
Tattooed in scars on the chests of the tars with a brand like the
    brand of Cain:
That none may woo the sea-born shrew save such as pay their
    way
With a kipperling netted at noon of night and cured ere the
    crack of day.

It was the woman Sal o' the Dune, and the men were three
to one,
Bill the Skipper and Ned the Nipper and Sam that was Son of a
Gun;
Bill was a Skipper and Ned was a Nipper and Sam was the Son
of a Gun,
And the woman was Sal o' the Dune, as I said, and the men were
three to one.

There was never a light in the sky that night of the soft mid-
summer gales,
But the great man-bloaters snorted low, and the young 'uns sang
like whales;
And out laughed Sal (like a dog-toothed wheel was the laugh that
Sal laughed she):
'Now who's for a bride on the shady side of up'ards of forty-
three?'

And Neddy he swore by butt and bend, and Billy by bend and
bitt,
And nautical names that no man frames but your amateur
nautical wit;
And Sam said: 'Shiver my topping-lifts and scuttle my foc's'le
yarn,
And may I be curst, if I'm not in first with a kipperling slued
astarn!'
Now the smack *Tommy This* and the smack *Tommy That* and
the *Fuzzy-Wuz* smack, all three,
Their captains bold, they were Bill and Ned and Sam re-
spectivelee.

And it's writ in the rules that the primary schools of kippers
should get off cheap
For a two-mile reach off Foulness beach when the July tide's
at neap;
And the lawless lubbers that lust for loot and filch the yearling
stock
They get smart raps from the coastguard chaps with their
blunderbuss fixed half-cock.

Now Bill the Skipper and Ned the Nipper could tell green
cheese from blue,
And Bill knew a trick and Ned knew a trick, but Sam knew a
trick worth two.

So Bill he sneaks a corporal's breeks and a belt of pipeclayed
hide,
And splices them on to the jibsail-boom like a troopship on the
tide.

And likewise Ned to his mast-head he runs a rag of the Queen's,
With a rusty sword and a moke on board to bray like the Horse
    Marines.

But Sam sniffs gore and he keeps off-shore and he waits for
    things to stir,
Then he tracks for the deep with a long fog-horn rigged up like
    a bowchasér.

Now scarce had Ned dropped line and lead when he spots the
    pipeclayed hide,
And the corporal's breeks on the jibsail-boom like a troopship on
    the tide;
And Bill likewise, when he ups and spies the slip of the rag of
    the Queen's,
And the rusty sword, and he sniffs aboard the moke of the Horse
    Marines.

So they each luffed sail, and they each turned tail, and they
    whipped their wheels like mad,
When the one he said: 'By the Lord, it's Ned!' and the other:
    'It's Bill, by Gad!'

Then about and about, and nozzle to snout, they rammed
    through breach and brace,
And the splinters flew as they mostly do when a Government
    test takes place.

Then up stole Sam with his little ram and the nautical talk
    flowed free,
And in good bold type might have covered the two front sheets
    of the *P. M. G.*

But the fog-horn bluff was safe enough, where all was weed and
    weft,
And the conger-eels were a-making meals, and the pick of the
    tackle left
Was a binnacle-lid and a leak in the bilge and the chip of a
    cracked sheerstrake
And the corporal's belt and the moke's cool pelt and a portrait of
    Francis Drake.

So Sam he hauls the dead men's trawls and he booms for the
    harbour-bar,
And the splitten fry are salted dry by the blink of the morning
    star.

And Sal o' the Dune was wed next moon by the man that paid
  his way
With a kipperling netted at noon of night and cured ere the crack
  of day;
For such is the law of the herring fleet that bloats on the northern
  main,
Tattooed in scars on the chests of the tars with a brand like the
  brand of Cain.

And still in the haunts of the Yang-tse-boo
Ever they tell the tale anew
  Of the chase for the kipperling swag;
How the smack *Tommy This* and the smack *Tommy That*
They broached each other like a whisky-vat,
  And the *Fuzzy-wuz* took the bag.

                     (1894)

III. A BALLAD OF A BUN
(After J. D.)

From Whitsuntide to Whitsuntide—
    That is to say, all through the year—
Her patient pen was occupied
    With songs and tales of pleasant cheer.

But still her talent went to waste
    Like flotsam on an open sea;
She never hit the public taste,
    Or knew the knack of Bellettrie.

Across the sounding City's fogs
    There hurtled round her weary head
The thunder of the rolling logs;
    'The Critics' Carnival!' she said.

Immortal prigs took heaven by storm,
    Prigs scattered largesses of praise;
The work of both was rather warm;
    'This is,' she said, 'the thing that pays!'

Sharp envy turned her wine to blood—
    I mean it turned her blood to wine;
And this resolve came like a flood—
    'The cake of knowledge must be mine!'

'I am in Eve's predicament—
    I sha'n't be happy till I've sinned;
Away!' She lightly rose and sent
    Her scruples sailing down the wind.

She did not tear her open breast,
  Nor leave behind a track of gore,
But carried flannel next her chest,
  And wore the boots she always wore.

Across the sounding City's din
  She wandered, looking indiscreet,
And ultimately landed in
  The neighbourhood of Regent Street.

She ran against a resolute
  Policeman standing like a wall;
She kissed his feet and asked the route
  To where they held the Carnival.

Her strange behaviour caused remark;
  They said: 'Her reason has been lost';
Beside her eyes the gas was dark,
  But that was owing to the frost.

A Decadent was dribbling by;
  'Lady,' he said, 'you seem undone;
You need a panacea; try
  This sample of the Bodley bun.

'It is fulfilled of precious spice,
  Whereof I give the recipe:
Take common dripping, stew in vice,
  And serve with vertu; taste and see!

'And lo! I brand you on the brow
  As kin to Nature's lowest germ;
You are sister to the microbe now,
  And second-cousin to the worm.'

He gave her of his golden store,
  Such hunger hovered in her look;
She took the bun, and asked for more,
  And went away and wrote a book.

To put the matter shortly, she
  Became the topic of the town;
In all the lists of Bellettrie
  Her name was regularly down.

'We recognize,' the critics wrote,
  'Maupassant's verve and Heine's wit';
Some even made a verbal note
  Of Shakespeare being out of it.

The seasons went and came again;
  At length the languid public cried:
'It is a sorry sort of Lane
  That hardly ever turns aside.

'We want a little change of air;
  On that,' they said, 'we must insist;
We cannot any longer bear
  The seedy sex-impressionist.'

Across the sounding City's din
  This rumour smote her on the ear:
'The publishers are going in
  For songs and tales of pleasant cheer!'

'Alack!' she said, 'I lost the art,
  And left my womanhood foredone,
When first I trafficked in the mart
  All for a mess of Bodley bun.

'I cannot cut my kin at will,
  Or jilt the protoplastic germ;
I am sister to the microbe still,
  And second-cousin to the worm!'

                                    (1894)

IV. TO A BOY-POET OF THE DECADENCE

But my good little man, you have made a mistake
  If you really are pleased to suppose
That the Thames is alight with the lyrics you make;
  We could all do the same if we chose.

From Solomon down, we may read, as we run,
  Of the ways of a man and a maid;
There is nothing that's new to us under the sun,
  And certainly not in the shade.

The erotic affairs that you fiddle aloud
  Are as vulgar as coin of the mint;
And you merely distinguish yourself from the crowd
  By the fact that you put 'em in print.

You're a 'prentice, my boy, in the primitive stage,
  And you itch, like a boy, to confess:
When you know a bit more of the arts of the age
  You will probably talk a bit less.

For your dull little vices we don't care a fig,
  It is *this* that we deeply deplore;
You were cast for a common or usual pig,
  But you play the invincible bore.

(1894)

Of the Stalking of the Stag

INTRODUCTION

In Scotland, where the porridge grows,
  And jokes demand a deal of care,
The stag, who has a nimble nose,
  Imbibes the pleasant mountain air;
He roams the forest at his ease,
And never knocks against the trees.

The colour of the beast is red,
  More sombre than the carrot's tone;
A most engaging quadruped
  When fairly hit, or left alone;
He really wouldn't hurt a child,
But crooked shooting drives him wild.

So eager is his sense of smell
  He knows you half a league away;
He also travels very well,
  How fast I hardly care to say;
But, though you take the train or drive,
You cannot catch the brute alive.

Your rifle's pace must be superb,
  And bullets built of common stuff
Are insufficient to disturb
  A frame incorrigibly tough;
It's best to penetrate his hide
With missiles made to burst inside.

OF THE PROCESS

Rules of the game as recognized:
  Your stalker comes the night before
To say that he has just surprised
  A herd of thirty head or more,
And in their midst a noble beast
With twelve or thirteen points at least.

This is a lie; but well I know
   You will believe it, every word,
And in your dreaming you will go
   And slay the whole astonished herd;
Then rise with blood upon the brain
And sally in a driving rain.

For miles and miles, soaked through and through,
   By barren braes you stoutly pound,
Your ardent body bent in two,
   An awful silence hovering round;
And so to lunch, with bated breath,
To drink the stag's ensuing death.

Your stalker, having had his fill
   Of undiluted mountain-dew,
Asserts that on a distant hill
   A ruddy patch arrests his view;
This representing, says the wag,
A portion of a splendid stag.

What seems to you the obvious track
   Is not the one by any means;
You have to turn about and tack
   Round three precipitous ravines;
Mere crows may steer an even flight,
Man stalks by faith and not by sight.

Emerging as the shadows fall,
   You find the reddish object there!
Your next manœuvre is to crawl
   Face downwards—*ventre*, in fact, *à terre*;
Or bury your excrescent head
Within a torrent's foaming bed.

OF THE DEATH

The gloaming deepens; all is dim!
   Now let the fatal bullet hum;
You fix your prey, your eye is grim,
   Your heart is going like a drum;
Crash! how the echoes rend the air!
The object doesn't turn a hair.

'Just over him!' your man observes;
 His duty is to seem to know;
At this you brace your shattered nerves
 And let the second barrel go;
Your stag is steady as a fence;
These beasts are really very dense.

With wary steps you now advance,
 Reloading swiftly on your way,
In case the stricken deer should chance,
 Being annoyed, to turn at bay;
And finally you come full-cock
Upon a ruddy patch of rock!

Well in its centre you derive
 Some solace from a splash of lead,
Which, had the target been alive,
 Would certainly have killed it dead;
Your stalker, meaning not to miss
His honorarium, tells you this.

He further says that what he spied
 Six miles away against the crag
(Speaking as one who never lied)
 Indubitably *was* a stag;
But in the darkness, while you stalked,
The stupid beast had been and walked.

OF THE HOME-COMING

Your pony waits you down below,
 Grazing at large with slackened girth;
At sight of you his features glow
 With pity, not untouched by mirth;
And where the quarry should have been
You mount and quit the painful scene.

'How many?' all the ladies cry;
 'One paltry Royal!' you remark;
'Sore wounded, he escaped to die
 Elsewhere in private after dark.'
This is your statement, terse but clear,
Describing how you killed the deer.

(189·)

MAY KENDALL
(1861–1943)

The Seraph and the Snob

IT was a draper eminent,
  A merchant of the land,
On lofty calculations bent,
Who raised his eyes, on cent per cent
  From pondering, in the Strand.

He saw a Seraph standing there,
  With aspect bright and sainted,
Ethereal robe of fabric fair,
And wings that might have been the pair
  Sir Noel Paton painted.

A real Seraph met his gaze—
  There was no doubt of that—
Irradiate with celestial rays.
Our merchant viewed him with amaze,
  And then he touched his hat.

I own, before he raised his hand,
  A moment he reflected,
Because in this degenerate land,
To meet a Seraph in the Strand
  Was somewhat unexpected.

Yet there one stood, as wrapt in thought,
  Amid the City's din,
No other eye the vision caught,
Not even a stray policeman sought
  To run that Seraph in.

But on the merchant curious eyes
  Men turned, and mocking finger,
For well they knew his mien and guise,
He was not wont, in moonstrick wise,
  About the Strand to linger.

Mute stood the draper for a space,
  The mystery to probe,
Alas! in that his hour of grace,
His eyes forsook the Seraph's face,
  And rested on his robe.

And wildly did he seek in vain
　　To guess the strange material,
And golden fancies filled his brain,
And hopes of unimagined gain
　　Woke at the sight ethereal.

Then, suffered not by fate austere
　　The impulse to discard,
He never paused to idly veer
About the bush; but calm and clear
　　He said: 'How much a yard?'

A bright and tremulous lustre shone
　　Through the dull, dingy Strand,
From parting wings seraphic thrown;
And then, mute, motionless, alone,
　　Men saw the merchant stand.

　　　.　　　.　　　.　　　.

In town to-day his memory's cold,
　　No more his name on 'Change is,
Idle his mart, his wares are sold,
And men forget his fame of old,
　　Who now in Earlswood ranges.

Yet evermore, with toil and care
　　He ponders on devices
For stuffs superlatively rare,
Celestial fabrics past compare,
　　At reasonable prices.

To him the padded wall and dead
　　With gorgeous colour gleams,
And huge advertisements are spread,
And lurid placards, orange, red,
　　Drive through his waking dreads.

                                        (1885)

The Lay of the Trilobite

A MOUNTAIN's giddy height I sought,
　　Because I could not find
Sufficient vague and mighty thought
　　To fill my mighty mind;
And as I wandered ill at ease,
　　There chanced upon my sight
A native of Silurian seas,
　　An ancient Trilobite.

So calm, so peacefully he lay,
    I watched him even with tears:
I thought of Monads far away
    In the forgotten years.
How wonderful it seemed and right,
    The providential plan,
That he should be a Trilobite,
    And I should be a Man!

And then, quite natural and free
    Out of his rocky bed,
That Trilobite he spoke to me,
    And this is what he said:
'I don't know how the thing was done,
    Although I cannot doubt it;
But Huxley—he if any one
    Can tell you all about it;

'How all your faiths are ghosts and dreams,
    How in the silent sea
Your ancestors were Monotremes—
    Whatever these may be;
How you evolved your shining lights
    Of wisdom and perfection
From Jelly-fish and Trilobites
    By natural selection.

'You've Kant to make your brains go round,
    Hegel you have to clear them,
You've Mr Browning to confound,
    And Mr Punch to cheer them!
The native of an alien land
    You call a man and brother,
And greet with hymn-book in one hand
    And pistol in the other!

'You've Politics to make you fight
    As if you were possessed;
You've cannon and you've dynamite
    To give the nations rest:
The side that makes the loudest din
    Is surest to be right,
And oh, a pretty fix you're in!'
    Remarked the Trilobite.

'But gentle, stupid, free from woe
    I lived among my nation,
I didn't care—I didn't know
    That I was a Crustacean.

I didn't grumble, didn't steal,
    I *never* took to rhyme:
Salt water was my frugal meal,
    And carbonate of lime.'

Reluctantly I turned away,
    No other word he said;
An ancient Trilobite he lay
    Within his rocky bed.
I did not answer him, for that
    Would have annoyed my pride:
I merely bowed, and raised my hat,
    But in my heart I cried:

' I wish our brains were not so good,
    I wish our skulls were thicker,
I wish that Evolution could
    Have stopped a little quicker;
For oh, it was a happy plight,
    Of liberty and ease,
To be a simple Trilobite
    In the Silurian seas.'

                               (1885)

Taking Long Views

H IS locks were wild, and wild his eye,
    Furrowed his brow with anxious thought.
Musing I asked him: 'Tell me why
    You look thus vacant and distraught?'
Sadly he gazed into my face:
    He said: 'I have no respite, none!
Oh, shall we wander into space
    Or fall into the sun?

' Astronomers I've sought in tears,
    And ah, 'tis terribly remiss
That after all these anxious years
    They cannot even tell us this!
Though each man seems to prove his case,
    Each contradicts the other one,
And—*do* we wander into space
    Or fall into the sun?'

Comfort!' I said, 'I can't discern
    The nature of our planet's end,
Nor should I greatly care to learn.
    We've many aeons left, my friend!

Whether we last from age to age
  A frozen ball, or turn to flame,
To me, at this inspiring stage,
  Is very much the same.

'Observe Humanity's advance,
  And Evolution's giant strides!
Remark on what a smooth expanse
  The nation's barque at anchor rides!
The march of Intellect retrace.'
  He moaned: 'I don't care what we've done.
Oh, shall we wander into space
  Or fall into the sun?

'If we should fall, you understand,
  Such heat the crash would generate
The solar system might expand
  Into its primal gaseous state.
It would be awkward, I maintain,
  The same old cycle to renew;
For once let things come round again
  And *we* should come round too!'

I cried: 'The prophecy forbear!
  Of finite woes we have enough.
What, travel through the old despair,
  Experience the old rebuff!
I'd rather haunt the void Afar,
  For endless ages, would rejoice
To be a harmless frozen star,
  If I might have my choice!'

He gazed at me with aspect strange.
  He only said: 'How would it be
If this poor planet should derange
  The solar system's equity;
If when the sun our planet met
  The sun himself began to fall,
Another system to upset,
  And so on through them all?'

'Peace, peace!' I said. 'However dark
  The destiny the aeons bear,
You won't be here the wreck to mark.'
  He cried: '*That* causes my despair.
I want to know what will take place,
  I want to see what will be done.
Oh, shall we wander into space
  Or fall into the sun?'

(1887)

ARTHUR THOMAS QUILLER-COUCH

(1863–1944)

De Tea Fabula

PLAIN LANGUAGE FROM TRUTHFUL JAMES

Do I sleep? Do I dream?
    Am I hoaxed by a scout?
Are things what they seem,
    Or is Sophists about?
Is our τὸ τί ἦν εἶναι a failure, or is Robert Browning played out?

    Which expressions like these
        May be fairly applied
    By a party who sees
        A Society skied
Upon tea that the Warden of Keble had biled with legitimate
    pride.

    'Twas November the third,
        And I says to Bill Nye:
    'Which it's true what I've heard:
        If you're, so to speak, fly,
There's a chance of some tea and cheap culture, the sort recom-
    mended as High.'

    Which I mentioned its name,
        And he ups and remarks:
    'If dress-coats is the game
        And pow-wow in the Parks,
Then I'm nuts on Sordello and Hohenstiel-Schwangau and
    similar Snarks.'

    Now the pride of Bill Nye
        Cannot well be express'd;
    For he wore a white tie
        And a cut-away vest:
Says I: 'Solomon's lilies ain't in it, and they was reputed well
    dress'd.'

But not far did we wend,
    When we saw Pippa pass
On the arm of a friend
    —Doctor Furnivall 'twas,
And he wore in his hat two half-tickets for London, return,
second-class.

'Well,' I thought, 'this is odd.'
    But we came pretty quick
To a sort of a quad
    That was all of red brick,
And I says to the porter: 'R. Browning: free passes; and kindly
look slick.'

But says he, dripping tears
    In his check handkerchief:
'That symposium's career's
    Been regrettably brief,
For it went all its pile upon crumpets and busted on gunpowder-
leaf!'

Then we tucked up the sleeves
    Of our shirts (that were biled),
Which the reader perceives
    That our feelings were riled,
And we went for that man till his mother had doubted the traits
of her child.

Which emotions like these
    Must be freely indulged
By a party who sees
    A Society bulged
On a reef the existence of which its prospectus had never
divulged.

But I ask—Do I dream?
    Has it gone up the spout?
Are things what they seem,
    Or is Sophists about?
Is our τὸ τί ἦν εἶναι a failure, or is Robert Browning played out?

        (1886)

Retrospection

(After c. s. c.)

WHEN the hunter-star Orion
    (Or, it may be, Charles his Wain)
Tempts the tiny elves to try on
    All their little tricks again;
When the earth is calmly breathing
    Draughts of slumber undefiled,
And the sire, unused to teething,
    Seeks for errant pins his child;

When the moon is on the ocean,
    And our little sons and heirs
From a natural emotion
    Wish the luminary theirs;
Then a feeling hard to stifle,
    Even harder to define,
Makes me feel I'd give a trifle
    For the days of Auld Lang Syne.

James—for we have been as brothers
    (Are, to speak correctly, twins),
Went about in one another's
    Clothing, bore each other's sins,
Rose together, ere the pearly
    Tint of morn had left the heaven,
And retired (absurdly early)
    Simultaneously at seven—

James, the days of yore were pleasant.
    Sweet to climb for alien pears
Till the irritated peasant
    Came and took us unawares;
Sweet to devastate his chickens,
    As the ambush'd catapult
Scattered, and the very dickens
    Was the natural result;

Sweet to snare the thoughtless rabbit;
    Break the next-door neighbour's pane;
Cultivate the smoker's habit
    On the not-innocuous cane;
Leave the exercise unwritten;
    Systematically cut
Morning school, to plunge the kitten
    In his bath, the water-butt.

Age, my James, that from the cheek of
    Beauty steals its rosy hue,
Has not left us much to speak of:
    But 'tis not for this I rue.
Beauty with its thousand graces,
    Hair and tints that will not fade,
You may get from many places
    Practically ready-made.

No; it is the evanescence
    Of those lovelier tints of Hope—
Bubbles, such as adolescence
    Joys to win from melted soap—
Emphasizing the conclusion
    That the dreams of Youth remain
Castles that are An delusion
    (Castles, that's to say, in Spain).

Age thinks 'fit,' and I say 'fiat.'
    Here I stand for Fortune's butt
As for Sunday swains to shy at
    Stands the stoic coco-nut.
If you wish it put succinctly,
    Gone are all our little games;
But I thought I'd say distinctly
    What I feel about it, James.

                                                (1887)

A Letter

Addressed during the Summer Term of 1888 *by* MR ALGERNON
DEXTER, *Scholar of* —— *College, Oxford, to his cousin,* MISS
KITTY TREMAYNE, *at* —— *Vicarage, Devonshire.*

          (After W. M. P.)

DEAR KITTY,
    At length the term's ending;
      I'm in for my Schools in a week;
And the time that at present I'm spending
      On you should be spent upon Greek:
But I'm fairly well read in my Plato,
      I'm thoroughly red in the eyes,
And I've almost forgotten the way to
      Be healthy and wealthy and wise.
So 'the best of all ways'—why repeat you
      The verse at 2.30 a.m.,
When I'm stealing an hour to entreat you
      Dear Kitty, to come to Commem.

Oh, come! You shall rustle in satin
   Through halls where Examiners trod:
Your laughter shall triumph o'er Latin
   In lecture-room, garden, and quad.
They stand in the silent Sheldonian—
   Our orators, waiting—for you,
Their style guaranteed Ciceronian,
   Their subject—'the Ladies in Blue.'
The Vice sits arrayed in his scarlet;
   He's pale, but they say he dissem-
bles by calling his Beadle a 'varlet'
   Whenever he thinks of Commem.

There are dances, flirtations at Nuneham,
   Flower-shows, the procession of Eights:
There's a list stretching *usque ad Lunam*
   Of concerts, and lunches, and fêtes:
There's the Newdigate all about 'Gordon,'
   —So sweet, and they say it will scan.
You shall flirt with a Proctor, a Warden
   Shall run for your shawl and your fan.
They are sportive as gods broken loose from
   Olympus, and yet very em-
inent men.   There are plenty to choose from,
   You'll find, if you come to Commem.

I know your excuses: Red Sorrel
   Has stumbled and broken her knees;
Aunt Phoebe thinks waltzing immoral;
   And 'Algy, you are such a tease;
It's nonsense, of course, but she *is* strict';
   And little Dick Hodge has the croup;
And there's no one to visit your 'district'
   Or make Mother Tettleby's soup.
Let them cease for a se'nnight to plague you;
   Oh, leave them to manage *pro tem.*
With their croups and their soups and their ague,
   Dear Kitty, and come to Commem.

Don't tell me Papa has lumbago,
   That you haven't a frock fit to wear,
That the curate 'has notions, and may go
   To lengths if there's nobody there,'
That the Squire has 'said things' to the Vicar,
   And the Vicar 'had words' with the Squire,

That the Organist's taken to liquor,
  And leaves you to manage the choir:
For Papa must be cured, and the curate
  Coerced, and your gown is a gem;
And the moral is—Don't be obdurate,
  Dear Kitty, but come to Commem.

'My gown?   Though, no doubt, sir, you're clever,
  You'd better leave fashions alone.
Do you think that a frock lasts for ever?'
  Dear Kitty, I'll grant you have grown;
But I thought of my 'scene' with McVittie
  That night when he trod on your train
At the Bachelor's Ball.   ''Twas a pity,'
  You said, but I knew 'twas Champagne.
And your gown was enough to compel me
  To fall down and worship its hem—
(Are 'hems' wearing?   If not, you shall tell me
  What is, when you come to Commem.)

Have you thought, since that night, of the Grotto?
  Of the words whispered under the palms,
While the minutes flew by and forgot to
  Remind us of Aunt and her qualms?
Of the stains of the old *Journalisten*?
  Of the rose that I begged from your hair?
When you turned, and I saw something glisten—
  Dear Kitty, don't frown; it *was* there!
But that idiot Delane in the middle
  Bounced in with 'Our dance, I—ahem!'
And—the rose you may find in my Liddell
  And Scott when you come to Commem.

Then, Kitty, let 'yes' be the answer.
  We'll dance at the 'Varsity Ball.
And the morning shall find you a dancer
  In Christ Church or Trinity hall.
And perhaps, when the elders are yawning
  And rafters grow pale overhead
With the day, there shall come with its dawning
  Some thought of that sentence unsaid.
Be it this, be it that—'I forget,' or
  'Was joking'—whatever the fem-
inine fib, you'll have made me your debtor
  And come—you *will* come? to Commem.

                                        (1888)

ROBERT FULLER MURRAY

(1863–1894)

The End of April

THIS is the time when larks are singing loud,
    And higher still ascending, and more high,
This is the time when many a fleecy cloud
    Runs lamb-like on the pastures of the sky,
This is the time when most I love to lie
    Stretched, on the links, now listening to the sea,
Now looking at the train that dawdles by;
    But James is going in for his degree.

James is my brother.   He has twice been ploughed,
    Yet he intends to have another try,
Hoping to pass (as he says) in a crowd.
    Sanguine is James, but not so sanguine I.
If you demand my reason, I reply:
    Because he reads no Greek without a key,
And spells Thucydides c-i-d-y;
    Yet James is going in for his degree.

No doubt, if the authorities allowed
    The taking in of Bohns, he might defy
The stiffest paper that has ever cowed
    A timid candidate and made him fly.
Without such aids, he all as well may try
    To cultivate the people of Dundee,
Or lead the camel through the needle's eye
    Yet James is going in for his degree.

Vain are the efforts hapless mortals ply
    To climb of knowledge the forbidden tree;
Yet still about its roots they strive and cry,
    And James is going in for his degree.

(1891)

Andrew M'Crie

(FROM THE UNPUBLISHED REMAINS OF
EDGAR ALLAN POE)

IT was many and many a year ago,
　　In a city by the sea,
That a man there lived whom I happened to know
　　By the name of Andrew M'Crie;
And this man he slept in another room,
　　But ground and had meals with me.

I was an ass and he was an ass,
　　In this city by the sea;
But we ground in a way which was more than a grind,
　　I and Andrew M'Crie;
In a way that the idle semis next door
　　Declared was shameful to see.

And this was the reason that, one dark night,
　　In this city by the sea,
A stone flew in at the window, hitting
　　The milk-jug and Andrew M'Crie.
And once some low-bred tertians came,
　　And bore him away from me,
And shoved him into a private house
　　Where the people were having tea.

Professors, not half so well up in their work,
　　Went envying him and me—
Yes!—that was the reason, I always thought
　　(And Andrew agreed with me),
Why they ploughed us both at the end of the year,
　　Chilling and killing poor Andrew M'Crie.

But his ghost is more terrible far than the ghosts
　　Of many more famous than he—
　　Of many more gory than he—
And neither visits to foreign coasts,
　　Nor tonics, can ever set free
Two well-known Profs from the haunting wraith
　　Of the injured Andrew M'Crie.

For at night, as they dream, they frequently scream,
  'Have mercy, Mr M'Crie!'
And at morn they will rise with bloodshot eyes,
  And the very first thing they will see,
When they dare to descend to their coffee and rolls,
Sitting down by the scuttle, the scuttle of coals,
  With a volume of notes on its knee,
  Is the spectre of Andrew M'Crie.

                                              (1891)

OLIVER HERFORD

(1863–1935)

The Music of the Future

THE politest musician that ever was seen
Was Montague Meyerbeer Mendelssohn Green.
So extremely polite he would take off his hat
When ever he happened to meet with a cat.

'It's not that I'm partial to cats,' he'd explain;
'Their music to me is unspeakable pain.
There's nothing that causes my flesh so to crawl
As when they perform a G-flat caterwaul.

'Yet I cannot help feeling—in spite of their din—
When I hear at a concert the first violin
Interpret some exquisite thing of my own,
If it were not for *cat gut* I'd never be known.

'And so, when I bow, as you see, to a cat,
It isn't to *her* that I take off my hat;
But to fugues and sonatas that possibly hide
Uncomposed in her—well—in her tuneful inside.'

                                              (1906)

The Missing Link

BESIDE the rail, despite the gale,
  Old Noah took each ticket,
And registered each beast and bird
  That passed inside the wicket.

And when at last they had made fast
  As much as they could stow away,
He cried 'Let go! cut loose! yo ho!
  Hoist gang! avast! heave ho—away!'

With heave and yank, up came the plank,
  A-straining and a-creaking,
When, rising o'er the wind and roar,
  They heard two voices shrieking—

'Take us aboard!   You can't afford
  So cruelly to flout us!
We are a pair extremely rare;
  No ark's complete without us.'

Down went the gang, and up there sprang
  Before them, through the curtain
Of blinding rain, the oddest twain,
  Of genus most uncertain.

They'd human shape, yet like the ape
  Were caudally appended;
And, strange to tell, their feet as well,
  Like apes', in fingers ended.

Quoth Noah: 'Pray, who are you—say?
  Human, or anthropoidal?'
'You takes your choice!' as with one voice
  They cried, which so annoyed all

The apes on board with one accord
  They screamed for indignation;
'Twas very clear *they* would not hear
  Of any such relation.

Said Noah: 'Though you're rare, I know
  You're not for my collection;
And though not vain, I must refrain
  From claiming the connection.'

With small regret the pair he set
  On shore mid cheers and hissing,
And that's the way it comes to-day
  The MISSING LINK is missing.

(1906)

ARTHUR ST JOHN ADCOCK
(1864–1930)

By Deputy

As Shakespeare couldn't write his plays
    (If Mrs Gallup's not mistaken)
I think how wise in many ways
    He was to have them done by Bacon;
They might have mouldered on the shelf
    Mere minor dramas (and he knew it!)
If he had written them himself
    Instead of letting Bacon do it.

And if it's true, as Brown and Smith
    In many learned tomes have stated,
That Homer was an idle myth
    He ought to be congratulated,
Since thus, evading birth, he rose
    For men to worship at a distance:
He might have penned inferior prose
    Had he achieved a real existence.

To him and Shakespeare men agree
    In making very nice allusions;
But no one thinks of praising me,
    For I compose my own effusions:
As others wrote *their* works divine
    And they immortal thus to-day are,
Perhaps had someone written mine
    I might have been as great as they are.

                          (1902)

RUDYARD KIPLING
(1865–1936)

The Post that Fitted

ERE the steamer bore him Eastward, Sleary was engaged t
    marry
An attractive girl at Tunbridge, whom he called 'my littl
    Carrie.'
Sleary's pay was very modest; Sleary was the other way.
Who can cook a two-plate dinner on eight poor rupees a day?

Long he pondered o'er the question in his scantly furnished
quarters—
Then proposed to Minnie Boffkin, eldest of Judge Boffkin's
daughters.
Certainly an impecunious Subaltern was not a catch,
But the Boffkins knew that Minnie mightn't make another match.

So they recognized the business and, to feed and clothe the bride
Got him made a Something Something somewhere on the
Bombay side.
Anyhow, the billet carried pay enough for him to marry—
As the artless Sleary put it: 'Just the thing for me and Carrie.'

Did he, therefore, jilt Miss Boffkin—impulse of a baser mind?
No! He started epileptic fits of an appalling kind.
[Of his *modus operandi* only this much I could gather:
'Pears' shaving sticks will give you little taste and lots of lather.']

Frequently in public places his affliction used to smite
Sleary with distressing vigour—always in the Boffkins' sight.
Ere a week was over Minnie weepingly returned his ring,
Told him his 'unhappy weakness' stopped all thought of
marrying.

Sleary bore the information with a chastened holy joy—
Epileptic fits don't matter in Political employ—
Wired three short words to Carrie—took his ticket, packed his
kit—
Bade farewell to Minnie Boffkin in one last, long, lingering fit.

Four weeks later, Carrie Sleary read—and laughed until she
wept—
Mrs Boffkin's warning letter on the 'wretched epilept.'
Year by year, in pious patience, vengeful Mrs Boffkin sits
Waiting for the Sleary babies to develop Sleary's fits.

(1886)

Pink Dominoes

JENNY and Me were engaged, you see,
    On the eve of the Fancy Ball;
So a kiss or two was nothing to you
    Or any one else at all.

Jenny would go in a domino—
    Pretty and pink but warm;
While I attended, clad in a splendid
    Austrian uniform.

Now we had arranged, through notes exchanged
    Early that afternoon,
At Number Four to waltz no more,
    But to sit in the dusk and spoon.

I wish you to see that Jenny and Me
    Had barely exchanged our troth;
So a kiss or two was strictly due
    By, from, and between us both.

When Three was over, an eager lover,
    I fled to the gloom outside;
And a Domino came out also
    Whom I took for my future bride.

That is to say, in a casual way,
    I slipped my arm around her:
With a kiss or two (which is nothing to you),
    And ready to kiss I found her.

She turned her head and the name she said
    Was certainly not my own;
But ere I could speak, with a smothered shriek
    She fled and left me alone.

Then Jenny came, and I saw with shame
    She'd doffed her domino;
And I had embraced an alien waist—
    But I did not tell her so.

Next morn I knew that there were two
    Dominoes pink, and one
Had cloaked the spouse of Sir Julian Vouse,
    Our big Political gun.

Sir J. was old, and her hair was gold,
    And her eye was a blue cerulean;
And the name she said when she turned her head
    Was not in the least like 'Julian.'

Now wasn't it nice, when want of *pice*
    Forbade us twain to marry,
That old Sir J., in the kindest way,
    Made me his Secre*tarry*?

                    (1886)

EDWARD VERRALL LUCAS

(1868–1938)

The Pedestrian's Plaint

WILL there never come a season
   Which shall rid us from the curse
Of a speed which knows no reason,
   And the too contiguous hearse;
When no longer shall we tremble
   As the motors leave their lair;
Meekly by the kerb assemble
   While the klaxon rends the air—

When the gladsome news will nerve us
   That the petrol-wells are dry
And the horse again must serve us,
   Safe and sure and stepping high?
That will be a day for fiddling,
   Fun and festival galore,
When the Armstrongs cease from siddling
   And the Royces roll no more!

(1925)

ST JOHN EMILE CLAVERING HANKIN

(1869–1909)

*An Elegy
on the late King of Patagonia*

THE generous man will not deny
   Few monarchs' paths in life were stonier
Than that one which was trodden by
   ACHILLES, King of Patagonia.

When he was crowned his subjects cheered,
   The bells were rung in every steeple,
From which it certainly appeared
   He was the Father of his People.

But envy of his peaceful sway
    And of his just administration
Inflamed in a disastrous way
    The rulers of the Chilian nation.

They drove ACHILLES from his throne
    To Paris, where his days were ended,
And all impartial men will own
    Their action cannot be defended.

A credible informant says
    This conduct on the part of Chili
Was much discussed for several days
    Both in Pall Mall and Piccadilly.

It shocked the virtuous English breast
    From Clapham Common to Belgravia,
And moved all classes to protest
    At such unprincipled behaviour.

For when the strong oppress the weak
    On either side of the Pacific,
You hear the British conscience speak
    And then its language is terrific!

So votes of sympathy were sent
    (As happened to Armenia lately),
But, though exceedingly well meant,
    They didn't help ACHILLES greatly.

He therefore made the best of things
    In Paris, where he lived contented—
Like many other exiled kings—
    In an *apartement* that he rented.

Lulled by the siren city's hum,
    Far from his former kingdom's borders,
He made a modest annual sum
    By selling Patagonian Orders.

The prices for the various ranks
    Suited alike the rich and thrifty;
A knighthood fetched a hundred francs,
    And other decorations fifty.

New Peers he made of every class,
    Counts, Barons, Viscounts he created;
His Order of the Golden Ass
    Was very much appreciated.

And so ACHILLES died in peace
    Chastened by Fate but not dejected,
His neighbours wept at his decease,
    For he was very much respected.

Grief-stricken thousands came to gaze
    Upon his corpse with lamentations,
Their manly breasts were all ablaze
    With Patagonian decorations.

And many a king I have in mind
    Will wait a longish time until he's
As much regretted by mankind
    As Patagonia's ACHILLES!

(1902)

Consolatory!

WHEN your feet are like lead
    (And so is your head)
And your temper is simply infernal,
    And your excellent wife,
    Worried out of her life,
Remarks on the fact in her journal—

When you growl like a bear,
    Or jump up and swear
If a plate is put down with a clatter,
    And are quite at a loss
    To explain why you're cross
And what in the world is the matter—

When you don't want to live,
    And the thought that you give
To your business is fretful and cursory,
    And you're sulky at meals,
    And can't bear the squeals
That (as usual!) proceed from the nursery—

When you snarl and you snap,
    And you don't care a rap
For the horrible way you're behaving,
    And you frequently mention
    Your rooted intention
Of cutting your throat while you're shaving—

When you ponder all day
On the easiest way
Of drowning yourself in the river,
It's a comfort, I find,
To keep clearly in mind
That it's probably only your liver!

(1902)

De Gustibus

I AM an unadventurous man,
And always go upon the plan
Of shunning danger where I can.

And so I fail to understand
Why every year a stalwart band
Of tourists go to Switzerland,

And spend their time for several weeks.
With quaking hearts and pallid cheeks,
Scaling abrupt and windy peaks.

In fact, I'm old enough to find
Climbing of almost any kind
Is very little to my mind.

A mountain summit white with snow
Is an attractive sight, I know,
But why not see it *from below*?

Why leave the hospitable plain
And scale Mont Blanc with toil and pain
Merely to scramble down again?

Some men pretend they think it bliss
To clamber up a precipice
Or dangle over an abyss,

To crawl along a mountain side,
Supported by a rope that's tied
—Not too securely—to a guide;

But such pretences, it is clear,
In the aspiring mountaineer
Are usually insincere.

And many a climber, I'll be bound,
Whom scarped and icy crags surround,
Wishes himself on level ground.

So I, for one, do not propose
To cool my comfortable toes
In regions of perpetual snows,

As long as I can take my ease,
Fanned by a soothing southern breeze
Under the shade of English trees.

And anyone who leaves my share
Of English fields and English air
May take the Alps for aught I care!

(1902)

The Editor's Tragedy

[Miss MARIE CORELLI has written to the *Gentlewoman* to complain
that her name was not mentioned among the distinguished persons
who were in the Royal Enclosure at Braemar.   Contrariwise—as
Tweedledum would say—the same lady has compelled Messrs GRAVES
& Co. to publish an apology in a conspicuous position in a daily paper
for having allowed a reproduction of a portrait of her to appear in a
magazine.]

THE Editor sat in his easy chair,
He seemed oppressed with a weight of care,
His eyes were wild.   There were straws in his hair.

'Twas clear from his look he was much distressed.
What was the anguish that wrung his breast?

What was it racked his soul with pain?
Listen a moment, and I'll explain.

This excellent person chanced to edit
A magazine—with conspicuous credit,
Thousands of pretty young ladies read it.

And month after month he filled its pages
With matter adapted to various ages.

There were photographs of noblemen's houses,
And notes on the latest fashion in blouses,

Paper patterns for making dresses,
And portraits of eminent authoresses,

Hints on the cradle and how to rock it,
A new design for a lady's pocket,
And part of a novel by S. R. CROCKETT!

But the time arrived—as such times will—
When the Editor had a page to fill,

And no one can envy an Editor's billet
With a page to fill and nothing to fill it!

Should he publish a note upon 'Knitted Purses'?
Or a few remarks on 'Hospital Nurses'?
Or some of the Laureate's faultless verses?

Or some 'Useful patterns for crochet mats'?
Or a paper on 'Lady BARKING's cats'?

Or 'A new receipt for blackberry jelly'?
Or 'The latest portrait of Miss CORELLI'?

The Editor's brow grew overcast.
He felt he would greatly prefer the last—
But if she objected—— He stopped aghast!

.   .   .   .

The Editor sat for several days,
And looked at the thing in a hundred ways;

Week after week he tried and tried
To settle the matter, but couldn't decide.

His once fine intellect grew less clear
As the weeks went by and the day drew near
When the fatal number ought to appear.

Fresh doubts on the subject daily racked him,
Symptoms of brain disease attacked him,
And at last, I'm told, his proprietors sacked him!

(1902)

ARCHIBALD STODART-WALKER
(1869–1934)

Selections from the Moxford Book of English Verse

1. COUNSEL TO GIRLS.   *By Robert Herrick*

GATHER ye soap-suds while ye may
The smuts are still a-flying:
And this same hair so bright to-day,
To-morrow may need dyeing.

The glorious Lamp of Oil, the wick,
The higher he's a-getting
The sooner will the smuts fly quick
And on your hair be setting.

That hair is best which is the first,
When youth and blood are warmer
But being spoilt, the worse, and worst
Hairs will succeed the former.

Then be not mean, good soap go buy;
And with it be not chary:
For having lost its bloom, you'll sigh,
'My hair for ever tarry.'

2. EARLY BACON.   *By Charles Kingsley*

EARLY bacon, early bacon!
   Oh, the pleasant sight to see,
Sires come down for early bacon,
   With an egg and pot of tea.

Early bacon, early bacon!
   Oh, the happy hours I fed,
Deep in joy on early bacon,
   Coming from a comfy bed.

Early bacon, early bacon!
   That's the breakfast dish for me,
All alone with early bacon,
   With the paper on my knee!

3. INFLICTIS. *By William Ernest Henley*

OUT of the mud which covers me,
Black as my hat from head to sole,
I thank the friendly referee
For our unconquerable goal.

In the fell clutch of quarter backs
I have not funked or swore aloud,
Under rough batterings and hacks
My head is bloody, but unbowed.

Beyond this game of kicks and mauls
Looms but the malice of the mob,
And yet the menace of their calls
Finds and shall find me 'on the job.'

It matters not how good their back,
How straight the drop towards the pole,
I am the captain of the pack;
I am the keeper of the goal.

(1913)

JOHN KAYE KENDALL
('Dum-Dum')

(1869–1952)

The Cat that followed his Nose

SCENE. *A London Square at night, surrounded by blocks of flats.
A solitary cat is gazing romantically up at one of the top floors.*

SERENADE

Come down, come down to the Square,
    For the midnight hour is near;
Why linger alone up there
    While I am alone down here?
Leave idle rest for the day;
    The time to be out is now
When the cats come forth to play;
    Miaow.
        [*Several other cats have strolled up behind him.*

ALL (*helpfully*). Miaow.
SERENADER. Never a sound.
ANOTHER CAT.   She is locked up all right;
  Her mistress never lets her out at night.
SERENADER. Curse on her mistress.
THIRD CAT.   They are all like that;
  Moral, they call it.
SERENADER (*bitterly*). Moral.   To a cat.

                                       [*A loud yell is heard.*
SECOND CAT. I know that voice.   Here comes our Uncle Tom
  Fresh from his battle with a loathsome Pom.
  Let's give him greeting.

                        CHORUS

              Lord of the flattened ears
                And of the spinal bow,
                  Whose unsheathed claw
                  Strikes fear and awe
              Into the canine foe;

              Lord of the rolling purr
                And the complacent beam
                  Whose smiles evoke
                  The pleasing stroke
              And, when it's handy, cream;

              Lord of the lustrous coat
                And the unrivalled tail,
                  Whose night-flung screech,
                  With luck, can reach
              From here to Fulham, hail!

                  [THOMAS, *a majestic black cat, has entered.*

THOMAS. Thanks, courteous friends.   I thought that, as I came,
  I heard a serenade from What's-his-name.
SERENADER. You did.   And she's locked in.
THOMAS.   And so it goes.
  My son——
SERENADER. Your *son*?
THOMAS.   You may be so; who knows?
              [*A female cat affects an elaborate unconsciousness.*
  I have seen this Square stiff with cats, have sung
  Half through the night with scores when I was young
  Where now you don't see seven; London cats
  Have fall'n off gravely in this age of flats.

SONG

THOMAS. Oh, gay were our carouses
             In the days not long ago
          When people lived in houses
             And had basements down below,
          And out of the walls came mice galore
          That frisked about on the kitchen floor,
          And every house had a cat or more
             For keeping their numbers low.

          And ah, for the excellent days gone by
             When we, as a race, were dear,
          And never a basement lacked some chink
          Through which a noctambulous cat could slink
             And join in the larks out here.
A VOICE (*without*). And join in the larks out here.

                The VOICE *proceeds.*

          There is never a star with a ray of light,
             And the dark town darker grows,
          But I am a cat on the road to-night,
             The cat that follows his nose.

SECOND CAT. Mark you yon stranger.   Is he friend or foe?
    Ho there to you, Sir.
STRANGER.   And to you, Sir, ho.
                [He leaps the railings and joins the party.
    Know you the way to Godalming?
SECOND CAT.   Not I.
STRANGER. No matter.   I shall find it.
THOMAS.   Yes, but why?

        SONG—'The Wanderer.'

STRANGER. They brought me up to London and they thought
    I'd settle down;
    I'm a country cat.
THOMAS. He's a country cat.
CHORUS. A country cat; that's so.
STRANGER. But there they made their blunder, for I can't get
    used to town,
    And be cooped up like a London cat.
CHORUS. Like a London cat.
STRANGER.   Why, no.
    So back I'm going to Godalming, my former country home.
THOMAS. He's going away to Godalming.
CHORUS. But Godalming—where's that?

STRANGER. For the people live in houses there and a cat has
  room to roam.
And I'll live my lives in Godalming.
ALL. Like a genuine country cat.
STRANGER. Yes, I'm off now to my country home.
THOMAS. But how will you find the way?
STRANGER. I'll follow my nose wherever it goes;
  It never leads cats astray.
THOMAS. But isn't it dull in a country town?
          I've frequently heard it mewed
        That a cultured mind would probably find
          Society somewhat crude.

SONG

STRANGER. A London cat came down to stay,
          And his London pride was strong,
        But he caught a mouse the very first day,
          And we passed the night in song;
        On the second day he tackled a rat,
          And before the third was through
        He'd fallen in love with a beautiful cat,
          As a matter of fact with two.

        And now he vows that for healthy sport,
          For keeping the mind in trim,
        And for social joys of the higher sort,
          The country's the place for him.

ALL (*confusedly*). And me—and me—we all agree;
  What a capital place it seems to be.
STRANGER. And now—the Road.   My London friends, good-
  night.
THOMAS. One moment.   Are there situations there?
  Cats wanted?
STRANGER.   Warmth and welcome, food and light.
THOMAS. Why then be damned to this flat-ruined Square.
  Are you all with me?
ALL.   All.
THOMAS.   No faltering;
  Lead on, Macduff.   Forward to Godalming.

CHORUS

        First with the left foot, then with the right,
          Onward the old club goes;
        We follow a cat on the Road to-night,
          The Cat that follows his nose.

                              [*They march out singing.*
                                          (1934)

ANTHONY CHARLES DEANE
(1870–1946)

Jack and Jill—as Kipling might have written it

Here is the tale—and you must make the most of it!
Here is the rhyme—ah, listen and attend!
Backwards—forwards—read it all and boast of it
If you are anything the wiser at the end!

Now Jack looked up—it was time to sup, and the bucket was yet to fill,
And Jack looked round for a space and frowned, then beckoned his sister Jill,
And twice he pulled his sister's hair, and thrice he smote her side;
'Ha' done, ha' done with your impudent fun—ha' done with your games!' she cried:
'You have made mud pies of a marvellous size—finger and face are black,
You have trodden the Way of the Mire and Clay—now up and wash you, Jack!
Or else, or ever we reach our home, there waiteth an angry dame—
Well you know the weight of her blow—the supperless open shame!
Wash, if you will, on yonder hill—wash, if you will, at the spring—
Or keep your dirt, to your certain hurt, and an imminent walloping!'

'You must wash—you must scrub—you must scrape!' growled Jack, 'you must traffic with cans and pails,
Nor keep the spoil of the good brown soil in the rim of your finger-nails!
The morning path you must tread to your bath—you must wash ere the night descends,
And all for the cause of conventional laws and the soapmakers' dividends!
But if 'tis sooth that our meal in truth depends on our washing, Jill,
By the sacred light of our appetite—haste—haste to the top of the hill!'

They have trodden the Way of the Mire and Clay, they have
    toiled and travelled far,
They have climbed to the brow of the hill-top now, where the
    bubbling fountains are,

They have taken the bucket and filled it up—yea, filled it up to
    the brim;
But Jack he sneered at his sister Jill, and Jill she jeered at him:
'What, blown already!' Jack cried out (and his was a biting
    mirth!)
'You boast indeed of your wonderful speed—but what is the
    boasting worth?
Now, if you can run as the antelope runs, and if you can turn
    like a hare,
Come, race me, Jill, to the foot of the hill—and prove your
    boasting fair!'
'Race? What is a race' (and a mocking face had Jill as she
    spoke the word)
'Unless for a prize the runner tries? The truth indeed ye
    heard,
For I can run as the antelope runs, and I can turn like the hare:
The first one down wins half a crown—and I will race you there!'
'Yea, if for the lesson that you will learn (the lesson of humbled
    pride)
The price you fix at two and six, it shall not be denied;
Come, take your stand at my right hand, for here is the mark
    we toe:
Now, are you ready, and are you steady? Gird up your petti-
    coats! Go!'

And Jill she ran like a winging bolt, a bolt from the bow released,
But Jack like a stream of the lightning gleam, with its pathway
    duly greased;
He ran down hill in front of Jill like a summer lightning flash—
Till he suddenly tripped on a stone, or slipped, and fell to earth
    with a crash.
Then straight did rise on his wondering eyes the constellations
    fair,
Arcturus and the Pleiades, the Greater and Lesser Bear,
The swirling rain of a comet's train he saw, as he swiftly fell—
And Jill came tumbling after him with a loud triumphant yell:
'You have won, you have won, the race is done! And as for the
    wager laid—
You have fallen down with a broken crown—the half-crown
    debt is paid!'
They have taken Jack to the room at the back where the family
    medicines are,
And he lies in bed with a broken head in a halo of vinegar;

While, in that Jill had laughed her fill as her brother fell to the
    earth,
She has felt the sting of a walloping—she hath paid the price
    of her mirth!

Here is the tale—and now you have the whole of it,
    Here is the story—well and wisely planned,
Beauty—Duty—these make up the soul of it—
    But ah, my little readers, will you mark and understand?

(1901)

HILAIRE BELLOC

(1870–1953)

Jim

WHO RAN AWAY FROM HIS NURSE, AND WAS EATEN BY A LION

THERE was a Boy whose name was Jim;
His Friends were very good to him.
They gave him Tea, and Cakes, and Jam,
And slices of delicious Ham,
And Chocolate with pink inside,
And little Tricycles to ride,
And read him Stories through and through,
And even took him to the Zoo—
But there it was the dreadful Fate
Befell him, which I now relate.

You know—at least you *ought* to know,
For I have often told you so—
That Children never are allowed
To leave their Nurses in a Crowd;
Now this was Jim's especial Foible,
He ran away when he was able,
And on this inauspicious day
He slipped his hand and ran away!
He hadn't gone a yard when—Bang!
With open jaws, a Lion sprang,
And hungrily began to eat
The Boy: beginning at his feet.

Now just imagine how it feels
When first your toes and then your heels,
And then by gradual degrees,
Your shins and ankles, calves and knees,
Are slowly eaten, bit by bit.
No wonder Jim detested it!
No wonder that he shouted 'Hi!'
The Honest Keeper heard his cry,
Though very fat he almost ran
To help the little gentleman.
'Ponto!' he ordered as he came
(For Ponto was the Lion's name),
'Ponto!' he cried, with angry Frown.
'Let go, Sir!   Down, Sir!   Put it down!'
The Lion made a sudden Stop,
He let the Dainty Morsel drop,
And slunk reluctant to his Cage,
Snarling with Disappointed Rage.
But when he bent him over Jim,
The Honest Keeper's Eyes were dim.
The Lion having reached his Head,
The Miserable Boy was dead!

When Nurse informed his Parents, they
Were more Concerned than I can say:
His Mother, as She dried her eyes,
Said: 'Well—it gives me no surprise,
He would not do as he was told!'
His Father, who was self-controlled,
Bade all the children round attend
To James's miserable end,
And always keep a-hold of Nurse
For fear of finding something worse.

(1907)

Henry King

WHO CHEWED BITS OF STRING, AND WAS EARLY
CUT OFF IN DREADFUL AGONIES

THE Chief Defect of Henry King
Was chewing little bits of String.
At last he swallowed some which tied
Itself in ugly Knots inside.
Physicians of the Utmost Fame
Were called at once; but when they came
They answered, as they took their Fees:
'There is no Cure for this Disease.

Henry will very soon be dead.'
His Parents stood about his Bed
Lamenting his Untimely Death,
When Henry, with his Latest Breath,
Cried: 'Oh, my Friends, be warned by me,
That Breakfast, Dinner, Lunch, and Tea
Are all the Human Frame requires . . .'
With that the Wretched Child expires.

(1907)

Matilda

WHO TOLD LIES, AND WAS BURNED TO DEATH

MATILDA told such Dreadful Lies,
It made one Gasp and Stretch one's Eyes;
Her Aunt, who, from her Earliest Youth,
Had kept a Strict Regard for Truth,
Attempted to Believe Matilda:
The effort very nearly killed her,
And would have done so, had not She
Discovered this Infirmity.
For once, towards the Close of Day,
Matilda, growing tired of play,
And finding she was left alone,
Went tiptoe to the Telephone
And summoned the Immediate Aid
Of London's Noble Fire-Brigade.
Within an hour the Gallant Band
Were pouring in on every hand,
From Putney, Hackney Downs, and Bow,
With Courage high and Hearts a-glow
They galloped, roaring through the Town:
'Matilda's House is Burning Down!'
Inspired by British Cheers and Loud
Proceeding from the Frenzied Crowd,
They ran their ladders through a score
Of windows on the Ball Room floor;
And took Peculiar Pains to Souse
The Pictures up and down the House,
Until Matilda's Aunt succeeded
In showing them they were not needed
And even then she had to pay
To get the Men to go away!

.   .   .   .   .

It happened that a few Weeks later
Her Aunt was off to the Theatre
To see that Interesting Play
The Second Mrs Tanqueray.
She had refused to take her Niece
To hear this Entertaining Piece:
A Deprivation Just and Wise
To punish her for Telling Lies.
That Night a Fire *did* break out—
You should have heard Matilda Shout!
You should have heard her Scream and Bawl,
And throw the window up and call
To People passing in the Street—
(The rapidly increasing Heat
Encouraging her to obtain
Their confidence)—but all in vain!
For every time She shouted: 'Fire!'
They only answered 'Little Liar!'
And therefore when her Aunt returned,
Matilda, and the House, were Burned.

(1907)

Godolphin Horne

WHO WAS CURSED WITH THE SIN OF PRIDE, AND BECAME A BOOT-BLACK

GODOLPHIN HORNE was Nobly Born;
He held the Human Race in Scorn,
And lived with all his Sisters where
His father lived, in Berkeley Square.
And oh! the Lad was Deathly Proud!
He never shook your Hand or Bowed,
But merely smirked and nodded thus:
How perfectly ridiculous!
Alas! That such Affected Tricks
Should flourish in a Child of Six!
(For such was Young Godolphin's age).
Just then, the Court required a Page,
Whereat the Lord High Chamberlain
(The Kindest and the Best of Men),
He went good-naturedly and took
A Perfectly Enormous Book
Called *People Qualified to Be
Attendant on His Majesty,*

And murmured, as he scanned the list
(To see that no one should be missed):
'There's William Coutts has got the Flue,
And Billy Higgs would never do,
And Guy de Vere is far too young,
And . . . wasn't D'Alton's Father hung?
And as for Alexander Byng!— . . .
I think I know the kind of thing,
A Churchman, cleanly, nobly born,
Come let us say Godolphin Horne?'
But hardly had he said the word
When Murmurs of Dissent were heard.
The King of Iceland's Eldest Son
Said: 'Thank you! I am taking none!'
The Aged Duchess of Athlone
Remarked, in her sub-acid tone,
'I doubt if He is what we need!'
With which the Bishops all agreed;
And even Lady Mary Flood
(*So* Kind, and oh! so *really* good)
Said: 'No! He wouldn't do at all,
He'd make us feel a lot too small.'
The Chamberlain said: '. . . Well, well, well!
No doubt you're right. . . . One cannot tell!'
He took his Gold and Diamond Pen
And Scratched Godolphin out again.
So now Godolphin is the Boy
Who blacks the Boots at the Savoy.

(1907)

Sarah Byng

SOME years ago you heard me sing
My doubts on *Alexander Byng*.
His sister SARAH now inspires
My jaded Muse, my failing fires.
Of Sarah Byng the tale is told
How though the child was twelve years old
She could not read or write a line.
Her sister Jane, though barely nine,
Could spout the Catechism through
And parts of Matthew Arnold too,
While little Bill, who came between
Was quite unnaturally keen
On *Athalie*, by *Jean Racine*.
But not so Sarah! Not so Sal!
She was a most uncultured girl

Who didn't care a pinch of snuff
For any literary stuff
And gave the classics all a miss.
Observe the consequence of this!
As she was walking home one day,
Upon the fields across her way
A gate, securely padlocked, stood,
And by its side a piece of wood
On which was painted plain and full
'BEWARE THE VERY FURIOUS BULL.'
Alas!   The young illiterate
Went blindly forward to her fate,
And ignorantly climbed the gate!

    .   .   .

Now happily the Bull that day
Was rather in a mood for play
Than goring people through and through
As Bulls so very often do;
He tossed her lightly with his horns
Into a prickly hedge of thorns,
And stood by laughing while she strode
And pushed and struggled to the road.

   .   .   .   .

The lesson was not lost upon
The child, who, since, has always gone
A long way round to keep away
From signs, whatever they may say,
And leaves a padlocked gate alone.
Moreover she has wisely grown
Confirmed in her instinctive guess
That letters always bring distress.

                                (1924)

ARTHUR GUITERMAN

(1871–1943)

The Shakespearean Bear
(*The Winter's Tale*, Act III, Scene 3)

WHEN, on our casual way,
  Troubles and dangers accrue
Till there's the devil to pay,
  How shall we carry it through?

Shakespeare, that oracle true,
Teacher in doubt and despair,
    Told us the best that he knew:
'Exit, pursued by a bear.'

That is the line of a play
    Dear to the cognisant few;
Hark to its lilt, and obey!
    Constantly keep it in view.
    Fate, the malevolent shrew,
Weaves her implacable snare;
    What is a fellow to do?
'Exit, pursued by a bear.'

Take to your heels while you may!
    Sinister tabby-cats mew,
Witches that scheme to betray
    Mingle their horrible brew,
    Thunderclouds darken the blue,
Beelzebub growls from his lair;
    Maybe he's hunting for *you*!
'Exit, pursued by a bear.'

ENVOI

Bores of the dreariest hue,
    Bringers of worry and care,
Watch us respond to our cue:
'Exit, pursued by a bear.'

(1936)

The Legend of the First Cam-u-el

AN ARABIAN APOLOGUE

ACROSS the sands of Syria,
    Or, possibly, Algeria,
Or some benighted neighbourhood of barrenness and drouth,
    There came the prophet Sam-u-el
    Upon the only Cam-u-el—
A bumpy, grumpy Quadruped of discontented mouth.

The atmosphere was glutinous;
    The Cam-u-el was mutinous;
He dumped the pack from off his back; with horrid grunts and
        squeals
    He made the desert hideous;
    With strategy perfidious
He tied his neck in curlicues, he kicked his paddy heels.

Then quoth the gentle Sam-u-el:
'You rogue, I ought to lam you well!
Though zealously I've shielded you from every grief and woe,
It seems, to voice a platitude,
You haven't any gratitude.
I'd like to know what cause you have for doing thus and so?'

To him replied the Cam-u-el:
'I beg your pardon, Sam-u-el.
I know that I'm a Reprobate, I know that I'm a Freak;
But oh! this utter loneliness!
My too distinguished Onliness!
Were there but other Cam-u-els I wouldn't be Unique.'

The Prophet beamed beguilingly.
'Aha,' he answered smilingly.
'You feel the need of company?   I clearly understand.
We'll speedily create for you
The corresponding mate for you—
Ho! presto, change-o, dinglebat!'—he waved a potent hand.

And, lo! from out Vacuity
A second Incongruity,
To wit, a Lady Cam-u-el was born through magic art.
Her structure anatomical,
Her form and face were comical;
She was, in short, a Cam-u-el, the other's counterpart.

As Spaniards gaze on Aragon,
Upon that Female Paragon
So gazed the Prophet's Cam-u-el, that primal Desert Ship.
A connoisseur meticulous,
He found her that ridiculous
He grinned from ear to auricle *until he split his lip*!

Because of his temerity
That Cam-u-el's posterity
Must wear divided upper lips through all their solemn lives!
A prodigy astonishing
Reproachfully admonishing
Those wicked, heartless married men who ridicule their wives.

(1939)

PATRICK REGINALD CHALMERS

(1872–1942)

My Woodcock

I STOOD in the ride, and the glamour
  Of autumn was gold on the trees,
While the far-away beaters' faint clamour
  Was borne on the whispering breeze,
When the voices that came through the cover
  With the tapping of stick upon stock,
Rang out with a roar: 'Woodcock over!
    Cock forward!   Mark cock!'

Like a leaf of last year that is lifted
  When March is in maddest of moods,
Through the tops of the beeches he drifted,
  A little brown ghost of the woods:
Bombarded with passionate vigour,
  He lazily dodged down the line,
And I knew, as I pressed on the trigger,
  I *knew* he was mine!

My pulses may fade and grow duller,
  My eyesight may weaken, but still
I shall see the soft pinion's warm colour,
  The length of that insolent bill;
And, till age leaves me withered and one-eyed
  At the ultimate end of my road,
I shall hear the click-click of the gun I'd
    Omitted to load!

(1908)

The Cuckoo

THE cuckoo, when the lambkins bleat,
Does nothing else but sing and eat.
The other birds in dale and dell
Sing also—but they work as well.

When daisies star the April sward,
His eggs he places out to board,
That when his nursery should be full
He may not be responsible.

When other birds, from rooks to wrens,
Good husbands are and citizens,
The cuckoo's little else beyond
A captivating vagabond.

The other birds who dawn acclaim,
Their songs are sweet but much the same;
The cuckoo has a ruder tone
But absolutely all his own.

Now where's the bard that it would irk
To eat his meals and not to work?—
And it's prodigiously worth while
To have an individual style.

So I would be the cuckoo bold
And loaf in meadows white-and-gold,
And make a song unique as his
And shirk responsibilities.

(1913)

The Tortoiseshell Cat

THE tortoiseshell cat
    She sits on the mat,
As gay as a sunflower she;
    In orange and black you see her blink,
    And her waistcoat's white, and her nose is pink,
And her eyes are green of the sea.
    But all is vanity, all the way;
    Twilight's coming and close of day,
    And every cat in the twilight's grey,
        Every possible cat.

    The tortoiseshell cat
        She is smooth and fat,
And we call her Josephine,
    Because she weareth upon her back
    This coat of colours, this raven black,
This red of the tangerine.
    But all is vanity, all the way;
    Twilight follows the brightest day,
    And every cat in the twilight's grey,
        Every possible cat.

(1914)

GUY WETMORE CARRYL

(1873–1904)

The Sycophantic Fox and the Gullible Raven

A RAVEN sat upon a tree,
　　And not a word he spoke, for
His beak contained a piece of Brie,
　　Or, maybe, it was Roquefort:
　　　　We'll make it any kind you please—
　　　　At all events, it was a cheese.

Beneath the tree's umbrageous limb
　　A hungry fox sat smiling;
He saw the raven watching him
　　And spoke in words beguiling:
　　　　'*J'admire*,' said he, '*ton beau plumage*.'
　　　　(The which was simply persiflage.)

Two things there are, no doubt you know,
　　To which a fox is used—
A rooster that is bound to crow,
　　A crow that's bound to roost,
　　　　And whichsoever he espies
　　　　He tells the most unblushing lies.

'Sweet fowl,' he said, 'I understand
　　You're more than merely natty:
I hear you sing to beat the band
　　And Adelina Patti.
　　　　Pray render with your liquid tongue
　　　　A bit from *Götterdämmerung*.'

This subtle speech was aimed to please
　　The crow, and it succeeded:
He thought no bird in all the trees
　　Could sing as well as he did.
　　　　In flattery completely doused
　　　　He gave the 'Jewel Song' from *Faust*.

But gravitation's law, of course,
　　As Isaac Newton showed it,
Exerted on the cheese its force,
　　And elsewhere soon bestowed it.
　　　　In fact, there is no need to tell
　　　　What happened when to earth it fell.

I blush to add that when the bird
   Took in the situation
He said one brief, emphatic word,
    Unfit for publication.
      The fox was greatly startled, but
      He only sighed and answered 'Tut!'

THE MORAL is: A fox is bound
   To be a shameless sinner.
And also: When the cheese comes round
   You know it's after dinner.
      But (what is only known to few)
      The fox is after dinner, too.

                      (1898)

WALTER DE LA MARE

(1873–1956)

Up and Down Rhymes

1. THE HUNTSMEN

THREE jolly gentlemen,
   In coats of red,
Rode their horses
   Up to bed.

Three jolly gentlemen
   Snored till morn,
Their horses champing
   The golden corn.

Three jolly gentlemen,
   At break of day,
Came clitter-clatter down the stairs
   And galloped away.

2. THE SHIP OF RIO

THERE was a ship of Rio
   Sailed out into the blue,
And nine and ninety monkeys
   Were all her jovial crew.

From bo'sun to the cabin boy,
  From quarter to caboose,
There weren't a stitch of calico
  To breech 'em—tight or loose;
From spar to deck, from deck to keel,
  From barnacle to shroud,
There weren't one pair of reach-me-downs
  To all that jabbering crowd.
But wasn't it a gladsome sight,
  When roared the deep-sea gales,
To see them reef her fore and aft,
  A-swinging by their tails!
Oh, wasn't it a gladsome sight,
  When glassy calm did come,
To see them squatting tailor-wise
  Around a keg of rum!
Oh, wasn't it a gladsome sight,
  When in she sailed to land,
To see them all a-scampering skip
  For nuts across the sand!

3. JIM JAY

Do diddle di do,
  Poor Jim Jay
Got stuck fast
  In Yesterday.
Squinting he was,
  On cross-legs bent,
Never heeding
  The wind was spent.
Round veered the weathercock,
  The sun drew in—
And stuck was Jim
  Like a rusty pin. . . .
We pulled and we pulled
  From seven till twelve,
Jim, too frightened
  To help himself.
But all in vain.
  The clock struck one,
And there was Jim
  A little bit gone.
At half past five
  You scarce could see
A glimpse of his flapping
  Handkerchee.

And when came noon,
    And we climbed sky-high,
Jim was a speck
    Slip—slipping by.
Come to-morrow,
    The neighbours say,
He'll be past crying for;
    Poor Jim Jay.

4. MISS T.

IT'S a very odd thing—
    As odd as can be—
That whatever Miss T. eats
    Turns into Miss T.;
Porridge and apples,
    Mince, muffins, and mutton,
Jam, junket, jumbles—
    Not a rap, not a button
It matters; the moment
    They're out of her plate,
Though shared by Miss Butcher
    And sour Mr Bate;
Tiny and cheerful,
    And neat as can be,
Whatever Miss T. eats
    Turns into Miss T.

(1913)

HARRY GRAHAM
(1874–1936)

Some Ruthless Rhymes

I

FATHER heard his children scream,
So he threw them in the stream,
Saying, as he drowned the third,
'Children should be seen, *not* heard!'

II

Billy, in one of his nice new sashes,
Fell in the fire and was burnt to ashes;
Now, although the room grows chilly,
I haven't the heart to poke poor Billy.

III

Auntie, did you feel no pain
  Falling from that apple-tree?
Will you do it, please, again?
  'Cos my friend here didn't see.

IV

Father, chancing to chastise
  His indignant daughter Sue,
Said: 'I hope you realize
  That this hurts me more than you.'

Susan straightway ceased to roar;
  'If that's really true,' said she,
'I can stand a good deal more;
  Pray go on, and don't mind me.'

V

Bob was bathing in the Bay,
When a Shark who passed that way
Punctured him in seven places;
—And he made *such* funny faces!

VI

O'er the rugged mountain's brow
  Clara threw the twins she nursed,
And remarked: 'I wonder now
  Which will reach the bottom first?'

VII

Philip, foozling with his cleek,
Drove his ball through Helen's cheek;
Sad they bore her corpse away,
Seven up and six to play.

VIII

'There's been an accident!' they said,
'Your servant's cut in half; he's dead!'
'Indeed!' said Mr Jones, 'and please
Send me the half that's got my keys.'

(1899)

Poetical Economy

WHAT hours I spent of precious time,
　　What pints of ink I used to waste,
Attempting to secure a rhyme
　　To suit the public taste,
Until I found a simple plan
Which makes the lamest lyric scan!

When I've a syllable de trop,
　　I cut if off, without apol.:
This verbal sacrifice, I know,
　　May irritate the schol.;
But all must praise my dev'lish cunn.
Who realize that Time is Mon.

My sense remains as clear as cryst.,
　　My style as pure as any Duch.
Who does not boast a bar sinist.
　　Upon her fam. escutch.;
And I can treat with scornful pit.
The sneers of ev'ry captious crit.

I gladly publish to the pop.
　　A scheme of which I make no myst.,
And beg my fellow scribes to cop.
　　This labour-saving syst.
I offer it to the consid.
Of ev'ry thoughtful individ.

The author, working like a beav.,
　　His readers' pleasure could redoub.
Did he but now and then abbrev.
　　The work he gives his pub.
(This view I most partic. suggest
To A. C. Bens. and G. K. Chest.)

If Mr Caine rewrote the Scape.,
　　And Miss Correll. condensed Barabb.,
What could they save in foolscap pape.
　　Did they but cult. the hab.,
Which teaches people to suppress
All syllables that are unnec.!

If playwrights would but thus dimin.
   The length of time each drama takes,
(The Second Mrs Tanq. by Pin.
   Or even Ham., by Shakes.)
We could maintain a watchful att.
When at a Mat. on Wed. or Sat.

Have done, ye bards, with dull monot.!
   Foll. my examp., O, Stephen Phill.,
O. Owen Seam., O, William Wat.,
   O. Ella Wheeler Wil.,
And share with me the grave respons.
Of writing this amazing nons.!

                         (1909)

The Cockney of the North
(W. B. YEATS)

I WILL arise and go now, and go to Inverness,
   And a small villa rent there, of lath and plaster built;
Nine bedrooms will I have there, and I'll don my native dress,
   And walk about in a d—— loud kilt.

And I will have some sport there, when the grouse come driven
     slow,
   Driven from purple hill-tops to where the loaders quail;
While midges bite their ankles, and shots are flying low,
   And the air is full of the grey-hen's tail.

I will arise and go now, for ever, day and night,
   I hear the taxis bleating and the motor-buses roar,
And over tarred macadam and pavements parched and white
   I've walked till my feet are sore!

                         (1913)

The Bath

Broad is the Gate and wide the Path
That leads man to his daily bath;
But ere you spend the shining hour
With plunge and spray, with sluice and show'r—

With all that teaches you to dread
The bath as little as your bed—
Remember, whereso'er you be,
To shut the door and turn the key!

I had a friend—my friend no more!—
Who failed to bolt the bath-room door;

A maiden-aunt of his, one day,
Walked in, as half-submerged he lay!

But did not notice nephew John,
And turned the boiling water on!

He had no time, or even scope,
To camouflage himself with soap,
But gave a yell and flung aside
The sponge, 'neath which he sought to hide!

It fell to earth, I know not where!
He beat his breast in his despair,

And then, like Venus from the foam,
Sprang into view, and made for home!

His aunt fell fainting to the ground!
Alas!   They never brought her round!

She died, intestate, in her prime,
The victim of another's crime;

And John can never quite forget
How, by a breach of etiquette,
He lost, at one fell swoop (or plunge)
His aunt, his honour, and his sponge!

                                        (1924)

GILBERT KEITH CHESTERTON

(1874–1936)

The Logical Vegetarian

YOU will find me drinking rum,
    Like a sailor in a slum,
You will find me drinking beer like a Bavarian,
    You will find me drinking gin
    In the lowest kind of inn,
Because I am rigid Vegetarian.

So I cleared the inn of wine,
And I tried to climb the sign,
And I tried to hail the constable as 'Marion.'
  But he said I couldn't speak
  And he bowled me to the Beak
Because I was a happy Vegetarian.

Oh, I knew a Doctor Gluck,
And his nose it had a hook,
And his attitudes were anything but Aryan;
  So I gave him all the pork
  That I had, upon a fork;
Because I am myself a Vegetarian.

I am silent in the club,
I am silent in the pub,
I am silent on a bally peak in Darien;
  For I stuff away for life
  Shoving peas in with a knife,
Because I am at heart a Vegetarian.

No more the milk of cows
Shall pollute my private house
Than the milk of the wild mares of the Barbarian;
  I will stick to port and sherry,
  For they are so very, very,
So very, very, very Vegetarian.

(1914)

Wine and Water

OLD Noah he had an ostrich farm and fowls on the largest scale,
He ate his egg with a ladle in an egg-cup big as a pail,
And the soup he took was Elephant Soup and the fish he took
    was Whale,
But they all were small to the cellar he took when he set out to sail,
And Noah he often said to his wife when he sat down to dine,
'I don't care where the water goes if it doesn't get into the wine.'

The cataract of the cliff of heaven fell blinding off the brink
As if it would wash the stars away as suds go down a sink,
The seven heavens came roaring down for the throats of hell to
    drink,
And Noah he cocked his eye and said: 'It looks like rain, I think,
The water has drowned the Matterhorn as deep as a Mendip
    mine,
But I don't care where the water goes if it doesn't get into the
    wine.'

But Noah he sinned, and we have sinned; on tipsy feet we trod,
Till a great big black teetotaller was sent to us for a rod,
And you can't get wine at a P.S.A., or chapel, or Eisteddfod,
For the Curse of Water has come again because of the wrath of
  God,
And water is on the Bishop's board and the Higher Thinker's
  shrine,
But I don't care where the water goes if it doesn't get into the
  wine.

                                                    (1914)

The Song against Grocers

GOD made the wicked Grocer
For a mystery and a sign,
That men might shun the awful shops
And go to inns to dine;
Where the bacon's on the rafter
And the wine is in the wood,
And God that made good laughter
Has seen that they are good.

The evil-hearted Grocer
Would call his mother 'Ma'am,'
And bow at her and bob at her,
Her aged soul to damn,
And rub his horrid hands and ask
What article was next,
Though *mortis in articulo*
Should be her proper text.

His props are not his children,
But pert lads underpaid,
Who call out 'Cash!' and bang about
To work his wicked trade;
He keeps a lady in a cage
Most cruelly all day,
And makes her count and calls her 'Miss'
Until she fades away.

The righteous minds of innkeepers
Induce them now and then
To crack a bottle with a friend
Or treat unmoneyed men,
But who hath seen the Grocer
Treat housemaids to his teas
Or crack a bottle of fish-sauce
Or stand a man a cheese?

He sells us sands of Araby
As sugar for cash down;
He sweeps his shop and sells the dust
The purest salt in town,
He crams with cans of poisoned meat
Poor subjects of the king,
And when they die by thousands
Why, he laughs like anything.

The wicked Grocer groces
In spirits and in wine,
Not frankly and in fellowship
As men in inns do dine;
But packed with soap and sardines
And carried off by grooms,
For to be snatched by duchesses
And drunk in dressing-rooms.

The hell-instructed Grocer
Has a temple made of tin,
And the ruin of good innkeepers
Is loudly urged therein;
But now the sands are running out
From sugar of a sort,
The Grocer trembles; for his time,
Just like his weight, is short.

(1914)

EDMUND CLERIHEW BENTLEY

(1875–1956)

Select Biography for Beginners

The Art of Biography
Is different from Geography.
Geography is about Maps,
But Biography is about Chaps.

1

SIR CHRISTOPHER WREN
Said: 'I am going to dine with some men.
If anybody calls,
Say I am designing St Paul's.'

2

The people of Spain think Cervantes
Equal to half a dozen Dantes:
An opinion resented most bitterly
By the people of Italy.

3

Sir Humphry Davy
Abominated gravy.
He lived in the odium
Of having discovered Sodium.

4

What I like about Clive
Is that he is no longer alive.
There is a great deal to be said
For being dead.

5

Dr Clifford
And I have differed.
He disapproves of gin:
I disapprove of sin.

6

Mr Hilaire Belloc
Is a case for legislation *adhoc*.
He seems to think nobody minds
His books being all of different kinds.

7

After dinner Erasmus
Told Colet not to be 'blas'mous.'
Which Colet, with some heat,
Requested him to repeat.

8

Sir Walter Raleigh
Bickered down the valley.
But he could do better than the rill,
For he could bicker uphill.

9

The intrepid Ricardo,
With characteristic bravado,
Alluded openly to Rent
Wherever he went.

10

If only Mr Roosevelt
Knew how officers in the Blues felt,
He wouldn't be so rife
With his Strenuous Life.

11

The great Duke of Wellington
Reduced himself to a skellington.
He reached seven stone two,
And then—Waterloo!

12

Mr Bernard Shaw
Was just setting out for the War,
When he heard it was a dangerous trade
And demonstrably underpaid.

(1905)

HERBERT GEORGE PONTING

(1878–1935)

The Sleeping-bag

ON the outside grows the furside, on the inside grows the skin-
side;
So the furside is the outside, and the skinside is the inside.
As the skinside is the inside, and the furside is the outside;
One 'side' likes the skinside inside, and the furside on the
outside.
Others like the skinside outside, and the furside on the inside;
As the skinside is the hardside, and the furside is the soft side.
If you turn the skinside outside, thinking you will side with that
'side,'
Then the soft side, furside's inside, which some argue is the
wrong side.
If you turn the furside outside, as you say it grows on that side;
Then your outside's next the skinside, which for comfort's not
the right side:
For the skinside is the cold side, and your outside's not your
warm side;

And two cold sides coming side by side are not right sides one
    'side' decides.
If you decide to side with that 'side,' turn the outside, furside,
    inside;
Then the hard side, cold side, skinside's, beyond all question,
    inside outside.

                            (1911)

EDMUND VALPY KNOX
('Evoe')

(1881–1971)

Inspiration

(A SUBURBAN RHAPSODY)

I SAID : 'Within the garden trimly bordered,
    Assisted by the merle, I mean to woo
The Heavenly Nine, by young Apollo wardered,'
    And Araminta answered: 'Yes, dear, do.
The deck chair's in the outhouse; lunch is ordered
        For twenty-five to two.'

I sat within the garden's island summer
    And heard far off the shunting of the trains,
Noises of wheels, and speech of every comer
    Passing the entrance—heard the man of brains
Talking of GEORGE's Budget, heard the plumber
        Planning new leaks for drains.

These things did not disturb me.   Through the fencing
    I liked to bear in mind that men less free
Must toil and tramp, whilst I was just commencing
    To court the Muses, foolscap on my knee,
Helped by the sweet bird in the shade-dispensing
        Something-or-other tree.

I wrote: 'Ah, who would be where rough men jostle
    In dust and grime, like porkers at a trough,
When here is May and May-time's blest apostle——
    Just then, without preliminary cough,
Suddenly, ere I knew, the actual throstle
        Tee'd up and started off.

It drowned the distant noise of motor-buses,
   It drowned the shunting trains, the traffic's roar,
The milk, the bread, the meat, the tradesmen's fusses,
   And the long secret tale told o'er and o'er
That all day long Eliza Jane discusses
     With the new girl next door.

So sweetly the bird sang.   Great thrills went through it.
   It seemed to say: 'The glorious sun hath shone,
Flooding the world like treacle wrapped round suet;
   Why should we harp of age and dull years gone?'
Time seemed to be no sort of object to it—
     It just went on and on.

Therefore I rose, and later (o'er the trifle),
   When Araminta with her tactful gush
Asked if the garden seemed to help or stifle
   The Muses' output, I responded: 'Tush;
When you go out, my dear, please buy a rifle;
     I want to shoot that thrush.'

                      (1914)

The Tryst

COME into the garden, Kate,
   For the green rat visions go;
Come into the garden, Kate,
   I am standing here in the snow;
And the seeds of the sunflower will not wait
   And the vodka is getting low.

For the dawn is beginning to drag
   His banner of hope on high,
And the stars and moon may be fain to lag,
   But the stars and moon must die
When the dawn comes up, like the People's Flag,
   Blood-red on the eastern sky.

All night long have I fired
   Rifle-shots over the town,
All night long, till I fainted and tired,
   Have the drinks gone down, down, down,
Till I fainted and fell with a coat bemired
   And a lump like an egg on the crown.

I said to the lamp-post: 'Tell me how
   I came to be here in the dirt,
When Katya is dancing, dancing now,
   Katya is playing the flirt.
The tavern windows are vomiting row;
   She is dancing there for a cert.,
My rosebud girl with a hexagon brow
   And a rectilinear skirt.'

I said to the moon: 'The night goes soon;
   Katya is false to me;
She is mine from her pointed head to her shoon
   By a Soviet law's decree,
But she flirts with Petka, the lousy loon,
   And Vanka the bourjoo-ee.'

And the face of the lamp said: 'Follow, follow,
   Be true to the people's will;
Don't lie there in the dirt and wallow,'
   And the moon said: 'Kill, kill, kill';
So I killed them and buried them here in the hollow,
   The hollow behind the hill.

I waited for both of them out in the street
   And I shot them between the eyes,
And buried them here where your arching feet,
   That are so much like your eyes,
May tread on them always when we meet
   In our garden of paradise.

The vampire bats in the lofty pine
   Scarce stirred from their nests to see,
For Petka was merely a friend of mine
   And Vanka a bourjoo-ee.
Now hushed and still is the were-wolf's whine;
   Come out to the trysting-tree,
And the sunflower-seed shall be thine, all thine,
   And the vodka reserved for me.

There has fallen a lump of ice
   From her window-sill on to the road,
She shall be in my arms in a trice
   Were it never so huge a load.
The sleigh-bells sing: 'She is nice, she is nice,'
   And the wind howls: 'Quite the mode';
But the carrion-crow call 'Cockatrice,'
   And the screech-owl answers: 'Toad.'

She is coming; I hear, I hear
    Her rhythmical rhomboid tread;
I am feeling uncommonly queer;
    My eyes see nothing but red—
See only the Soviet rose sprung clear
    From the dust of centuries dead.
Trak-tak! . . .   I must bury you, Kate my dear;
    My bullet has gone through your head.

                                                    (1921)

ALAN ALEXANDER MILNE

(1882–1956)

The Ballad of Private Chadd

I sing of George Augustus Chadd,
Who'd always from a baby had
A deep affection for his Dad—
    In other words, his Father;
Contrariwise, the father's one
And only treasure was his son,
Yes, even when he'd gone and done
    Things which annoyed him rather.

For instance, if at Christmas (say)
Or on his parent's natal day
The thoughtless lad forgot to pay
    The customary greeting,
His father's visage only took
That dignified reproachful look
Which dying beetles give the cook
    Above the clouds of Keating.

As years went on such looks were rare;
The younger Chadd was always there
To greet his father and to share
    His father's birthday party;
The pink 'For auld acquaintance' sake'
Engraved in sugar on the cake
Was his.   The speech he used to make
    Was reverent but hearty.

The younger Chadd was twentyish
When War broke out, but did not wish
To get an A.S.C. commish
    Or be a rag-time sailor;
Just Private Chadd he was, and went
To join his Dad's old regiment,
While Dad (the dear old dug-out) sent
    For red tabs from the tailor.

To those inured to war's alarms
I need not dwell upon the charms
Of raw recruits when sloping arms
    Nor tell why Chadd was hoping
That 'if his sloping-powers increased,
They'd give him two days' leave at least
To join his Father's birthday feast' . . .
    And so resumed his sloping.

One morning on the training-ground,
When fixing bayonets, he found
The fatal day already round
    And, even as he fixed, he
Decided then and there to state
To Sergeant Brown (at any rate)
His longing to congratulate
    His sire on being sixty.

'Sergeant,' he said, 'we're on the eve
Of Father's birthday; grant me leave'
(And here his bosom gave a heave)
    'To offer him my blessing;
And, if a Private's tender thanks—
Nay, do not blank my blanky blanks!
I could not help but leave the ranks;
    Birthdays are more than dressing.'

The Sergeant was a kindly soul,
He loved his men upon the whole,
He'd also had a father's role
    Pressed on him fairly lately.
'Brave Chadd,' he said, 'thou speakest sooth!'
O happy day!   O pious youth!
'Great,' he extemporized, 'is Truth,
    And it shall flourish greatly.'

The Sergeant took him by the hand
And led him to the Captain, and
The Captain tried to understand,
    And (more or less) succeeded;
'Correct me if you don't agree,
But one of you wants *what?*' said he,
'And also which?'   And Chadd said: 'Me!'
    Meaning of course that *he* did.

The Captain took him by the ear
And gradually brought him near
The Colonel, who was far from clear,
    But heard it all politely,
And asked him twice: 'You want a *what?*'
The Captain said that *he* did not,
And Chadd saluted quite a lot
    And put the matter rightly.

The Colonel took him by the hair
And furtively conveyed him where
The General inhaled the air,
    Immaculately booted;
Then said: 'Unless I greatly err
This private wishes to prefer
A small petition to you, Sir,'
    And so again saluted.

The General inclined his head
Towards the two of them and said:
'Speak slowly, please, or shout instead;
    I'm hard of hearing, rather.'
So Chadd, that promising recruit,
Stood to attention, clicked his boot,
And bellowed, with his best salute,
    '*A happy birthday, Father!*'   (1918)

The King's Breakfast

The King asked
The Queen, and
The Queen asked
The Dairymaid:
'Could we have some butter for
The Royal slice of bread?'
The Queen asked
The Dairymaid,

The Dairymaid
Said: 'Certainly,
I'll go and tell
The cow
Now
Before she goes to bed.'

The Dairymaid
She curtsied,
And went and told
The Alderney:
'Don't forget the butter for
The Royal slice of bread.'
The Alderney
Said sleepily:
'You'd better tell
His Majesty
That many people nowadays
Like marmalade
Instead.'

The Dairymaid
Said: 'Fancy!'
And went to
Her Majesty.
She curtsied to the Queen, and
She turned a little red:
'Excuse me,
Your Majesty,
For taking of
The liberty,
But marmalade is tasty, if
It's very
Thickly
Spread.'

The Queen said:
'Oh!'
And went to
His Majesty:
'Talking of the butter for
The Royal slice of bread,
Many people
Think that
Marmalade
Is nicer.
Would you like to try a little
Marmalade
Instead?'

The King said:
'Bother!'
And then he said:
'Oh, deary me!'
The King sobbed: 'Oh, deary me!'
And went back to bed.
'Nobody,'
He whimpered,
'Could call me
A fussy man;
I *only* want
A little bit
Of butter for
My bread!'

The Queen said:
'There, there!'
And went to
The Dairymaid.
The Dairymaid
Said: 'There, there!'
And went to the shed.
The cow said:
'There, there!
I didn't really
Mean it;
Here's milk for his porringer
And butter for his bread.'

The Queen took
The butter
And brought it to
His Majesty;
The King said:
'Butter, eh?'
And bounced out of bed.
'Nobody,' he said,
As he kissed her
Tenderly,
'Nobody,' he said,
As he slid down
The banisters,
'Nobody,
My darling,
Could call me
A fussy man—
BUT
I do like a little bit of butter to my bread!'

                                        (1924)

The Old Sailor

THERE was once an old sailor my grandfather knew
Who had so many things which he wanted to do
That, whenever he thought it was time to begin,
He couldn't because of the state he was in.

He was shipwrecked, and lived on an island for weeks,
And he wanted a hat, and he wanted some breeks;
And he wanted some nets, or a line and some hooks
For the turtles and things which you read of in books.

And, thinking of this, he remembered a thing
Which he wanted (for water) and that was a spring;
And he thought that to talk to he'd look for, and keep
(If he found it) a goat, or some chickens and sheep.

Then, because of the weather, he wanted a hut
With a door (to come in by) which opened and shut
(With a jerk, which was useful if snakes were about),
And a very strong lock to keep savages out.

He began on the fish-hooks, and when he'd begun
He decided he couldn't because of the sun.
So he knew what he ought to begin with, and that
Was to find, or to make, a large sun-stopping hat.

He was making the hat with some leaves from a tree,
When he thought: 'I'm as hot as a body can be,
And I've nothing to take for my terrible thirst;
So I'll look for a spring, and I'll look for it *first*.'

Then he thought as he started: 'Oh, dear and oh, dear!
I'll be lonely to-morrow with nobody here!'
So he made in his note-book a couple of notes:
'*I must first find some chickens*' and '*No, I mean goats*.'

He had just seen a goat (which he knew by the shape)
When he thought: 'But I must have a boat for escape.
But a boat means a sail, which means needles and thread;
So I'd better sit down and make needles instead.'

He began on a needle, but thought as he worked,
That, if this was an island where savages lurked,
Sitting safe in his hut he'd have nothing to fear,
Whereas now they might suddenly breathe in his ear!

So he thought of his hut . . . and he thought of his boat,
And his hat and his breeks, and his chickens and goat,
And the hooks (for his food) and the spring (for his thirst) . . .
But he *never* could think which he ought to do first.

And so in the end he did nothing at all,
But basked on the shingle wrapped up in a shawl.
And I think it was dreadful the way he behaved—
He did nothing but basking until he was saved!

(1927)

JOHN COLLINGS SQUIRE

(1884–1958)

If Pope had written 'Break, Break, Break'

FLY, Muse, thy wonted themes, nor longer seek
The consolations of a powder'd cheek;
Forsake the busy purlieus of the Court
For calmer meads where finny tribes resort.
So may th' Almighty's natural antidote
Abate the worldly tenour of thy note,
The various beauties of the liquid main
Refine thy reed and elevate thy strain.
See how the labour of the urgent oar
Propels the barks and draws them to the shore.
Hark! from the margin of the azure bay
The joyful cries of infants at their play.
(The offspring of a piscatorial swain,
His home the sands, his pasturage the main.)
Yet none of these may soothe the mourning heart,
Nor fond alleviation's sweets impart;
Nor may the pow'rs of infants that rejoice
Restore the accents of a former voice,
Nor the bright smiles of ocean's nymphs command
The pleasing contact of a vanished hand.

So let me still in meditation move,
Muse in the vale and ponder in the grove,
And scan the skies where sinking Phoebus glows
With hues more rubicund than Cibber's nose. . . .

(1917)

EMILE VICTOR RIEU

(1887–1972)

The Lesser Lynx

THE laughter of the lesser Lynx
  Is often insincere:
It pays to be polite, he thinks,
  If Royalty is near.

So when the Lion steals his food
  Or kicks him from behind,
He smiles, of course—but oh, the rude
  Remarks that cross his mind!

(1933)

RONALD ARBUTHNOT KNOX

(1888–1957)

'*Horace: Book V, Ode III*'[1]

MISERANDUS vir amicis hymenaei tamen expers,
patitur continuo qui sine solamine Bacchi
      studiosae iuga neptis:
pia ludos adit omnes, revocantesque Camenas
animo respicit aequo Neobule, neque pacem
      patrui dat furia oti.
Dryas et Naïas aeque, freta quae tranatat Helles,
et eques Penthesileam, pede vincens Atalanten
      iuvenes urit et angit:
calathis non vacat umquam sapientique Minervae:
oculus me tamen ardens et iniquae flagra linguae
      agitant exanimatum.

(1920)

[1] See page 152 for 'translation' by C. L. Graves.

Absolute and Abitofhell

(BEING A SATIRE IN THE MANNER OF MR JOHN DRYDEN
UPON A NEWLY ISSU'D WORK ENTITLED FOUNDATIONS)

IN former Times, when Israel's ancient Creed
Took Root so widely that it ran to Seed;
When Saints were more accounted of than Soap,
And MEN in happy Blindness serv'd the POPE:
Uxorious JEROBOAM, waxen bold,
Tore the Ten Tribes from DAVID's falt'ring Hold,
And, spurning Threats from Salem's Vatican,
Set gaiter'd Calves in Bethel and in Dan.
So, Freedom reign'd: so, Priests, dismay'd by naught,
Thought what they pleas'd, and mention'd what they thought.
Three hundred Years, and still the Land was free'd,
And Bishops still, and Judges disagreed,
Till men began for some Account to call,
What was believ'd, or why believ'd at all?
The thing was canvass'd, and it seem'd past doubt
Much we adher'd to we could do without;
First, ADAM fell; then NOAH's ARK was drown'd,
And SAMSON under close inspection bound;
For DANIEL's Blood the Critick Lions roar'd,
And trembling Hands threw JONAH overboard.
    Lux Mundi came, and here we found indeed
A Maximum and Minimum of Creed:
But still the Criticks, bent on MATTHEW's Fall,
And setting PETER by the Ears with PAUL,
Brought unaccustom'd Doctrines oversea
Suggesting rather, Caeli Tenebrae.
So, while our Ark let in, through Seams ill-join'd
And gaping Timbers, Bilge of ev'ry Kind,
Ran to and fro, and like a Drunkard shook,
Seven of the Younger Men compos'd a Book.
    Seven Men, in Views and Learning near ally'd,
Whom Forms alone and Dogmas did divide,
Their Differences sunk, in Conclave met,
And each his Seal (with Reservations) set:
Each in his Turn subscrib'd the fateful Scroll,
And stamp'd his Nihil Constat on the whole.
    Sing, Heavenly MUSE, from high Olympus bowing,
Their Names, their Training, and their Weltanschauung.
Say, why did Magdala, renown'd in Ships,
Withhold the Tribute of his dauntless Lips,

Who, setting out the Gospel Truths t'explain,
Thought all that was not German, not germane:
Whose queasy Stomach, while it tried in vain
Recorded Miracles to entertain,
Eschewing LUKE, JOHN, MATTHEW, and the rest,
Read MARK, but could not inwardly digest?
Why did Neapolis, aloof like ASHER,
Withhold—the Name is in the Book of Jasher—
Where, 'mid the Thunders of a boisterous Quad,
He ponders on the Raison d'Être of God?
Not such the Arms, not such the vain Defence,
That rallied to thy Standard, Common Sense.

    First, from the Public Schools—*Lernaean* Bog—
No paltry Bulwark, stood the Form of OG.
A man so broad, to some he seem'd to be
Not one, but all Mankind in Effigy:
Who, brisk in Term, a Whirlwind in the Long,
Did everything by turns, and nothing wrong,
Bill'd at each Lecture-hall from Thames to Tyne
As Thinker, Usher, Statesman, or Divine.
Born in the Purple, swift he chose the Light,
And Lambeth mark'd him for a Nazirite:
Discerning *Balliol* snatch'd him in his teens,
And mourn'd him, early forfeited to *Queen's.*
His name suffic'd to leave th'insidious tome
A household word in every English Home:
No academick Treatise, high and dry,
Canvass'd in Walks round Mesopotamy,
Or where in Common Room, when days are short,
Soulless Professors gulp disguested Port.
'Not from the few, the learned, and the pale'
—So ran his message—'we expect our Sale;
Man in the Street, our Publication con—
What matter, if the Street be Ashkelon?'

    In Weight not less, but more advanc'd in Height,
Gigantic ELIPHAZ next hove in Sight:
Who 'mid the Prophets' Sons his Trade did ply
In teaching Wells to bless and magnify.
The Pomegranate upon his Helm display'd
His Prebendarial Dignity betray'd:
Magdalen to *Univ.* gave him, and from there
He rapidly achiev'd a wider sphere;
Grey Hairs alone he wanted, but for that
Ripe for the Apron and the shovel Hat.
Those other Six, in punier arms array'd,
Crouch'd in his Shadow, and were not afraid.

    Yet something marr'd that order'd Symmetry:
Say, what did STRATO in their company?

Who, like a Leaven, gave his Tone to all,
'Mid prophet Bands an unsuspected Saul.
For he, discerning with nice arguings
'Twixt non-essential and essential Things,
Himself believing, could not reason see
Why any other should believe, but he.
(Himself believing, as believing went
In that wild Heyday of th' Establishment,
When suave Politeness, temp'ring bigot Zeal,
Corrected 'I believe,' to 'One does feel.')
He wish'd the *Bilge* away, yet did not seek
To man the *Pumps*, or plug the treach'rous Leak:
Would let into our Ark the veriest Crow,
That had the measliest Olive-branch to show.
Who has not known how pleasant 'tis to sigh,
'Others, thank God, are less correct than I'?
    From such Conclusion (so men said) averse,
A Balaam, blessing what he dared not curse,
A Scaeva, raising Powers he could not quell,
Dragging their Coat-tails, followed ABDIEL.
In Height magnificent, in Depth profound,
Bless'd with more Sense than some, than all more sound,
Gifted as if with Tongues, were there but wit
Among his Audience to interpret it:
Still, like a clumsy Falconer, he'd untie
Tradition's Hood from Reason's piercing Eye,
And then complain, because she soar'd too high.
So labour'd he, in Devorguilla's Pile,
Jowett's and Manning's views to reconcile:
Beneath his Rule (I quote from Dryden's Rhyme)
'The Sons of Belial had a glorious Time,'
And, when he shook his Fist and talk'd of Eve,
Like Devils trembled, but did not believe.
    With sunnier Faith, with more unclouded Brow,
Brilliant ARCTURUS did the Fates endow:
Who cried, as joyfully he bound his Sheaves,
'What I believe is what the Church believes':
Yet some might find it matter for Research,
Whether the Church taught him, or he the Church.
Corpus had trained him reason's Truth to doubt,
And Keble added Faith, to do without.
What matter, whether two and two be four,
So long as none account them to be more?
What difference, whether black be black or white,
If no officious Hand turn on the Light?
Whether our Fact be Fact, no Man can know,
But, Heav'n preserve us, we will treat it so.
    Yet, lest some envious Critick might complain

The BIBLE had been jettisoned as vain,
Pellucid JABBOK show'd us, how much more
The Bible meant to us then e'er before.
Twelve *Prophets* our unlearn'd forefathers knew,
We are scarce satisfy'd with twenty-two:
A single *Psalmist* was enough for them,
Our list of Authors rivals A. and M.:
They were content MARK, MATTHEW, LUKE, and JOHN
Should bless th' old-fashion'd Beds they lay upon:
But we, for ev'ry one of theirs, have two,
And trust the Watchfulness of blessed Q.
    The last, EPIGONUS, but not the least,
Levite by Birth, yet not by Calling Priest,
Woo'd coy Philosophy, reluctant Maid,
To bring her troubl'd Sister timely aid.
His Views on Punishment what need to tell?
Poor, proctor'd Victims lately knew them well,
His pregnant Logick fill'd their only Want,
Temp'ring EZEKIEL with a Dash of KANT.
    Hail, dauntless Mariners, that far outstrip
Previous Attempts to undergird the Ship!
To you this Rhyme, now falt'ring to its End,
Is dedicated by an humble Friend,
Praying that Providence this Wind may use
To puff your Sales, and to confound your Views.

                                                (1928)

THOMAS STEARNS ELIOT

(1888–1965)

Macavity : the Mystery Cat

MACAVITY's a Mystery Cat: he's called the Hidden Paw—
For he's the master criminal who can defy the Law.
He's the bafflement of Scotland Yard, the Flying Squad's
   despair:
For when they reach the scene of crime—*Macavity's not there!*

Macavity, Macavity, there's no one like Macavity,
He's broken every human law, he breaks the law of gravity.
His powers of levitation would make a fakir stare,
And when you reach the scene of crime—*Macavity's not there!*
You may seek him in the basement, you may look up in the air—
But I tell you once and once again, *Macavity's not there!*

Macavity's a ginger cat, he's very tall and thin;
You would know him if you saw him, for his eyes are sunken in.
His brow is deeply lined with thought, his head is highly domed;
His coat is dusty from neglect, his whiskers are uncombed.
He sways his head from side to side, with movements like a
     snake;
And when you think he's half asleep, he's always wide awake.

Macavity, Macavity, there's no one like Macavity,
For he's a fiend in feline shape, a monster of depravity.
You may meet him in a by-street, you may see him in the
     square—
But when a crime's discovered, then *Macavity's not there*!

He's outwardly respectable.   (They say he cheats at cards.)
And his footprints are not found in any file of Scotland Yard's.
And when the larder's looted, or the jewel-case is rifled,
Or when the milk is missing, or another Peke's been stifled,
Or the greenhouse glass is broken, and the trellis past repair—
Ay, there's the wonder of the thing!   *Macavity's not there*!

And when the Foreign Office find a Treaty's gone astray,
Or the Admiralty lose some plans and drawings by the way,
There may be a scrap of paper in the hall or on the stair—
But it's useless to investigate—*Macavity's not there*!
And when the loss has been disclosed, the Secret Service say:
'It *must* have been Macavity!'—but he's a mile away.
You'll be sure to find him resting, or a-licking of his thumbs,
Or engaged in doing complicated long division sums.

Macavity, Macavity, there's no one like Macavity,
There never was a Cat of such deceitfulness and suavity.
He always has an alibi, and one or two to spare:
At whatever time the deed took place—MACAVITY WASN'T
     THERE!
And they say that all the Cats whose wicked deeds are widely
     known
(I might mention Mungojerrie, I might mention Griddlebone)
Are nothing more than agents for the Cat who all the time
Just controls their operations: the Napoleon of Crime!

                                                          (1939)

Gus: the Theatre Cat

GUS is the Cat at the Theatre Door.
His name, as I ought to have told you before,
Is really Asparagus.   That's such a fuss
To pronounce, that we usually call him just Gus.

His coat's very shabby, he's thin as a rake,
And he suffers from palsy that makes his paw shake.
Yet he was, in his youth, quite the smartest of Cats—
But no longer a terror to mice and to rats.
For he isn't the Cat that he was in his prime;
Though his name was quite famous, he says, in its time.
And whenever he joins his friends at their club
(Which takes place at the back of the neighbouring pub)
He loves to regale them, if someone else pays,
With anecdotes drawn from his palmiest days.
For he once was a Star of the highest degree—
He has acted with Irving, he's acted with Tree.
And he likes to relate his success on the Halls,
Where the Gallery once gave him seven cat-calls.
But his grandest creation, as he loves to tell,
Was Firefrorefiddle, the Fiend of the Fell.

'I have played,' so he says, 'every possible part,
And I used to know seventy speeches by heart.
I'd extemporize back-chat, I knew how to gag,
And I knew how to let the cat out of the bag.
I knew how to act with my back and my tail;
With an hour of rehearsal, I never could fail.
I'd a voice that would soften the hardest of hearts,
Whether I took the lead, or in character parts.
I have sat by the bedside of poor Little Nell;
When the Curfew was rung, then I swung on the bell.
In the Pantomime season I never fell flat,
And I once understudied Dick Whittington's Cat.
But my grandest creation, as history will tell,
Was Firefrorefiddle, the Fiend of the Fell.'

Then, if someone will give him a toothful of gin,
He will tell how he once played a part in *East Lynne*.
At a Shakespeare performance he once walked on pat,
When some actor suggested the need for a cat.
He once played a Tiger—could do it again—
Which an Indian Colonel pursued down a drain.
And he thinks that he still can, much better than most,
Produce blood-curdling noises to bring on the Ghost.
And he once crossed the stage on a telegraph wire,
To rescue a child when a house was on fire.
And he says: 'Now, these kittens, they do not get trained
As we did in the days when Victoria reigned.
They never get drilled in a regular troupe,
And they think they are smart, just to jump through a hoop.'
And he'll say, as he scratches himself with his claws,
'Well, the Theatre's certainly not what it was.

These modern productions are all very well,
But there's nothing to equal, from what I hear tell,
   That moment of mystery
    When I made history
As Firefrorefiddle, the Fiend of the Fell.'

                        (1939)

ALAN PATRICK HERBERT
(1890–1971)

Cupid's Darts

Do not worry if I scurry from the grill-room in a hurry,
   Dropping hastily my curry and retiring into baulk;
Do not let it cause you wonder if, by some mischance or blunder
   We encounter on the Underground and I get out and walk.

If I double as a cub'll when you meet him in the stubble,
   Do not think I am in trouble or attempt to make a fuss;
Do not judge me melancholy or attribute it to folly
   If I leave the Metropolitan and travel in a bus.

Do not quiet your anxiety by giving me a diet,
   Or by base resort to *vi et armis* fold me to your arms,
And let no suspicious tremor violate your wonted phlegm, or
   Any fear that Harold's memory is faithless to your charms.

For my passion as I dash on in that disconcerting fashion
   Is as ardently irrational as when we forged the link,
When you gave your little hand away to me, my own Amanda,
   And we sat in the veranda till the stars began to wink.

And I am in such a famine when your beauty I examine,
   That it lures me as the jam invites a hungry little brat,
But I fancy that, at any rate, I'd rather waste a penny
   Than be spitted by the many pins that bristle from your hat.

                        (1910)

The Farmer

The Farmer will never be happy again;
   He carries his heart in his boots;
For either the rain is destroying his grain
   Or the drought is destroying his roots.

You may speak, if you can, to this querulous man,
    Though I should not attempt to be funny,
And if you insist he will give you a list
    Of the reasons he's making no money.

He will tell you the Spring was a scandalous thing,
    For the frost and the cold were that bad;
While what with the heat and the state of the wheat
    The Summer was nearly as sad.

The Autumn, of course, is a permanent source
    Of sorrows as black as your hat;
And as for the Winter, I don't know a printer
    Who'd pass his opinion of *that*.

And, since (to our shame) the seasons I name
    Keep happening year after year,
You can calculate out to a minute about
    How much he enjoys his career.

No wonder he eyes the most roseate skies
    With a mute inexpressible loathing;
No wonder he swears, and no wonder he wears
    Such extremely peculiar clothing.

Poor fellow! his pig declines to grow big
    (You know what these animals are);
His favourite heifer is very much deafer,
    The bull has a chronic catarrh.

In fact, when you meet this unfortunate man,
    The conclusion is only too plain
That Nature is just an elaborate plan
    To annoy him again and again.

Which makes it so difficult not to be rude,
    As you'll find when you're lunching together;
He is certain to brood if you speak of the food,
    And it's fatal to mention the weather.

You must never, I beg, refer to an egg,
    However deplorably done,
And it's cruel to say: 'It's a very fine day!'
    When he's probably sick of the sun.

But under what head to address him instead
  I cannot pretend to be sure,
Though no doubt there are many good things to be said
  Concerning the price of manure.

While if you are short of appropriate themes
  There is always the State of the Nation,
And Drama and Art, and the Meaning of Dreams,
  And Proportional Representation.

But you cannot go wrong if you stick to this song
  And assume that his heart's in his boots,
For either the rain is destroying his grain
  Or the drought is destroying his roots.

(1922)

The Centipede

THE centipede is not quite nice;
He lives in idleness and vice;
  He has a hundred legs.
He also has a hundred wives,
And each of these if she survives
  Has just a hundred eggs;
So that's the reason if you pick
Up any boulder, stone, or brick
  You nearly always find
A swarm of centipedes concealed;
They scatter far across the field,
  But *one* remains behind.
And you may reckon then, my son,
That not alone that luckless one
  Lies pitiful and torn,
But millions more of either sex—
100 multiplied by X—
  Will never now be born;
I dare say it will make you sick,
But so does all Arithmetic.
The gardener says, I ought to add,
The centipede is not so bad;
  He rather *likes* the brutes.
The millipede is what he loathes;
He uses wild bucolic oaths
  Because it eats his roots;

And every gardener is agreed
That if you see a centipede
   Conversing with a milli—
On one of them you drop a stone,
The other one you leave alone—
   I think that's rather silly;
They may be right, but what I say
Is 'Can one stand about all day
   And *count* the creature's legs?'
It has too many any way,
And any moment it may lay
   Another hundred eggs!
So if I see a thing like *this*
I murmur 'Without prejudice,'
   And knock it on the head;
And if I see a thing like *that*
I take a brick and squash it flat;
   In either case it's dead.

(1920)

GUY BOAS

(1896– 1966)

The Underground

THE Underground
   Goes round and round,
And also to and fro;
   And men in blue
   Look after you
And tell you how to go.
   They never quite
   Direct you right,
Although, of course, they know

   The lift-man's whim
   Is being grim;
He is extremely strict;
   He fines the folk
   Who dare to smoke
When once his gates have clicked;
   Nor are his crowd
   Ever allowed
To have their pockets picked.

The platform-man
Has got a plan
For dealing with a queue;
He makes men wait
Behind a gate
Until their train is due;
They watch their train
Depart again,
And then he lets them through.

But on the car
Take place by far
The most convulsive scenes;
The car-men gnash
Their teeth and clash
Their double-jointed screens;
And those for whom
There is no room
Are smashed to smithereens.

The Underground
Goes round and round
And makes a lot of fuss;
And men in blue
Make fools of you,
Which is ridiculous.
So that is why
For my part I
Am sitting in a bus.

(1925)

CLIVE STAPLES LEWIS

(1898–1963)

Awake, my Lute

I STOOD in the gloom of a spurious room
  Where I listened for hours (on and off)
To a terrible bore with a beard like a snore
  And a heavy rectangular cough,
Who discoursed on the habits of orchids and rabbits
  And how an electron behaves,
And a way to cure croup with solidified soup
  In a pattern of circular waves;

Till I suddenly spied that what stood at his side
  Was a richly upholstered baboon
With paws like the puns in a poem of Donne's
  And a tail like a voyage to the Moon.
Then I whispered: 'Look out! For I very much doubt
  If your colleague is really a man.'
But the lecturer said, without turning his head:
  'Oh, that's only the Beverage Plan!'
As one might have foreseen, the whole sky became green
  At this most injudicious remark,
For the Flood had begun and we both had to run
  For our place in the queue to the Ark.
Then, I hardly know how (we were swimming by now),
  The sea got all covered with scum
Made of publishers' blurbs and irregular verbs
  Of the kind which have datives in -um;
And the waves were so high that far up in the sky
  We saw the grand lobster, and heard
How he snorted: 'Compare the achievements of Blair
  With the grave of King Alfred the Third,
And add a brief note and if possible quote,
  And distinguish and trace and discuss
The probable course of a Methodist horse
  When it's catching a decimal bus.'
My answer was Yes. But they marked it N.S.,
  And a truffle-fish grabbed at my toe,
And dragged me deep down to a bombulous town
  Where the traffic was silent and slow.
Then a voice out of heaven observed: 'Quarter past seven!'
  And I threw all the waves off my head,
For that voice beyond doubt was the voice of my scout,
  And the bed of that sea was my bed.

                              (1943)

NOEL COWARD

(1899– 1973)

Mad Dogs and Englishmen

IN tropical climes there are certain times of day
  When all the citizens retire
  To tear their clothes off and perspire
It's one of those rules that the greatest fools obey.
  Because the sun is much too sultry
  And one must avoid its ultry-
              violet ray.

It's such a surprise for Eastern eyes to see
   That though the English are effete,
   They're quite impervious to heat.
When the whiteman rides every native hides in glee,
   Because the simple creatures hope he
   Will impale his solar topee
                on a tree.

The natives grieve when the whitemen leave their huts,
Because they're obviously, definitely Nuts!
It seems such a shame when the English claim the earth
That they give rise to such hilarity and mirth.

Mad dogs and Englishmen
Go out in the midday sun.
The Japanese don't care to,
The Chinese wouldn't dare to,
Hindoos and Argentines sleep firmly from twelve to one.
But Englishmen detest a siesta.
In the Philippines there are lovely screens
To protect you from the glare.
In the Malay States there are hats like plates
Which the Britishers won't wear.
At twelve noon the natives swoon
And no further work is done.
But mad dogs and Englishmen
Go out in the midday sun.

Mad dogs and Englishmen
Go out in the midday sun.
The toughest Burmese bandit
Can never understand it.
In Rangoon the heat of noon is just what the natives shun.
They put their Scotch or Rye down and lie down.
In a jungle town where the sun beats down
To the rage of man or beast
The English garb of the English Sahib
Merely gets a bit more creased.
In Bangkok at twelve o'clock
They foam at the mouth and run.
But mad dogs and Englishmen
Go out in the midday sun.

Mad dogs and Englishmen
Go out in the midday sun.
The smallest Malay rabbit
Deplores this stupid habit.

In Hong Kong they strike a gong
And fire off a noonday gun
To reprimand each inmate who's in late.
In the mangrove swamps where the python romps
There is peace from twelve till two.
Even Caribous lie around and snooze,
For there's nothing else to do.
In Bengal to move at all
Is seldom if ever done.
But mad dogs and Englishmen
Go out in the midday sun.

(1932)

OGDEN NASH

(1902–1971)

The Boy who laughed at Santa Claus

In Baltimore there lived a boy.
He wasn't anybody's joy.
Although his name was Jabez Dawes,
His character was full of flaws.
In school he never led his classes,
He hid old ladies' reading glasses,
His mouth was open when he chewed,
And elbows to the table glued.

He stole the milk of hungry kittens,
And walked through doors marked No ADMITTANCE.
He said he acted thus because
There wasn't any Santa Claus.
Another trick that tickled Jabez
Was crying 'Boo!' at little babies.
He brushed his teeth, they said in town,
Sideways instead of up and down.

Yet people pardoned every sin,
And viewed his antics with a grin,
Till they were told by Jabez Dawes,
'There isn't any Santa Claus!'
Deploring how he did behave,
His parents swiftly sought their grave.
They hurried through the portals pearly,
And Jabez left the funeral early.

Like whooping cough, from child to child,
He sped to spread the rumour wild:
'Sure as my name is Jabez Dawes
There isn't any Santa Claus!'
Slunk like a weasel or a marten
Through nursery and kindergarten,
Whispering low to every tot:
'There isn't any, no there's not!'

The children wept all Christmas Eve
And Jabez chortled up his sleeve.
No infant dared hang up his stocking
For fear of Jabez' ribald mocking.
He sprawled on his untidy bed,
Fresh malice dancing in his head,
When presently with scalp a-tingling,
Jabez heard a distant jingling;
He heard the crunch of sleigh and hoof
Crisply alighting on the roof.

What good to rise and bar the door?
A shower of soot was on the floor.
What was beheld by Jabez Dawes?
The fire-place full of Santa Claus!
Then Jabez fell upon his knees
With cries of 'Don't,' and 'Pretty please.'
He howled: 'I don't know where you read it,
But anyhow, I never said it!'

'Jabez,' replied the angry saint,
'It isn't I, it's you that ain't.
Although there is a Santa Claus,
There isn't any Jabez Dawes!'
Said Jabez then with impudent vim,
'Oh, yes there is! and I am him!
Your magic don't scare me, it doesn't'—
And suddenly he found he wasn't!

From grimy feet to grimy locks,
Jabez became a Jack-in-the-box,
An ugly toy with springs unsprung,
For ever sticking out his tongue.
The neighbours heard his mournful squeal;
They searched for him but not with zeal.
No trace was found of Jabez Dawes,
Which led to thunderous applause,
And people drank a loving cup
And went and hung their stockings up.

All you who sneer at Santa Claus,
Beware the fate of Jabez Dawes,
The saucy boy who mocked the saint.
Donder and Blitzen licked off his paint.

(1950)

Adventures of Isabel

ISABEL met an enormous bear,
Isabel, Isabel, didn't care;
The bear was hungry, the bear was ravenous,
The bear's big mouth was cruel and cavernous.
The bear said, Isabel, glad to meet you,
How do, Isabel, now I'll eat you!
Isabel, Isabel, didn't worry,
Isabel didn't scream or scurry.
She washed her hands and she straightened her hair up,
Then Isabel quietly ate the bear up.

Once in a night as black as pitch
Isabel met a wicked old witch.
The witch's face was cross and wrinkled,
The witch's gums with teeth were sprinkled.
Ho ho, Isabel! the old witch crowed,
I'll turn you into an ugly toad!
Isabel, Isabel, didn't worry,
Isabel didn't scream or scurry,
She showed no rage and she showed no rancour,
But she turned the witch into milk and drank her.

Isabel met a hideous giant,
Isabel continued self-reliant.
The giant was hairy, the giant was horrid,
He had one eye in the middle of his forehead.
Good morning Isabel, the giant said,
I'll grind your bones to make my bread.
Isabel, Isabel, didn't worry,
Isabel didn't scream or scurry.
She nibbled the zwieback that she always fed off,
And when it was gone, she cut the giant's head off.

Isabel met a troublesome doctor,
He punched and he poked till he really shocked her.
The doctor's talk was of coughs and chills
And the doctor's satchel bulged with pills.
The doctor said unto Isabel,
Swallow this, it will make you well.

Isabel, Isabel, didn't worry,
Isabel didn't scream or scurry.
She took those pills from the pill concocter,
And Isabel calmly cured the doctor.

                                    (1950)

'I want a Pet . . .'

THE CAMEL

THE camel has a single hump;
The dromedary, two;
Or else the other way around.
I'm never sure.   Are you?

THE POULTRIES

Let's think of eggs.
They have no legs.
Chickens come from eggs
But they have legs.
The plot thickens;
Eggs come from chickens,
But have no legs under 'em.
What a conundrum!

THE GERM

A mighty creature is the germ,
Though smaller than the pachyderm.
His customary dwelling place
Is deep within the human race.
His childish pride he often pleases
By giving people strange diseases.
Do you, my poppet, feel infirm?
You probably contain a germ.

THE COW

The cow is of the bovine ilk;
One end is moo, the other milk.

THE RHINOCEROS

The rhino is a homely beast,
For human eyes he's not a feast.
Farewell, farewell, you old rhinoceros,
I'll stare at something less prepoceros.

THE PHOENIX

Deep in the study
Of eugenics
We find that fabled
Fowl the Phoenix.
The wisest bird
As ever was,
Rejecting other
Mas and Pas,
It lays one egg,
Not ten or twelve,
And when it's hatched,
Out pops itselve.

THE WOMBAT

The wombat lives across the seas,
Among the far Antipodes.
He may exist on nuts and berries,
Or then again, on missionaries;
His distant habitat precludes
Conclusive knowledge of his moods.
But I would not engage the wombat
In any form of mortal combat.

THE SHREW

Strange as it seems, the smallest mammal
Is the shrew, and not the camel.
And that is all I ever knew,
Or wish to know, about the shrew.

THE SQUIRREL

A squirrel to some is a squirrel,
To others, a squirrel's a squirl.
Since freedom of speech is the birthright of each,
I can only this fable unfurl:

A virile young squirrel named Cyril,
In an argument over a girl,
Was lambasted from here to the Tyrol
By a churl of a squirl named Earl.

THE TERMITE

Some primal termite knocked on wood
And tasted it, and found it good,
And that is why your Cousin May
Fell through the parlour floor to-day.

THE LION

Oh, weep for Mr and Mrs Bryan!
He was eaten by a lion;
Following which, the lion's lioness
Up and swallowed Bryan's Bryaness.

(1950)

JOHN BETJEMAN

(1906–   )

Potpourri from a Surrey Garden

MILES of pram in the wind and Pam in the gorse track,
   Coco-nut smell of the broom and a packet of Weights
Press'd in the sand.   The thud of a hoof on a horse track—
A horse-riding horse for a horse-track—
      Conifer county of Surrey approached
Through remarkable wrought-iron gates.

Over your boundary now, I wash my face in a bird-bath,
   Then which path shall I take?   That over there by the pram?
Down by the pond? or else, shall I take the slippery third path,
      Trodden away with gymn. shoes,
     Beautiful fir-dry alley that leads
To the bountiful body of Pam?

Pam, I adore you, Pam, you great big mountainous sports girl,
   Whizzing them over the net, full of the strength of five;
That old Malvernian brother, you zephyr and khaki shorts girl,
      Although he's playing for Woking,
Can't stand up to your wonderful backhand drive.

See the strength of her arm, as firm and hairy as Hendren's;
   See the size of her thighs, the pout of her lips as, cross,
And full of a pent-up strength, she swipes at the rhododendrons,
      Lucky the rhododendrons,
     And flings her arrogant love-lock
Back with a petulant toss.

Over the redolent pinewoods, in at the bath-room casement,
One fine Saturday, Windlesham bells shall call
Up at Butterfield aisle rich with Gothic enlacement,
Licensed now for embracement,
Pam and I, as the organ
Thunders over you all.

(1940)

PATRICK BARRINGTON
(1908–)

I had a Hippopotamus

I HAD a hippopotamus; I kept him in a shed
And fed him upon vitamins and vegetable bread;
I made him my companion on many cheery walks
And had his portrait done by a celebrity in chalks.

His charming eccentricities were known on every side,
The creature's popularity was wonderfully wide;
He frolicked with the Rector in a dozen friendly tussles,
Who could not but remark upon his hippopotamuscles.

If he should be afflicted by depression or the dumps,
By hippopotameasles or the hippopotamumps,
I never knew a particle of peace till it was plain
He was hippopotamasticating properly again.

I had a hippopotamus; I loved him as a friend;
But beautiful relationships are bound to have an end.
Time takes, alas! our joys from us and robs us of our blisses;
My hippopotamus turned out a hippopotamissis.

My housekeeper regarded him with jaundice in her eye;
She did not want a colony of hippopotami;
She borrowed a machine-gun from her soldier-nephew, Percy,
And showed my hippopotamus no hippopotamercy.

My house now lacks the glamour that the charming creature gave,
The garage where I kept him is as silent as the grave;
No longer he displays among the motor-tyres and spanners
His hippopotamastery of hippopotamanners.

No longer now he gambols in the orchard in the Spring
No longer do I lead him through the village on a string;
No longer in the mornings does the neighbourhood rejoice
To his hippopotamusically-modulated voice.

I had a hippopotamus; but nothing upon earth
Is constant in its happiness or lasting in its mirth.
No joy that life can give me can be strong enough to smother
My sorrow for that might-have-been-a-hippopotamother.

(1933)

I had a Duck-billed Platypus

I HAD a duck-billed platypus when I was up at Trinity,
With whom I soon discovered a remarkable affinity.
He used to live in lodgings with myself and Arthur Purvis,
And we all went up together for the Diplomatic Service.
I had a certain confidence, I own, in his ability,
He mastered all the subjects with remarkable facility;
And Purvis, though more dubious, agreed that he was clever,
But no one else imagined he had any chance whatever.
I failed to pass the interview, the Board with wry grimaces
Took exception to my boots and then objected to my braces,
And Purvis too was failed by an intolerant examiner
Who said he had his doubts as to his sock-suspenders' stamina.
The bitterness of failure was considerably mollified,
However, by the ease with which our platypus had qualified.
The wisdom of the choice, it soon appeared, was undeniable;
There never was a diplomat more thoroughly reliable.
He never made rash statements his enemies might hold him to,
He never stated anything, for no one ever told him to,
And soon he was appointed, so correct was his behaviour,
Our Minister (without Portfolio) to Trans-Moravia.
My friend was loved and honoured from the Andes to Esthonia,
He soon achieved a pact between Peru and Patagonia,
He never vexed the Russians nor offended the Rumanians,
He pacified the Letts and yet appeased the Lithuanians,
Won approval from his masters down in Downing Street so
    wholly, O,
He was soon to be rewarded with the grant of a Portfolio.

When, on the Anniversary of Greek Emancipation,
Alas!   He laid an egg in the Bulgarian Legation.
This untoward occurrence caused unheard-of repercussions,
Giving rise to epidemics of sword-clanking in the Prussians.
The Poles began to threaten, and the Finns began to flap at him,
Directing all the blame for this unfortunate mishap at him;

While the Swedes withdrew entirely from the Anglo-Saxon
    dailies
The right of photographing the Aurora Borealis,
And, all efforts at rapprochement in the meantime proving
    barren,
The Japanese in self-defence annexed the Isle of Arran.
My platypus, once thought to be more cautious and more
    tentative
Than any other living diplomatic representative,
Was now a sort of warning to all diplomatic students
Of the risks attached to negligence, the perils of imprudence,
And, branded in the Honours List as 'Platypus, Dame Vera,'
Retired, a lonely figure, to lay eggs at Bordighera.

(1933)

The Air Sentry

I ATE my fill of army bread,
    I drank my pint of army tea,
I set my helmet on my head
    And girt my ground-sheet over me.

I laid my gas-mask on my chest,
    I took my musket in my hand,
And full of meat and martial zest
    Went out to guard my native land.

My bayonet was bared to hack
    The innards out of an attacker.
Above my head the night was black,
    But in my heart the hate was blacker.

I was as full of martial ire
    As any newspaper reporter.
My soldier's heart was full of fire
    And both my boots were full of water.

Like some sea-rover on his deck
    I paced, and mused on life with loathing,
While water trickled down my neck
    And nestled in my underclothing.

The meadows squelched beneath my tread,
    The streams were rapids and I shot 'em;
The rain came down upon my head,
    And I came down upon my bottom.

And as in solemn thought I stood
　　And brooded on the Past and Present
And whether Purgatory would
　　Be more prolonged or more unpleasant,

Or dreaming of a heaven as dry
　　And bright as earth was damp and sickly,
A sergeant came and asked me why
　　I hadn't challenged him more quickly.

He scorned my 'Wherefor' and 'Because':
　　In accents neither kind nor cooing
He asked me who I thought I was
　　And what I thought that I was doing.

I answered that in my belief
　　So far as I could read the mystery,
I was a transitory, brief,
　　Damp episode in cosmic history.

I said that he and I were blind
　　Insensate tools for Fate to batter—
Two pale projections of the mind
　　Of God upon the screen of Matter.

He answered—(sergeants can be fools,
　　Like other military gentry)—
That wasn't in the army rules
　　For challenging a cove on sentry.

I said that he should understand
　　That men who were allied together
Against the foemen of their land
　　Should be allied against the weather.

I pointed out that in our king's
　　And country's service all were brothers.
I pointed out a lot of things:
　　He pointed out a lot of others.

He said he'd put me on a charge
　　(He worded it more impolitely),
And I'd no longer be at large
　　To roam the fields and pastures nightly.

I said that if the prison cell
　　Were dryer—it could not be wetter—
Than those green fields I knew so well,
　　There's nothing that would please me better.

He launched at me those words of shame
    With which the army loves to plague you
He said he'd got my ——ing name.
    I said I'd got the ——ing ague.

And while we argued, as the dead
    Will argue after their damnation,
An aeroplane flew overhead
    And dropped a bomb on Euston Station.

The sergeant went.   The morning broke.
    Dark as a song by D. H. Lawrence
The day came, and the world awoke;
    And still the rain came down in torrents.

But though some weeks have passed away,
    And many suns and moons have risen
Behind those banks of cloudy grey,
    I have not yet been put in prison.

And that is why I wander here
    So wet and wild in my apparel,
With water gleaming on my gear
    And glittering on my rifle-barrel.

Stray rustics, passing me at night,
    Believing that these fields are haunted,
Mistake me for a water-sprite
    And pass upon their ways undaunted.

I dwell beside untrodden ways
    By banks the Past and Future meet on——
A living door-mat of the days
    For Time to wipe his weary feet on.

Alone beneath the leaden sky
    From which a leaden stream is falling
I challenge cattle with a cry
    And tree-stumps like a trumpet calling.

Sometimes I hear a sea-bird snore
    And hail it with a mournful bellow,
Like banshee calling banshee or
    The satyr crying to his fellow.

And when the section-sergeant comes,
    Through pools and puddles softly stepping,
My voice is like a roll of drums
    And percolates from here to Epping.

I wander lonely as a cloud
   Or some forgotten West-end waiter.
An anti-gas-cape is my shroud;
   My death-mask is a respirator.

The rain streams from my finger-tips,
   About me life is at a standstill:
From hedge and tree the water drips,
   And thus I guard my native land still.

                    (1939)

ROGER LANCELYN GREEN
(1918–   )

On First looking into the Dark Future

MUCH have I travail'd in the realms of gold,
   And many dull and portly volumes seen;
   To many dreary lectures have I been
Which dry professors in the *Taylor* hold;
Oft of the wide expanse had I been told
   That *Nichol Smith* then ruled as his demesne,
   Yet ever did I tread my way serene—
Till thoughts of coming Finals turned me cold.

Then felt I like some urger of the punt
   Left on the pole to dangle in dismay;
Or like some climber when the treacherous drain
Eludes his grasp—and nearer draws the hunt,
   Proctors and Bulldogs, till they sight their prey
Silent upon a spike in *Magpie Lane.*

                    (1941)

APPENDIX

A

FROM 'THE MASQUE OF BALLIOL'
(1881)

FIRST come I. My name is JOWETT.
There's no knowlege but I know it.
I am Master of this College,
What I don't know isn't knowledge.

Henry Charles Beeching (1859–1919)

Roughly, so to say, you know,
I am NETTLESHIP or so;
You are gated after Hall,
That's all. I mean that's nearly all.

John William Mackail (1859–1945)

Upright and shrewd, more woo'd of fame
Than wooing, MATHESON's my name;
I'm not what you would call intense,
But I've uncommon common sense.

Henry Charles Beeching (1859–1919)

Old tips come out as good as new
From me, for I am MONTAGUE;
With head aslant I softly cram
The world into an epigram.

John William Mackail (1859–1945)

I am HUXLEY, blond and merry,
Fond of jokes and laughter, very;
If I laughed at what was witty,
I should laugh less, which were a pity,

John Bowyer Buchanan Nichols (1859–1939)

I am featly-tripping LEE,
Learned in modern history.
My gown, the wonder of beholders,
Hangs like a footnote from my shoulders.

Henry Charles Beeching (1859–1919)

I am a most superior person,
My name is GEORGE NATHANIEL CURZON.
My face is soft, my hair is sleek,
I dine at Blenheim twice a week.

Henry Charles Beeching (1859–1919)

Later Additions

I am ANDREW CECIL BRADLEY:
When my liver's acting badly,
I take refuge from 'the brute'
In the blessed Absolute.

Cecil Arthur Spring-Rice (1859–1918)

I am the Dean of Christ Church, Sir;
This is my wife—look well at her.
She is the Broad; I am the High:
We are the University.

(I am the Dean, and this is Mrs Liddell:
She plays the first, and I the second fiddle.)

Cecil Arthur Spring-Rice (1859–1918)

B

Stray Verses

IF I were a Cassowary
On the plains of Timbuctoo,
I would eat a missionary,
Cassock, band, and hymn-book too.

Samuel Wilberforce (1805–73)

I TAKES and paints
Hears no complaints,
And sells before I'm dry;
Till savage Ruskin
He sticks his tusk in,
Then nobody will buy.   (1856)

Shirley Brooks (1816–74)

INSTRUCTION sore long time I bore,
And cramming was in vain;
Till Heaven did please my woes to ease
With water on the brain.

(1863)
Charles Kingsley (1819–75)

IF ever you go to Dolgelly
Don't dine at the Lion Hotel;
For there's nothing to put in your belly
And no one to answer the bell.

Thomas Hughes (1822–96)

FROUDE informs the Scottish youth
That parsons do not care for truth.
The Reverend Canon Kingsley cries:
'History is a pack of lies!'
What cause for judgements so malign?
A brief reflection solves the mystery—
Froude believes Kingsley a divine,
And Kingsley goes to Froude for history.

(1871)
William Stubbs (1825–1901)

I NEVER had a piece of toast
Particularly long and wide,
But fell upon the sanded floor,
And always on the buttered side.

(1884)
James Payn (1830–98)

THE rain it'raineth on the just
And also on the unjust fella:
But chiefly on the just, because
The unjust steals the just's umbrella.

Charles, Baron Bowen (1835–94)

THE little tigers are at rest,
Coiled within their cosy nest;
The sympathetic crocodile
Is sleeping with a placid smile;
The all-embracing bounteous bear
Dreams sweetly in his lowly lair.

(1875)
Tom Hood (1835–74)

BUT now the dentist cannot die
And leave his forceps as of old,
But round him, e'er he scarce be cold,
Begins the vast biography.

(1901)
Andrew Lang (1844–1912)

WHEN I am grown to man's estate
I shall be very proud and great,
And tell the other girls and boys
Not to meddle with my toys.

(1885)
Robert Louis Stevenson (1850–94)

TO know thy bent and then pursue,
  Why, that is genius, nothing less;
But he who knows what not to do,
  Holds half the secret of success.

(1894)
Ella Wheeler Wilcox (1850–1919)

THE ordinary valour only works
At those rare intervals when peril lurks;
There is a courage, scarcer far, and stranger,
Which nothing can intimidate but danger.

(1902)

Thomas Anstey Guthrie ('F. Anstey') (1856–1934)

MAN, matron, maiden,
Please call it Baden;
Further for Powell,
Rhyme it with Noel.

Robert Baden-Powell (1857–1941)

MR Ody met a body
Hanging from a tree;
And what was worse
He met a hearse
As black as black could be.
Mr Ody said: 'By God, he
Ought to have a ride!'
Said the driver: 'I'd oblige yer,
But we're full inside!'

(1921)

Edith Nesbit (1858–1924)

W'EN you see a man in woe,
Walk right up and say 'hullo';
Say 'hullo' and 'how d'ye do?
How's the world a-usin' you?'

Sam Walter Foss (1858–1911)

I RAN for a catch
With the sun in my eyes, sir,
Being sure at a 'snatch,'
I ran for a catch . . .
Now I wear a black patch
And a nose *such* a size, sir,
I ran for a catch
With the sun in my eyes, sir.

Coulson Kernahan (1858–1943)

Heaven and Hell

THE burning—at first—would be probably worst,
But habit the anguish might soften,
While those who are bored by praising the Lord
Would be more so by praising Him often.

James Kenneth Stephen (1859–92)

THE Grizzly Bear is huge and wild,
He has devoured the infant child.
The infant child is not aware
He has been eaten by the bear.

A. E. Housman (1859–1936)

AND this is good old Boston,
The home of the bean and the cod,
Where the Lowells talk to the Cabots,
And the Cabots talk only to God.

John Collins Bossidy (1860–1928)

KING DAVID and King Solomon
Led merry, merry lives,
With many, many lady friends
And many, many wives;
But when old age crept over them,
With many, many qualms,
King Solomon wrote the Proverbs
And King David wrote the Psalms.

James Ball Naylor (1860–1945)

I WISH I loved the Human Race;
I wish I loved its silly face;
I wish I liked the way it walks;
I wish I liked the way it talks;
And when I'm introduced to one
I wish I thought *What Jolly Fun!*

(1923)
Walter A. Raleigh (1861–1922)

'WHAT hundred books are best, think you?' I said,
Addressing one devoted to the pen.
He thought a moment, then he raised his head:
'I hardly know—I've only written ten.'

(1890)
John Kendrick Bangs (1862–1922)

Macaulay at Tea

POUR, varlet, pour the water,
The water steaming hot!
A spoonful for each man of us,
Another for the pot!

(1892)
Barry Pain (1864–1928)

CHILDREN, behold the Chimpanzee:
He sits on the ancestral tree
From which we sprang in ages gone.
I'm glad we sprang: had we held on,
We might, for aught that I can say,
Be horrid Chimpanzees to-day.

(1899)
Oliver Herford (1863–1935)

THE lion is a beast to fight:
    He leaps along the plain,
And if you run with all your might,
    He runs with all his mane.

(1897)
Arthur T. Quiller-Couch (1863–1944)

I SHOOT the Hippopotamus
With bullets made of platinum,
Because if I use leaden ones
His hide is sure to flatten 'em.

(1896)
Hilaire Belloc (1870–1953)

Curtain!

VILLAIN shows his indiscretion;
Villain's partner makes confession;
Juvenile with golden tresses
Finds her pa, and dons long dresses;
Scapegrace comes home money-laiden;
Hero comforts tearful maiden;
Soubrette marries loyal chappie;
Villain skips, and all are happy.

(1895)
Paul Laurence Dunbar (1872–1906)

THOU should'st be living at this hour,
Milton, and enjoying power.
England hath need of thee, and not
Of Leavis and of Eliot.

(1946)

Heathcote William Garrod (1878–   )

NO teacher I of boys or smaller fry,
No teacher I of teachers, no, not I.
Mine was the distant aim, the longer reach,
To teach men how to teach men how to teach.

(1946)

Allen Beville Ramsay (1872–1955)

AMONG the anthropophagi
One's friends are one's sarcophagi.

Ogden Nash (1902–71)

C

ROOTLESS RHYMES

Oral and Anonymous

'TWAS an evening in November,
As I very well remember,
I was strolling down the street in drunken pride,
But my knees were all a-flutter,
So I landed in the gutter,
And a pig came up and lay down by my side.

Yes, I lay there in the gutter,
Thinking thoughts I could not utter,
When a colleen passing by did softly say:
'Ye can tell a man that boozes
By the company he chooses.'
At that the pig got up and walked away!

• • •

AS I was coming down the stair
I met a man who wasn't there.
He wasn't there again to-day:
I *wish* that man would go away!

• • •

ONE fine day in the middle of the night
Two dead men got up to fight;
Two blind men to see fair play,
Two dumb men to shout: 'Hurray!'
And two lame men to carry them away.

• • •

I EAT my peas with honey,
I've done it all my life;
It makes the peas taste funny,
But it keeps them on the knife.

• • •

I THREW a penny in the air,
It fell again—I know not where.
But if it had been half a crown
I would have watched where it came down.

• • •

275

I KNOW two things about the horse,
And one of them is rather coarse.

.　　　　.　　　　.

LIZZIE BORDEN took an axe
And gave her mother forty whacks;
When she saw what she had done
She gave her father forty-one!

(U.S.A., *c.* 1890)

.　　　　.　　　　.

MISS BUSS and Miss Beale
Cupid's darts do not feel.
How different from us
Miss Beale and Miss Buss.

(Late Nineteenth Century) [*Cheltenham Ladies College*]

.　　　　.　　　　.

TWO men wrote a lexicon, Liddell and Scott;
Some parts were clever but some parts were not.
Hear, all ye learned, and read me this riddle:
Which part wrote Scott, and which part wrote Liddell?

(Mid Nineteenth Century)

.　　　　.　　　　.

THE boy stood in the supper-room
　　Whence all but he had fled;
He'd eaten seven pots of jam
　　And he was gorged with bread.

'Oh, one more crust before I bust!'
　　He cried in accents wild;
He licked the plates, he sucked the spoons—
　　He was a vulgar child.

There came a burst of thunder-sound—
　　The boy—oh! where was he?
Ask of the maid who mopped him up,
　　The bread-crumbs and the tea!

.　　　　.　　　　.

SPEAK when you're spoken to,
　　Do as you're bid,
Shut the door after you,
　　Good little kid.

[After *Maria Edgeworth*]

.　　　　.　　　　.

SULK when you're spoken to,
Cry when you're chid,
Slam the door after you,
Bad little kid.

. . .

ROCK away, passenger, in the Third Class,
When your train shunts a faster will pass;
When your train's late your chances are small—
Crushed will be carriages, engine and all.

Punch (9 October 1852)

. . .

THERE was an old owl lived in an oak,
The more he heard, the less he spoke;
The less he spoke, the more he heard—
Oh, if men were all like that wise bird!

Punch (10 April 1875)

. . .

THE greatest bore is boredom,
The greatest nuisance known
Is he who talks about himself
And *his* affairs alone,
When you want *him* to listen
While you talk about your own.

Fun (4 March 1885)

. . .

SEE the happy moron,
He doesn't give a damn.
I wish I were a moron:
My God! perhaps I am!

Eugenics Review (July 1929)

D

BY KNOWN AUTHORS

THE Reverend Henry Ward Beecher
Called a hen a most elegant creature.
  The hen, pleased with that,
  Laid an egg in his hat—
And thus did the hen reward Beecher.

Oliver Wendell Holmes (1809–94)

.   .   .

THERE was an Old Man of the coast,
Who placidly sat on a post;
  But when it was cold
  He relinquished his hold
And called for some hot buttered toast.

(1861)

There was an Old Man of Thermopylae,
Who never did anything properly;
  But they said: 'If you choose
  To boil Eggs in your Shoes,
You shall never remain in Thermopylae.'

(1872)

There was an Old Person of Ware
Who rode on the back of a Bear;
  When they ask'd, 'Does it trot?'—
  He said: 'Certainly not!
He's a Moppsikon Floppsikon Bear!'

(1872)

There was an Old Man on the Border,
Who lived in the utmost disorder;
  He danced with the Cat,
  And made tea in his Hat,
Which vexed all the folks on the Border.

(1872)

279

There was a Young Lady of Corsica,
Who purchased a little brown, Saucy-cur,
    Which she fed upon Ham
    And hot Raspberry Jam,
That expensive Young Lady of Corsica.

                                  (1872)
                          Edward Lear (1812–88)

         •   •   •

THERE was a queer fellow named Woodin
Who always ate pepper with puddin';
    Till, one day, 'tis said,
    He sneezed off his head!
That imprudent old fellow named Woodin.

                                  (1868)
     Edward Bradley ('*Cuthbert Bede*') (1827–89)

         •   •   •

THERE's a combative Artist named Whistler
Who is, like his own hog-hairs, a bristler:
    A tube of white lead
    And a punch on the head
Offer varied attractions to Whistler.

There's a Portuguese person named Howell
Who lays on his lies with a trowell:
    Should he give over lying,
    'Twill be when he's dying,
For living is lying with Howell.

There once was a painter named Scott
Who seemed to have hair, but had not.
    He seemed to have sense:
    'Twas an equal pretence
On the part of the painter named Scott.

There's an Irishman, Arthur O'Shaughnessy—
On the chessboard of poets a pawn is he:
    Though a bishop or king
    Would be rather the thing
To the fancy of Arthur O'Shaughnessy.

There is an old he-wolf named Gambart,
Beware of him if thou a lamb art;
    Else thy tail and thy toes
    And thine innocent nose
Will be ground by the grinders of Gambart.

There was a poor chap called Rossetti;
As a painter with many kicks met he—
  With more as a man—
  But sometimes he ran,
And that saved the rear of Rossetti.

> *Dante Gabriel Rossetti* (1828–82)

.   .   .

THERE was a young lady of station,
'I love man,' was her sole exclamation;
  But when men cried: 'You flatter,'
  She replied: 'Oh! no matter,
Isle of Man is the true explanation!'

> *Charles Lutwidge Dodgson*
> (*'Lewis Carroll'*) (1832–98)

.   .   .

IL était un Hébreu de Hambourg,
Qui creva d'un mauvais calembourg,
  Qu'il eut l'audace extrême
  De commettre en carême,
Un Dimanche, au milieu d'Edimbourg.

> (1877)

Chaque époque a ses grands noms sonores;
Or, de tous les défunts cockolores,
  Le moral *Fénélon*,
  Michel Ange et *Johnson*
(Le Docteur), sont les plus awful bores!

> (1877)

À *Potsdam*, les totaux absteneurs,
Comme tant d'autres titotalleurs,
  Sont gloutons, omnivores,
  Nasorubicolores,
Grands manchons, et terribles duffeurs.

> (1877)
> *George du Maurier* (1834–1896)

.   .   .

THERE was a young lady of Limerick
Who stole from a farmer named Tim a rick.
  When the priest at the altar
  Suggested a halter,
She fled from the county of Limerick.

> (1909)

There was an auld birkie ca'ed Milton
Who lo'ed na the lads wi' a kilt on;
   Gie'd Colkitto a rasp,
   Ca'd Gillespie 'Galasp,'
Sae slicht was the Gaelic he built on.

                     (1912)
             Andrew Lang (1844–1912)

     •   •   •   •

My name's Mister Benjamin Bunny,
And I travel about without money.
   There are lots I could name
   Do precisely the same—
It's convenient, but certainly funny!

                   (*c.* 1890)
      Frederick Edward Weatherley (1848–1929)

     •   •   •   •

THERE was a young genius of Queens',
Who was fond of explosive machines.
   He once blew up a door,
   But he'll do it no more
For it chanced that that door was the Dean's.

                   (1872)

There was a young gourmand of John's,
Who'd a notion of dining on swans,
   To the Backs he took big nets
   To capture the cygnets,
But was told they were kept for the Dons.

                   (1872)

There was an old Fellow of Trinity,
A Doctor well versed in Divinity,
   But he took to free thinking
   And then to deep drinking,
And so had to leave the vicinity.

                   (1872)

There was a young critic of King's,
Who had views on the limits of things;
   With the size of his chapel
   He would frequently grapple,
And exclaim: 'It *is* biggish for King's!'

                   (1872)
        Arthur Clement Hilton (1851–77)

     •   •   •   •

THERE was an old man of Bengal,
Who purchased a bat and a ball,
  Some gloves and some pads:
  It was one of his fads,
For he never played cricket at all.

(1907)
Thomas Anstey Guthrie ('F. Anstey') (1856–1934)

· · ·

I WISH that my room had a floor!
I don't so much care for a door,
  But this crawling around
  Without touching the ground
Is getting to be quite a bore!

(1914)
Gelett Burgess (1860–1951)

· · ·

THERE was a good Canon of Durham
Who fished with a hook and a worrum.
  Said the Dean to the Bishop,
  'I've brought a big fish up,
But I fear we may have to inter'm.'

William Ralph Inge (1860–1954)

· · ·

A PRETTY young actress, a stammerer,
Knew acting in theatres would damn her.   A
  Producer (film genus)
  Engaged her as 'Venus'—
The rest of the story's 'in camera.'

Eille Norwood (1861–1948)

· · ·

THERE was a young man of Devizes
Whose ears were of different sizes;
  The one that was small
  Was no use at all,
But the other won several prizes.

(1904)
Archibald Marshall (1866–1934)

· · ·

THERE was a young man of Montrose,
Who had pockets in none of his clothes.
  When asked by his lass
  Where he carried his brass,
He said, 'Darling, I pay through the nose.'

Arnold Bennett (1867–1931)

· · ·

An angry young husband called Bicket
Said: 'Turn yourself round and I'll kick it;
    You have painted my wife
    In the nude to the life:
Do you think, Mr Greene, it was cricket?'

                   John Galsworthy (1867–1933)

        •   •   •

A certain young gourmet of Crediton
Took some *pâté de fois gras* and spread it on
    A chocolate biscuit
    Then murmured, 'I'll risk it!'
His tomb bears the date that he said it on.

                 Charles Cuthbert Inge (1868–)

        •   •   •

An eccentric old person of Slough,
Who took all his meals with a cow,
    Always said: 'It's uncanny,
    She's so like Aunt Fanny.'
But he never would indicate how.

                 George Robey (1869–1954)

        •   •   •

There was a young lady named Bright
Whose speed was far faster than light.
    She set out one day
    In a relative way,
And returned home the previous night.

                          (1923)
                 Arthur Buller (1874–1944)

        •   •   •

A wonderful bird is the pelican;
His bill can hold more than his belican.
    He can take in his beak
    Food enough for a week;
But I'm damned if I see how the helican!

                 Dixon Lanier Merritt (1879–)

        •   •   •

There was a young curate of Hants,
Who suddenly took off his pants.
    When asked why he did,
    He replied: 'To get rid
Of this regular army of ants!'

                 Edmund Valpy Knox (1881–1971)

        •   •   •

EVANGELICAL Vicar in want
Of a portable, second-hand font.
   Would dispose of the same
   For a portrait (in frame)
Of the Bishop-Elect of Vermont.

Ronald Arbuthnot Knox (1888–1957)

THERE once was a man who said: 'Damn!
It is borne in upon me I am
   An engine that moves
   In predestinate grooves,
I'm not even a bus, I'm a tram.'

(1905)
Maurice Evan Hare (1889–)

CONSIDER the lowering Lynx:
He's savage and sullen and stynx,
   Though he never has stunk
   Like the scandalous skunk—
That's a task far beyond him, methynx.

(1927)
Langford Reed (1889–1954)

THERE was an old man in a trunk,
Who inquired of his wife: 'Am I drunk?'
   She replied with regret:
   'I'm afraid so, my pet.'
And he answered: 'It's just as I thunk.'

Ogden Nash (1902–71)

Limericks—II

ANONYMOUS AND TRADITIONAL

THERE was a young lady of Riga
Who went for a ride on a tiger;
   They returned from the ride
   With the lady inside,
And a smile on the face of the tiger.

i.e.

Puella Rigensis ridebat
Quam tigris in tergo vehebat;
   Externa profecta,
   Interna revecta,
Risusque cum tigre manebat.

There was a young lady of Bude
Who ran through the town in the nude.
The Policeman said 'What a m—
'Agnificent bottom!'
And smacked it as hard as he could.

or

Κόρη τις ἐνναίουσα Μεθύμνῃ
ὁδούς περιέδραμε γυμνή
    ὁ Σκύθης 'ὅσην'
    ἔφη 'ἔχει πυγήν'
καὶ νῦν ῥοδοδάκτυλος πρύμνη.

*

There was an old Tailor of Bicester,
He went out to walk with his sister,
    When a bird called a Jay
    Took the old girl away
Before the old gentleman missed her.

(Punch, 7 January 1860)

There was a young lady of Ryde
Who ate a green apple and died;
    The apple fermented
    Inside the lamented,
And made cider inside her inside.

There was an old man of Boulogne,
Who sang a most topical song;
    It wasn't the words
    Which frightened the birds,
But the horrible *double entendre*.

There was a young lady of Kent,
Who said that she knew what it meant
    When men asked her to dine,
    Gave her cocktails and wine,
She knew what it meant—but she went!

There was a young lady of Lynn
Who was so uncommonly thin
    That when she essayed
    To drink lemonade,
She slipped through the straw and fell in.

An epicure, dining at Crewe,
Found quite a large mouse in his stew;
    Said the waiter: 'Don't shout
    And wave it about,
Or the rest will be wanting one, too!'

There was a young fellow of Ceuta
Who rode into church on his scooter;
   He knocked down the Dean
   And said: 'Sorry, old bean,
I ought to have sounded my hooter.'

There once were two cats of Kilkenny,
Each thought there was one cat too many;
   So they fought and they fit,
   And they scratched and they bit,
Till instead of two cats there weren't any.

There was a kind Curate of Kew
Who kept a large cat in a pew,
   Where he taught it each week
   Alphabetical Greek,
But it never got further than $\mu\nu$.

                          (*Punch*, 7 May 1924)

There was a young lady called Starky
Who had an affair with a darky;
   The result of her sins
   Was quadruplets, not twins—
One black, and one white, and two khaki.

There was a young lady of Ealing
Who walked upside down on the ceiling;
   She shouted: 'Oh, Hec!
   I've broken my neck,
And it is a peculiar feeling!'

There once was a girl of Pitlochry
Whose morals were merely a mochry,
   For under her bed
   She'd a young man, instead
Of the ten times more usual crochry.

There once was a man of Bengal
Who was asked to a Fancy Dress Ball;
   He murmured: 'I'll risk it
   And go as a biscuit!'
But the dog ate him up in the hall.

There was an old man of Blackheath
Who sat on his set of false teeth.
   Said he, with a start,
   'O Lord, bless my heart!
I have bitten myself underneath!'

There was an old man of Peru,
Who dreamt he was eating his shoe.
  He woke in the night
  In a terrible fright,
And found it was perfectly true.

There was a young lady of Flint,
Who had a most horrible squint.
  She could scan the whole sky
  With her uppermost eye,
While the other was reading small print.

They say that I was in my youth
Uncouth and ungainly, forsooth!
  I can only reply,
  'Tis a lie! 'Tis a lie!
I was couth—I was perfectly couth.

                        (*Punch*, 11 September 1907)

There was a young fellow called Green,
Whose musical sense was not keen.
  He said: 'It's most odd,
  But I cannot tell *God*
Save the Weasel from *Pop goes the Queen*'!

There was an old person of Lyme
Who married three wives at a time.
  When asked: 'Why the third?'
  He replied: 'One's absurd,
And bigamy, sir, is a crime.'

There was a faith-healer of Deal,
Who said: 'Although pain isn't real,
  If I sit on a pin
  And it punctures my skin,
I dislike what I fancy I feel.'

There was a young bard of Japan
Whose limericks never would scan;
  When they said it was so,
  He replied: 'Yes, I know,
But I make a rule of always trying to get just
    as many words into the last line as I
    possibly can.'

EPILOGUE

LAST come I, my name is GREEN—
That so much Humorous Verse has seen.
I hope here's value for your money,
And what I've missed—just isn't funny!

EVERYMAN'S LIBRARY AND EVERYMAN PAPERBACKS: A Selection

indicates the volumes also in paperback: for their series numbers in Everyman paperbacks add 1000 to the EML numbers given.

BIOGRAPHY

ESSAYS AND CRITICISM

FICTION

HISTORY

LEGENDS AND SAGAS

POETRY AND DRAMA

RELIGION AND PHILOSOPHY

SCIENCES: POLITICAL AND GENERAL

TRAVEL AND TOPOGRAPHY